Yes

The
Tormato
Story

This book is dedicated to every individual who has been involved in any way with creating the multifaceted idea we call Yes music.

https://tormatobook.com/book-owners-only

Yes

The Tormato Story

Kevin Mulryne

Foreword by
Oliver Wakeman

Five Per Cent For Something Publishing
tormatobook.com
Email: show@yesmusicpodcast.com

First Published in the United Kingdom 2023
First Published in the United States 2023
British Library Cataloguing in Publication Data:
A Catalogue record for this book is available from the British Library

Copyright © Kevin Mulryne 2023

ISBN 978-1-7392133-0-5

The right of Kevin Mulryne to be identified as the author of this work has been asserted by him in accordance with the Copyright, Designs and Patents Act 1988.

All rights reserved. No part of this publication may be reproduced, stored in a retrieval system or transmitted in any form or by any means, electronic, mechanical, photocopying, recording or otherwise, without prior permission in writing from Five Per Cent For Something Publishing.

Typesetting: Bob Carling
Cover Design: Iszi Lawrence
Cover Photography: Barry Plummer
Foreword: © copyright Oliver Wakeman, 2022

Contents

i. Executive Producers viii

ii. Foreword by Oliver Wakeman ix

iii. Introduction xiv

iv. The Context xviii

PART 1 – RECORDING THE ALBUM 1

   HE TURNED UP AT RECEPTION WITH A CROW ON HIS SHOULDER .2

   THE TIME DAVE AND HIS BROTHER JOINED YES . . . 22

PART 2 – THE INSTRUMENTS AND TECHNICALITIES . . . 33

   THE RAREST MUSICAL INSTRUMENT IN THE WORLD 34

   THE OTHER TORMATO KEYBOARDS 49

   STEVE HOWE'S GUITARS (AND A BIT ABOUT JON ANDERSON). 66

   THE 'FLARED TROUSERS' OF 70S DRUMS 78

   THE OTHER DRUMS 85

   CHRIS SQUIRE'S TECHNICAL SETUP. 95

   WHERE ARE THE MASTER TAPES? 105

PART 3 – THE SONGS 113
SONG REVIEWS. 114
THE LYRICS 133

PART 4 – ALBUMS AND SINGLES 143
TORMATO ARTWORK 144
PROMOTIONAL ALBUM COPIES. 165
SINGLES 169
VINYL ALBUM VERSIONS 179
DEEP INTO THE DEAD WAX 185
CASSETTES AND 8-TRACK CARTRIDGES . . . 193
CD VERSIONS. 202
JAPANESE VERSIONS 209
WHICH VERSION SOUNDS BEST? 217
SHEET MUSIC 228

PART 5 – PROMOTION AND RECEPTION 237
ADVERTISEMENTS AND PROMOTIONAL ITEMS. . . 238
ALBUM RECEPTION 249
PROMOTIONAL VIDEOS 254
SALES FIGURES. 262

PART 6 – TORMATO LIVE 265
THE TOURMATO TOUR, THE TEN TRUE SUMMERS TOUR AND BEYOND. 266
TORMATO OFFICIAL LIVE RELEASES AND COVERS. 271

TOUR BOOKS/PROGRAMMES	283
FAN RECOLLECTIONS	286
CONCERT MEMORABILIA	293
THE 'REVOLUTIONARY' ROTATING STAGE	295
WEMBLEY STADIUM RECORDING, 1978	302
PART 7 – EPILOGUE	307
EPILOGUE	308
ACKNOWLEDGEMENTS	312

Yes: The Tormato Story

i. Executive Producers

who made this book possible

Aaron Steelman
Ariel E. Copetti
Clifford Wayne Irwin Jr
Doug Curran
James McQuinn
John S Kuehne
John Thomson
Joseph Cottrell
Marc Troyan
Michael O'Connor
Paul Tomei
Preston Frazier
Rachel Hadaway
Ray Riethmeier
Robert C Nasir
Sean H. McCarthy
Simon Stopher

Thank you
Kevin Mulryne 2023

ii. Foreword by Oliver Wakeman

Oliver Wakeman was keyboardist for Yes 2008–11

Long before I became a member of Yes, I was often asked, "Which is your favourite Yes album?" to which I would always reply, "*Tormato*".

There would then follow a short, almost imperceptible silence followed by one of three responses:

"Really?"
  "I wasn't expecting you to say that!"

... or very occasionally from a fellow aficionado ...

"Wow, I love that album too."

Admittedly, more often than not, it's one of the first two responses.

So why do I seem to go against the standard wisdom of the majority of Yes fans? Well, this goes back really to my childhood and early teenage years when I started to discover 'real' music ...

My mum and dad split up when I was about five. Dad relocated to Switzerland and my mum, brother and I, along with our stepdad moved into a small semi-detached cottage where my mum kept a multitude of animals. Lots of chickens and ducks, a sheep they brought back from the pub one day, a horse and a duckling which lived in the downstairs bathroom.

By the time I got to my teenage years we had moved again and I now had my own room with a small record player. I had a few Adam and the Ants singles, but I didn't have any full-length albums. My mum went into the loft and brought down a few records which had survived the various moves and gave them to me.

I can still remember them to this day. There were four. *The Grand Illusion* by Styx, *Myths and Legends of King Arthur* by dad, *Tales From Topographic Oceans* and *Going for the One* by Yes.

The Grand Illusion has remained one of my favourite records ever and I often credit Styx as being one of my all-time favourite bands. I really loved *King Arthur* and was so pleased to be asked to perform it with dad at the O2 in 2016. *Going for the One* I really enjoyed (and in particular 'Turn of the Century').

However, *Tales* had a different effect on me. I didn't have my dad's well-publicised aversion to the record and I enjoyed listening to it, but I never 'got' *Tales* as a record like some YES fans do. But I have listened to it lots of times over the years and never felt the need to turn it into an ashtray as my father has threatened to do on multiple occasions.

By the time I reached twelve years-of-age, my dad was back living in the UK and my brother and I started to visit him again. He was living with his soon to be third wife, Nina, and they had bought and were converting an old nursing home. This was to become the family home where Adam and I could visit at weekends along with occasional visits *ii. Foreword by Oliver Wakeman*

from my Swiss brother, Ben. This was in addition to the new family they had with the arrival of Jemma and then Oscar a few years later.

Anyway, one of the items my dad had retained from his divorce with my mum was, oddly enough, a six-foot snooker table. It was put at the top of the house on the third floor where all of us visiting kids had bedrooms and so the small snooker room became our hanging out place.

On the windowsill was a record player and Dad had put loads of different records up there on the off chance we might listen to some of them.

I can distinctly remember, around the age of thirteen, saying to Nina, "What's the *Journey to the Centre of the Earth* record that I keep hearing about?" Nina looked at Dad and said, "Rick, how come your son hasn't heard your most famous record?" to which he said he didn't know but he'd sort out a few records for me to listen to.

So, by the next time I visited for a weekend, there by the side of the record player in the snooker room was a copy of *Journey* along with some of his more current records. But nestled behind them all was a copy of '*Tormato*'.

I listened to (and enjoyed) *Journey* but I found myself coming back to *Tormato* again and again. I loved playing snooker on my own, just practising for hours and would put on *Tormato* as my first choice more often than not. Over the years I got to know the record really well but then dad moved to the Isle of Man and so I didn't see him as often. Also, the copy of *Tormato* ended up moving there too. I moved down to Devon with my mum and while there discovered secondhand record stores and would spend hours and hours buying and discovering new bands (new to me anyway). I managed to find my own copy of *Tormato* which I played over and over again.

Sometimes it's really difficult to put your finger on why a record resonates with an individual so much. I mean, how often have you put on a record to play to someone close to you and excitedly watched for their reaction?

You wait to see their emotions start to show as an exciting solo approach or a wonderful melody is performed exquisitely.

You prepare for them to turn and say how they finally understand all the reasons why you are so enamoured with the record – only to end up disappointed as they look at you blankly and say, "Yeah, it's okay."

You desperately try to explain why they aren't getting it and they must listen to it again and really focus on this bit – but it's too late – the moment has gone. It doesn't make sense, but we all absorb music into our lives in different ways.

Which brings me full circle to the opening part of this narrative. Why is this my favourite Yes record? A question to which I'll honestly say, I don't know the answer.

Maybe it's the memory of being back as a part of my dad's life in the 80s. Maybe it was just there at the right time during my formative years of discovering my musical taste. But as I listen to it again now while writing this (on my latest, remastered version with extra tracks) I think the main reason is that I found it a very exciting record musically and I love the songs.

I loved the fact that the keyboards and guitars were going at it all the time, I loved the way the songs were of a more reasonable length but were crammed full of musical changes and ideas (remember this was the mid 80s and the charts was full of music which was very verse chorus led). Maybe it was Chris's great bass with Alan's energetic drumming driving the record forward. Maybe it was Jon's angelic voice as he sang 'Circus Of Heaven' and 'Madrigal'. This music seemed to break every mould of the conventional music that I was hearing on the chart shows and I loved it.

Every time I play it, I still get the same feelings of excitement and anticipation I used to get back then. I am transported back to that small room at the top of the house where I would spend long periods of time knocking snooker balls around listening to the record over and over. And that, I think, is the magic of music. It can transport us away from the here and now and take us to a point in our past where the discovery of the music began.

So, to finish with, here is one story from the more immediate past.

ii. Foreword by Oliver Wakeman

During my many years of being a musician, there is only one album sleeve image I have gone out of my way to re-create. During a tour with Barclay James Harvest (where Gordon Giltrap and I were the special guests) we were en route to a show in Tavistock, Devon. As we were passing close to Dartmoor, I convinced everyone that it would be a great idea to divert the tour bus and head up to *Yes Tor* so that we could recreate the band image from the back sleeve of *Tormato*.

We all took poses similar to the original sleeve and I positioned myself as Dad had done 34 years earlier with the same style of sunglasses. The photo was taken, emailed to me, and before that evening's show I spent some time in my hotel room with my laptop and Photoshop, matching the colours to the original sleeve's blue hue. I then searched the internet for a picture of a splattered tomato to place over the top.

And so how would I answer that question if I was asked it today, having been in the band and played music from almost every Yes album? (To avoid favouritism, I am going to omit the *From a Page* record which I was very involved in and is very close to my heart.)

Something must be pretty special to me – to be at the forefront of my mind – to be searching for a splattered tomato before preparing for a show. So my answer remains the same – *Tormato*.

iii. Introduction

In March 2018, I attended the Yes 50th Anniversary Fan Convention[1] in London. It was a fantastic event, organised by Dave Watkinson and Brian Neeson to celebrate half a century of the world's greatest progressive rock band.

One of my favourite parts of the weekend was the Yes bus tour. The route was developed by Dave with transport and guide supplied by London Rock Tours. We visited many important Yes sites including Advision and RAK studios where *Tormato* was recorded, as well as the original 'Yes houses' and the sites of La Chasse cafe (where Chris Squire met Jon Anderson) and The Marquee Club. The in-depth, expert commentary helped us to understand the geography and the historical context of the various sites. It was an unforgettable experience.

Two minibuses were required to accommodate Yes fans on the Sunday morning. I travelled with the redoubtable Geoff Bailie and others and we all enjoyed a highly appropriate soundtrack of Yes albums. I'm glad I took that particular minibus for a reason closely connected with one of the themes of this book. As the first notes of 'Future Times/Rejoice' sounded from the audio system, our guide asked us if it was okay to let *Tormato* continue playing. Apparently, his passengers on the previous day's tour had banned Yes' 1978 masterwork from the trip. It's a viewpoint I have encountered many times over the years. In fact, Yes themselves seemed to want to dissociate themselves from *Tormato* at one point. The record went out of print in the 1980s and was omitted from official discographies in the 1984 *90125*, the 1987 *Big Generator* and the 1991 *Union* tour books. Was this some kind of *Tormato*-washing?

---

1   https://tormatobook.com/50

iii. Introduction

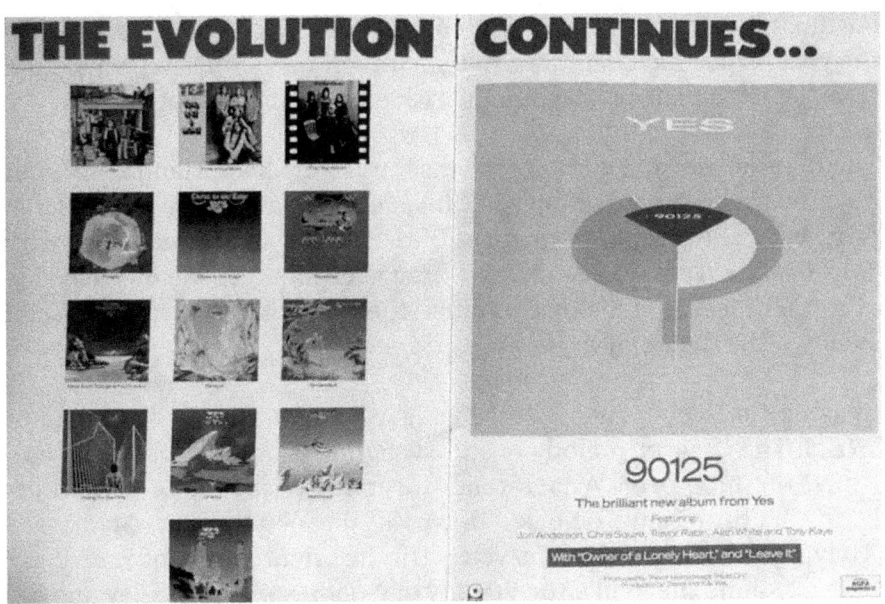

90125 Tour Book, note the lack of Tormato, author's collection

Union Tour Book, author's collection and Big Generator Tour Book, Eddie Lee from Forgotten-Yesterdays.com[1]

---

1   https://tormartobook.com/tourbook

Fortunately for us, *Tormato* has enjoyed somewhat of a resurgence in the years since *Big Generator*, but you might be wondering why I hold it so close to my heart, despite the risk of staining my clothes.

The first Yes music I ever heard was lent to me by a friend who went on to be the best man at my wedding, decades later. Back in 1983, the practice was to record vinyl discs onto cassette tapes and share with your friends. This is how I received two Yes albums, one on each side of a C90 cassette. Side one contained the recently released *90125* and side two the then only 5-year-old *Tormato*.

Imagine the scene. I'm 13 and I've just listened for the first time to *90125*. The 'Hearts' melody is still swashing around in my head, and I turn the tape over. What's this? Tormato? A spelling error? Track listing, 'Future Times Rejoice', 'Don't Kill the Whale', okay, 'Madrigal'? 'Arriving UFO'? 'Circus of Heaven'? 'On the Silent Wings of Freedom'? Doesn't sound much like the *90125* song names ... I press play and my jaw hits the ground. What on earth is this?

I had no frame of reference for what I heard – no *The Yes Album*, no *Close To The Edge*, no *Tales From Topographic Oceans*, no *Relayer*, no *Going For The One*, not even *Drama*. I did know, however, that I loved it from the first note to the last. It sparked my interest in Yes and I started to collect as many albums as I could, with little understanding of how *Tormato* fitted into the whole catalogue. In those pre–internet days, it was very difficult to find any information about the band. All I had to go on was sleeve notes. Try as I might, I couldn't find anything in the music press of the time beyond some *90125* information or in the local library. My friends were able to buy T-shirts and other memorabilia from bands like The Smiths, The Cure, The Sisters of Mercy and many others but I couldn't find a single item containing Roger Dean's Yes logo. I'm sure you can sympathise with my predicament. I knew Yes music was special, but I simply had to guess how it all fitted together.

So *Tormato* was my gateway album, my golden ticket to a world of sonic possibilities I hardly dared imagine might exist. Branching out through *Drama, Close To The Edge, Fragile* and *The Yes Album* followed by all the others was a true voyage of discovery, extended and widened by the appearance of *Big Generator, ABWH, Union(!), Talk* and everything up to and including *Mirror To The sky*. However, *Tormato* remains my favourite album of all time – the acorn (pip) from which my outrageously extensive but strangely restricted album, single and memorabilia collection has grown. I do have a small number of other albums, singles and miscellaneous Yes items but I seem to have accumulated no fewer than fifty-seven (at the last count) copies of *Tormato* in various formats and over a dozen different versions of 'Don't Kill The Whale' (not to mention several variations of the Canadian-only 'Release, Release' single – see chapter 14).

Nevertheless, it may still seem an odd choice to embark on writing a whole book about one album, particularly this one which is widely regarded as 'not great', 'mediocre' or 'sounds terrible'. Of course, *Tormato* has its supporters, some of whom are vocal on social media, but perhaps even they might struggle to imagine how an entire tome could be produced around this record.

Throughout this book, I will share with you a large number of surprising and fascinating topics, which shed light on the Yes story and not just on *Tormato*. In a sense, I'm using this album as a starting point, a way to pull together seemingly disparate aspects of the world's greatest progressive rock band.

I hope you enjoy joining me in this endeavour to spy into the music of Yes via the lens of *Tormato*.

Kevin Mulryne, March 2023

iv. The Context

In his essential Yes companion book, *Yes Perpetual Change*, David Watkinson says that the UK success of the 1977 album *Going For The One* and its single 'Wonderous Stories' was somewhat surprising during the ascendance of punk rock, led by The Sex Pistols (about whose Yes connection we will learn more in chapter 12).

After the months-long tour in support of the album, the band were reportedly tired and nervous about how to sustain their career in a world where a significant part of the musical press had written off old-fashioned stadium bands like Yes. On the other hand, as pointed out by Dan Hedges in his authorised biography of the band, Steve Howe had recently been voted best guitarist in the *Guitarist* magazine readers' poll. Yes had also once again won the best band spot in the international section of the *Melody Maker* readers' poll and Anderson, Wakeman and Squire had won their respective categories as well. Chris Welch, the *Melody Maker* journalist and author of *Close To The Edge The Story Of Yes*, points out that, despite actions like the cancellation of BBC Radio 1's progressive rock show, Yes fans appeared to be 'fighting a rearguard action' in supporting their heroes.

The final date on the *Going For The One* tour was on 6th December 1977 in Paris. When the band reconvened in mid-February 1978 to rehearse at Sound Associates in London's Bayswater, they didn't appear to be resting on their laurels or suffering from paralysis and uncertainty about the future. I asked Rick Wakeman if the band were exhausted and worried about starting work on *Tormato* and he said:

> "Not really. We were all still in our late twenties or early thirties and in good health, so we were always excited about starting a

new project. Rehearsals for the album went well, if I recall, and there was a good mood except for the fact that none of us could agree on a producer!"

This paints a different picture to the generally accepted one of a band at loggerheads and teetering on the brink of collapse.

In his authorised biography of Yes, Dan Hedges says they recorded enough rough material for about one and a half albums. One of the original ideas was to make the new album a two-part record, with the second part being released at the end of 1978 or in 1979. When I asked Rick Wakeman about the two-album plan, however, he responded with, "News to me," and his recollection of rehearsing lots of songs differed as well – "Also news to me." Hedges quotes Steve Howe who says the band needed a lot of material because of the process they then undertook to shape it into a complete album. Chris Squire was renowned for his attention to detail, despite always being the last to turn up at the studio. Yes hadn't abandoned their 'composition by committee' approach, with seemingly every individual note being discussed and analysed to make sure it was perfect for the song.

Dave Watkinson tells us that even the recording location was an issue. Some band members wanted to return to Switzerland (partly for tax reasons) and others wanted to work in London. London won that battle and Advision was chosen. After all, it was the site of great success in the past with *Time And A Word*, *The Yes Album*, *Fragile* and *Close To The Edge* all being recorded there. There was certainly a desire not simply to recreate past Yes glories, however. Many commentators point out that the process of making Yes music shorter, less complex and therefore more commercial and accessible to a changing music-buying public began with *Going For The One* and reached its 1970s peak with *Tormato*. This is clear on songs like 'Don't Kill The Whale', which could have been a big hit with its catchy, melodic approach and its topical, conservation angle. 'Arriving UFO' tries to latch onto the science fiction zeitgeist of the time with its weird sound effects and otherworldly tone. 'Release, Release' attempts to bring a little of the abandon of punk to the album and 'Onward' is, if nothing else, a beautiful, memorable love song. Clearly, eight songs is significantly more than the three on *Close To The Edge* and *Relayer* and four on the double-album *Tales From Topographic Oceans*, but these attempts to appeal to a perceived changing audience are balanced, I suggest, by some other aspects of the record. For example, consider the extravagant bass-driven mini-epic 'On The Silent Wings Of Freedom', the strange (but wonderful) soundscape of 'Madrigal' and the proliferation of fanciful and, at times, traditionally opaque lyrics, contributed by Jon Anderson – "Hot metal will abound the land ... As the form regards our blazing hand." 'Future Times' isn't exactly about cars and girls or the aggressive nihilism of punk and 'Circus Of Heaven' nestles slightly uncomfortably in its own, unique universe.

This perceived move by the band towards shorter, more accessible songs in order to fend off the threat from new bands and changing attitudes is now challenged by Rick Wakeman. As he said to me:

> "[It was] not deliberate, but that's just the way it worked out. Record companies were getting more concerned about a lack of radio play and so it's more than likely they said something!"

I also asked Rick about the idea that Yes were against the new musical movements and that punk was taking over and pushing them out. His response was:

> "I can't speak for the others but I never felt like that. It's often overlooked by media who say that I hated punk [but] I was the guy who championed The Tubes and got them signed to A&M records."

Efforts were certainly made by more than one member of the band to do things differently on *Tormato*. This ranged from their choice of instruments (and electronic devices) to relying on their own production skills rather than working with a separate producer – after all, this had worked well on *Going For The One* – but, in the end, who would be buying *Tormato*? Was it even possible to appeal to the people who were spending their money on bands like The Ruts and The Damned? *Tormato* did indeed sell very well and Yes did manage to reinvent themselves for the 1980s, but not for another five years and under very different circumstances. When *90125* came along in 1983, the band mounted a serious bid for chart success, albeit minus Wakeman and Howe.

iv. The Context

What follows is an analysis of how *Tormato* was created and whether this contributed to its success.

PART 1 – RECORDING THE ALBUM

1

HE TURNED UP AT RECEPTION WITH A CROW ON HIS SHOULDER

" ... it was a nightmare to make that record. It was ... almost impossible to make it."

Steve Howe, *Yes Music Podcast*, October 2022

It was a rare privilege to welcome Peter Woolliscroft onto the *Yes Music Podcast*. If you take a look at your copy of *Tormato*, you'll see his name listed as one of two assistant engineers. He refers to himself as a 'tape op' when he worked at Advision studios in London from 1978. Peter went on to work with many of the top musicians of the 1980s including Joy Division, Frank Zappa, Orchestral Manoeuvres In The Dark, Thin Lizzie, ABC, Kate Bush, Peter Gabriel, Elton John, Squeeze, Tina Turner, Jeff Beck, Def Leppard, Bill Wyman, Simon Phillips and Jeff Wayne.

Originally an apprentice engineer and then a BBC film recordist, Peter wrote many letters to different studios and Advision was the one to give him a chance. Starting at the bottom of the studio structure, he was there, " ... for the artists and the clients because they're the ones that are paying your salary."

Advision Studios today, photo by William Mulryne

Advision was a very popular, even legendary recording location in central London. The Fitzrovia studios could easily be seen as Yes' natural home as they had already recorded four classic albums there. After that they changed studios repeatedly – *Tales From Topographic Oceans* was rerecorded at Morgan Studios, London, *Relayer* was famously recorded at Chris Squire's home studio (but mixed at Advision) and *Going For The One* was put together at Mountain Studios in Montreux, Switzerland.

Yes: The Tormato Story

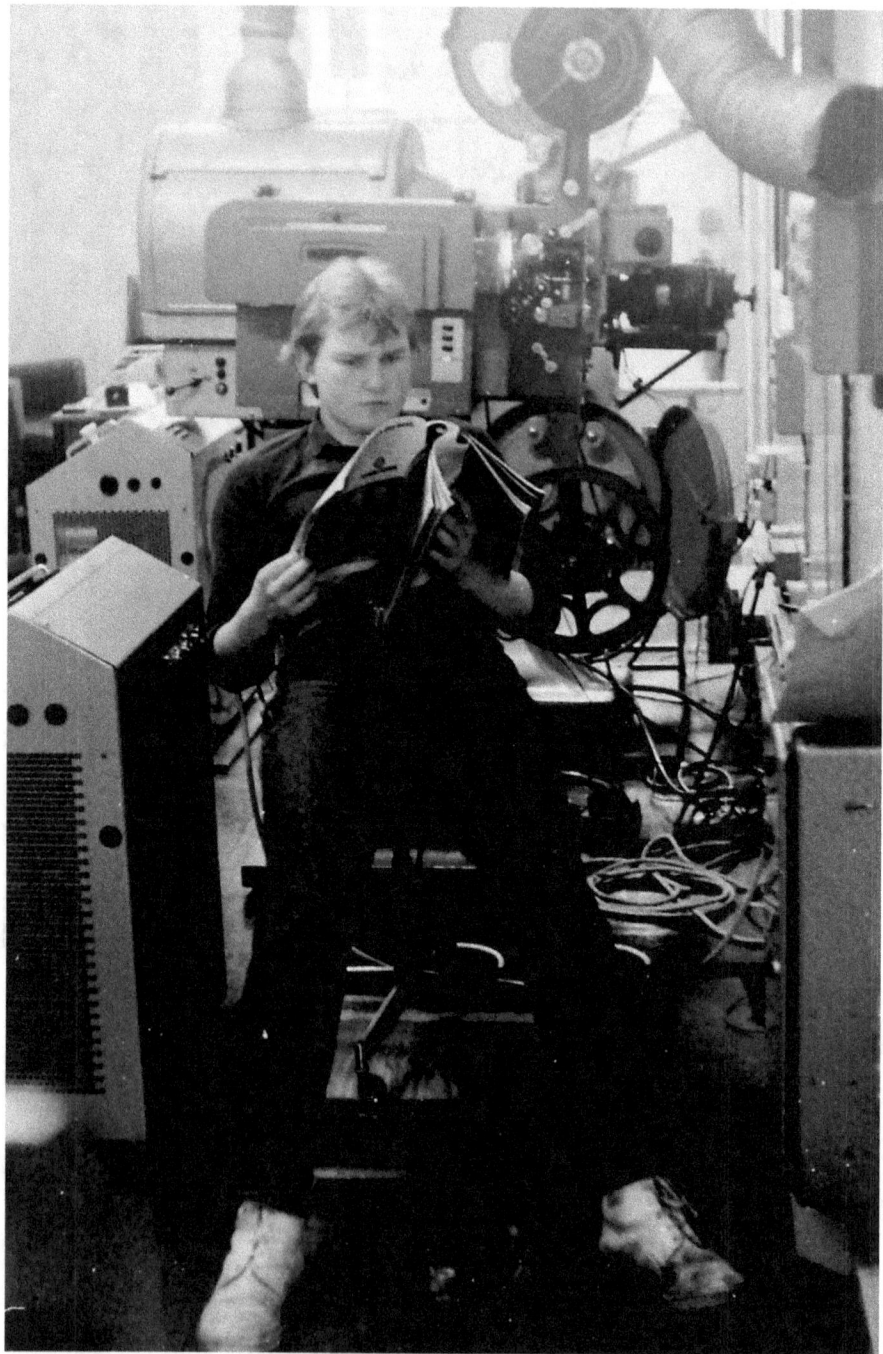

The young Kevin in the projection room at Advision, photo courtesy of Kevin Pyne

Advision had certain advantages over other recording studios in the area. For example, studios like RAK had wooden floors throughout whereas Advision had half wooden and half softer material. Advision's large Studio 1 also sported a huge cinema screen which made it perfect for recording sizeable ensembles such as orchestras to synchronise soundtracks to movies and TV programmes.

Kevin Pyne contacted me when he heard the *Yes Music Podcast* interview with Peter Woolliscroft, and sent me the fantastic photograph above. He remembers working with Peter and explained his own role at Advision:

> "That's me at 17 reading *Studio Magazine* in 1978, upstairs in the dubbing theatre in Advision, as a projectionist. That's where Martin Rushent [iconic 1970s and 80s producer] started. I loved hanging out with the engineers downstairs in studio 1 and the mix room, studio 2. Stayed late after work and asked so many questions. All the amazing engineers at Advision were so supportive to a young whipper snapper like me. I was so lucky to work through the amazing analogue days of multi-track through MIDI and into digital. As an interesting point, digital recording experiments started at Advision because of Feldon Audio, who were Advision's technical team, based in the basement. Sony digital recording onto video tape. 1's and 0's on video tape. Umatic if I remember. Andy Whetstone was the dubbing mixer when I joined Advision, and Roger Cameron was the other guy who interviewed me. Advision was an amazing place, at the top of its game when I was lucky enough to be there.
>
>   The dubbing theatre had another projection room upstairs that serviced Studio 1, for music to picture sessions, film scoring and commercials, as you could get a full orchestra in there. The academy wide screen can be seen now and again in the 'On Silent Wings' video. I remember once projecting sections of *Flash Gordon* when Queen were at Advision recording the soundtrack. The guys were down in Studio 1, sometimes playing to picture, while I was eagerly watching through a small projection porthole. Great memories."

According to Chris Squire, interviewed at Advision by Chris Welch for *Melody Maker*, the band had rehearsed plenty of material at Sound

Associates in Bayswater:

> years: "There was a time when tracks were laid down to evolve upon, and it was a case of music growing out of music. But now, on this album, we've got a pretty clear idea of the end product to start with. We rehearsed over 25 songs before we started to record. And we're hoping to record as much of that material as possible."
>
> *Chris Welch article, Melody Maker, 6th May 1978*

In fact, as mentioned above, the plan was to release *Tormato* as a two-part album, with the second record coming at the end of 1978 or in 1979. Squire again:

> "We have so much material there may well be a second album at the end of the year. There is nothing
>
> *Chris Welch article, Melody Maker, 6th May 1978*

After three months at Advision, the band had run out of time and had to move everything to RAK Studios to finish the overdubs and additional tracks.

Yes came through the door only about a month and a half into Peter's time at Advision and, as a huge Yes fan himself, it was a profound experience. He refers to the way the band played in the studio as 'clean' and 'tight' and he ranks their professional attitude to studio work alongside Frank Zappa and Kate Bush, both known for their perfectionist natures. This is more than could be said about his colleagues on the production side at Advision, however. He says that people tended to be employed on their personalities rather than any knowledge of the recording process and if you wanted to work there you had to be able to, " ... fit in and take the knocks of everyday life in the studio – have the stamina for doing very, very long hours." It was essential to give whoever you were working for the impression that theirs was the only project that mattered.

Studio	Address & Tel.	Tracks & Price	Demos Cut?	Capacity	Comments
Acorn	Church Road, Stonesfield, Oxon. Tel. 099-389-444	2, 4, and 16 (all £12 per hour)	Yes	7	Small but willing; "endless free tea, coffee, and coke"; a mobile unit.
Advision	23 Gosfield St., London W1 Tel. 01-580-5707	16, 24; (£30 per hour)	No	60	Ultra-modern technology, compu-mixing and a wealth of comforts.

A list of studios in the UK from International Musician and Recording World, October 1978, author's collection

The Yes project got off to what Peter calls a 'rocky start' and not in a good way. The late Nigel Luby was Yes' live sound engineer and the week before the band were scheduled to come in and start recording,

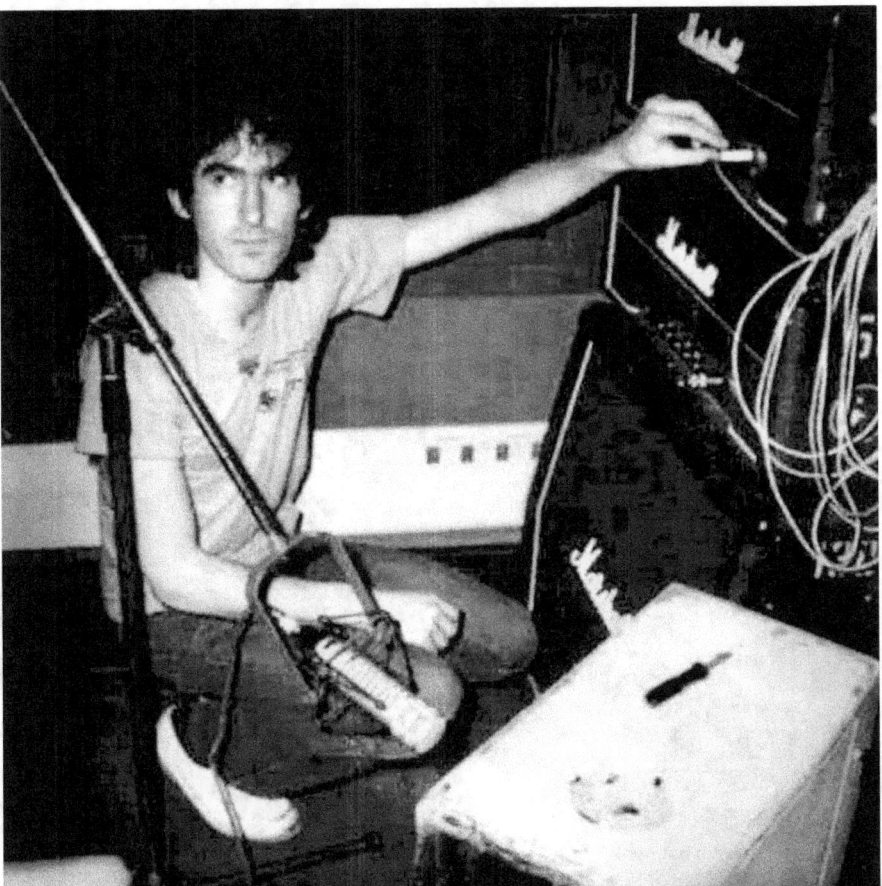

Nigel Luby (RIP) in Advision Studios at work on Tormato, photo courtesy of Jan Halley via Jon Dee

they arrived at Studio 2 with Nigel and, " ... did a rough mix of a live take of 'Parallels'," from *Going For The One*. The idea was that *Tormato* would be recorded as a live album at Advision, complete with a mock stage constructed in Studio 1. Peter was to assist Nigel in engineering the recording because he knew the studio well.

Arriving back at the studio on Monday morning, Peter found that Yes' roadies had been there over the weekend and set up the two thousand five hundred square foot Studio 1. They had literally nailed the drums to the floor – in completely the wrong place, under the huge cinema screen. Next to the drums were six Sunn bass cabinets set up for Chris Squire and it was all somewhat chaotic. After it became clear the band were also refusing to use headphones for the recording, Peter informed everyone that the configuration was just not going to work. At this point he sneaked off and collared Geoff Young, imploring him to come and help. Young is another name mentioned on the sleeve notes, a colleague of Peter's who had worked at Advision for several years.

Having been assistant engineer on *Fragile*, also recorded at Advision, and therefore knowing the band, Geoff was able to show them the error of their ways and convince them the setup needed to be changed.

Rick Wakeman with Geoff Young in Studio 1 at Advision, photo courtesy of Chris Hoskins

Had they wanted to record the album 'live', Advision wasn't going to work for them. Fortunately, it was agreed that the instruments would have to be set up more like they would be for a standard studio album. Alan's drums were moved to the 'live' area, five of Chris' bass cabinets were removed completely and the remaining one was put in a booth for sound separation. Jon was given a pair of headphones with a separate feed from the mixing console so he would at least have control over what was coming into his own 'cans'. Rick set up his keyboards in the corner and didn't care where he was positioned as long as he was able to turn up, play and then go home.

The arrangement eventually agreed on was: Alan's kit set up on the wooden floor and screened off, Steve tucked away in the live booth, Rick's huge keyboard setup in the main studio, Jon sitting on a high chair in front of the control room 'conducting things' while playing the cuatro (see chapter 5), and Chris in his sound booth with the single bass cabinet. This is the setup seen in the 'On The Silent Wings Of Freedom' behind-the-scenes video.

Jon Anderson, Steve Howe and his guitar technician, Claude Johnson-Taylor in front of the cinema screen in Studio 1 at Advision, photo courtesy of Chris Hoskins, who explains below how he took these photos:

"As a teenager I was a huge Yes fan and I was attending college in London one day when I spotted Steve Howe getting out of his Bristol car and going into the Advision Studio. The next day I was hanging around outside with my camera when Rick Wakeman walked up. I asked if it might be possible to come and say hi and take a few photos. He couldn't have been nicer and I got to go into the studio for about 20 mins. The whole band were there and allowed me to take some pictures, the next day I popped back with prints for them and also got some copies signed for myself. Sadly a few years later I offered the signed copies to be auctioned at a Yes fan club convention and the organiser sold them and kept the money! Recently whilst clearing the loft I found my original negatives; many are not great it was very low lighting in the studio and I expect my hands were shaking at the time."

In some sources, Eddy Offord is credited with early engineering or production work on *Tormato* so I asked Peter at this point whether Eddy was present at the Advision sessions. Peter's response was enlightening:

" ... there's a lot of stories about it, but as far as I know ... he was never going to do this album. He tried to do some location recording with them when they were rehearsing songs, but he never arrived [at Advision] and he was never expected. I only saw Eddy once, about a month or so later when he turned up at reception with a ... crow on his shoulder. Reception said, "I've got this guy out here. He's [got] this bird on his shoulder. His name's Eddy." I went, "Okay". So he just came and looked round and left. That's the only time I ever saw him."

I also asked Rick Wakeman if he remembered Eddy doing any recording at the rehearsals and he responded, "Not that I recall."

Peter says the band were well-rehearsed before arriving at Advision and perhaps that was necessary because, "We turned up at 10 o'clock. Alan would drift in, Jon would drift in, Fish [Chris] would turn up at about half past two and then Jon had to go home at eight o'clock to read his son a bedtime story. So, we only had a very narrow window to get the backing tracks down ... after six, seven o'clock, Rick would stay behind and do all the keyboard overdubs." Advision cost £70/hr at this time and Yes had it booked out 24hrs a day. Clearly, the time was somewhat underused. However, it did give Peter the opportunity to work late into the evening with the hilarious Rick Wakeman who told me he had, "rented a small place in London," because he was living in Switzerland at the time. Peter recalls Rick's Birotrons (see chapter 3) kept sticking and breaking down, making comical descending, whining noises. At these points Rick would shout for his personal roadie, Toby, who was invariably in the pub, so Peter had to go and get him. As expected, Rick kept everyone amused with what amounted to a stand-up comedy routine and Peter has fond memories of Rick recording his famous Denis Healey improvised routine over the top of the song 'Money'. It was eventually released on the expanded and remastered *Tormato* CD in 2004.

All the band played on the backing tracks recorded in Studio 1 with Jon's vocals there mostly as a guide. There were quite a few takes – for example, Peter recalls they did 32 takes of 'On The Silent Wings Of Freedom'. The tape was running at the standard thirty inches per second which meant about three takes on one reel, if he was lucky. Peter says he was 'drowning in reels of tape'. This was exacerbated when, for example, Chris Squire would come along and ask Peter to join take fourteen to take thirty-two so he had to do a multi-track edit as the basis for the band to do all the overdubs on.

I mentioned to Peter that when we were talking to Brian Kehew about the *Tormato* master tapes (see chapter 9), he claimed that the main reason the mixes sound 'muddy' is because there was a mistake over the use of Dolby noise reduction. The story goes that Eddy Offord used Dolby on the initial recordings which later engineers didn't realise and, when it was switched back on, the masters sounded much better. Now, after speaking to Peter, we know that Eddy wasn't involved in any of the recording at Advision so that part of the story cannot be correct. Also, Peter points out above that the Advision recording was done at thirty inches per second with no Dolby. He was in charge of the tapes so surely there can be no misunderstanding. Advision never used Dolby at this tape speed because there was no need to – the good signal to noise ratio made it unnecessary. This means that any mistake over the use of Dolby can only have happened in the RAK sessions where overdubs and mixing were done. Peter says he was disappointed when he heard how the album sounded after the RAK mixing and he's not sure what happened. He does remember Steve Howe discussing the way his guitars and Rick Wakeman's Polymoog didn't 'gel' together and that they would have to sort it out when mixing. After three months, the band ran out of time at Advision and when they moved to RAK, Peter was not involved. Mixing and overdubs were handled by Nigel Luby and Geoff Young who had been there throughout the sessions at Advision, so Peter can't see why there might have been a problem at that stage either. It was perhaps an issue of not getting proper monitoring in the control room at RAK because at Advision the recordings, " ... blew your trousers off when you did playback." So, unfortunately, we didn't reach a definitive answer on the 'muddy' sound of the album but at least we confirmed that the Dolby issue couldn't have happened at Advision 'on Peter's watch'.

Squire, Howe, White and Anderson compare notes, photo by Barry Plummer

Next, we went on to talk about some of the instruments and how they were recorded at Advision, beginning with Chris Squire. I asked Peter whether Squire had arrived at the session with everything sorted out or whether he worked on his sound in the studio. Peter assured us that Squire had it all worked out in advance. In chapter 8, Miguel Falcão mentions Chris' use of the Eventide H910 Harmonizer unit, but Peter says it was actually the Eventide 1745M Digital Delay. These sorts of

HE TURNED UP AT RECEPTION WITH A CROW ON HIS SHOULDER

The site of Feldon Audio (now partly a nail bar) as it appears today from My Own TOURMATO in 2023, photo by William Mulryne

contradictory details are what makes all the detective work fun! Peter points out that the reasons they used the 1745M included better shift registers, a toggle switch to increment delay by milliseconds and a four-digit readout rather than three digits on the H910. Chris specified this device before the Advision sessions – however, see chapter 8 for photographic evidence of an Eventide 1745A Digital Delay in use rather than the 1745M. As the studio was connected to the Feldon Audio hire company, who were based in Gt. Portland Street literally just round the corner, they were able to provide the machine for Squire. In fact, Peter told me that technical staff from Feldon Audio worked in the basement of Advision Studios. They set the unit up to 0.997 with a 40-millisecond delay and managed to record clean bass onto one track and harmonized bass onto another, in stereo.

This was an entirely new technique which Peter was to use again a couple of years later when he was producing an album for another band – but with less success because of the phasing issues when cutting stereo bass to vinyl. This is perhaps another reason why the Tormato record sounds less punchy than it should do, suggests Peter. When being mastered, stereo bass has to be 'closed in' in order to cut the record as loudly as possible. As my co-host Mark Anthony K says, the received wisdom is always to place bass frequencies of 300Hertz or lower in mono, not stereo, precisely because of the phasing issues which can reduce or even eliminate the sound. It's a problem of physics, whereby sound waves can cancel each other out if they are out of phase. This only becomes apparent when the sound sources are joined up or 'summed' in the process of mastering to vinyl. The damaging effect can be impossible to hear when you are listening to the stereo mix from a recording console. In the late 70s, solving this problem was mainly a case of trialling and testing different approaches. Another example of this is the fact that, despite having lots of fantastic (but by then rather old-fashioned) valve microphones, the only one used in the recording of *Tormato* was a Neumann M49, which was great for capturing Squire's bass. The trend at the time was to use the newer, transistor microphones (note the Electro-Voice RE20 in the photo of Jon Anderson below), despite the arguably superior sound quality provided by the older equipment.

We were also interested in the approach to recording Alan White's hybrid drum kit. Sometimes there is a 'minimalist' setup of only two or

HE TURNED UP AT RECEPTION WITH A CROW ON HIS SHOULDER

Jon Anderson on his habitual chair in Advision Studio 1 for the Tormato sessions (note the standard guitar in use and the cuatro behind – see chapter 5), photo by Barry Plummer

three microphones to cover the whole set, but Peter says that the approach here was to use separate mics for bass drum, snare and hi-hats, all on their own tracks. Then there was a stereo tom track and stereo overhead setup as well as a stereo ambience approach with a Neumann U47 microphone against the control room window and (Peter thinks) another in the ceiling. This extensive setup was also enlarged further for particular songs like 'Future Times' where a shotgun mic was positioned pointing down over Alan's head. Shotgun at his head – now there's an incentive to keep in time!

When we asked Peter about the rumour that Jon Anderson had played along to every song on a guitar and then decided that he needed it removed from the mix, Peter confirmed that they did indeed have to do that. "As soon as we possibly could, it would go." Peter describes Jon's guitar as some sort of a 'multi-stringed instrument' which fits in well with the idea it was the Spanish cuatro (see Chapter 5). This instrument is credited on 'Future Times' (not 'Rejoice'), 'Arriving UFO' and 'On The Silent Wings Of Freedom' so, clearly, there is some strumming left in the mix on those songs. Studio outtakes can also be heard which feature a lot more of Anderson's guitar work, which personally I don't find that off-putting. It tends to fill out the texture pleasingly.[1]

Jon's use of the cuatro didn't go unnoticed by the rest of the band and was, perhaps, a bone of contention between him and Chris Squire at times. Peter recalls that on more than one occasion manager Brian Lane needed to send the musicians to have a break because of personality clashes. Peter overheard Chris saying to Jon, "All you do is sit there with that f***ing guitar, singing and you're never happy."

On the theme of (lack of) band harmony, Peter also confirmed the impression a lot of fans and critics have had over the years that there were 'too many hands on the faders' during the recording process at Advision. The band came into the control room a lot, rather like (as suggested by Peter) the old story of Jack Bruce appearing at the mixing desk with a ten inch bowie knife, setting it on top of the board and saying, "Now, let's discuss the level of the bass." I don't think Chris Squire – or any of the others – wielded knives during the recording of *Tormato* to get their points across. However, quite a few hands were actually

---

[1] https://tormatobook.com/outtakes

Jon Anderson "...strumming that f***ing guitar, singing..." in front of the control room in Studio 1 at Advision, from the 'On The Silent Wings Of Freedom' behind-the-scenes video

needed in those days to operate the mixing desk, as there were no programmable computer tools to help. The job of the producer is to find ways to convince the band what's best for the music. Of course, in this situation, the producer and the band were one and the same. Despite this, Peter recalls that all the Yes musicians were good to work with, as long as you kept up with what they wanted, and the atmosphere was only ever spoiled by friction between Chris and Jon. As Brian Lane put it, "[So] they could have a barney about whatever they chose to argue about that day."

To appease the gear nerds, such as my podcast co-host Mark Anthony K, we asked Peter to describe the equipment which was used to record the band at Advision. The tape machine was a Studer A80 24-track which was quite new. The previous machines had been 3M ones, used most recently to record Jeff Wayne's *War of the Worlds* album and they were pretty worn out (surely not exclusively through the rigours of the *War of the Worlds*?) A new machine had to be bought in time for *Tormato* to be recorded. The console in use at the time at RAK was an

API but the mixing desk at Advision was a rather obscure Quad Eight from the US. Recently resurrected, the original Quad Eight company was in operation from the 1960s to the late 80s. Peter believes Advision may have made this unusual purchase because they thought quadraphonic recording would take off and the Quad Eight had four output groups so was capable of mixing quadraphonic sound. According to Peter, this functionality was never used.

Alan White and Nigel Luby in Advision Studio 1 control room, photo courtesy of Chris Hoskins

As can be seen in the still from the 'Silent Wings' video opposite, Peter recalls Steve Howe having a large collection of guitars, lined up in their cases below Studio 1's projection screen. Each one of these guitars had to be tuned up and ready to go each session so that Steve could choose the one he wanted to use, as the mood took him. Peter also says that Steve was keen on the concept of biorhythms, now classed as pseudoscience, and used his biorhythm calculator to inform what he should do.

Steve's Fender amps were put in a live booth with the door slightly ajar so he could still hear the guitar sound, but it didn't interfere too much with the drum mics by 'bleeding' through to those. The same was true of Squire's bass amp. Peter points out that, as we might have imagined,

Steve Howe's guitar case collection, from the behind-the-scenes video for 'On The Silent Wings of Freedom'

Chris wasn't pleased about his bass amp being put in a dead booth. As mentioned above, the original idea was that his six bass cabinets were to be set up in a 'live' format in the studio, so this restriction was approaching the final straw. Peter remembers being in the booth setting things up when Chris struck a chord and, " ... nearly ended my career." The sound level was *fairly* high in the booth, as you can imagine. "Oh, sorry," said Chris. However, as we know, this incident didn't finish Peter off and the band completed the three-month stint at Advision before having to decamp to RAK. It's almost unheard of nowadays to spend three months in a central London studio working on a single record, but the perfectionist nature of Yes led to more and more time being eaten up. *Going For The One* had taken seven months to record, after all.

Peter might have gone with the band and Geoff Young to RAK and Jon Anderson was keen that he did, mainly because he was the only one who knew where all the takes were. However, his employers at Advision couldn't justify losing a tape-op to another studio while still paying his

Yes: The Tormato Story

Rick Wakeman in a (rare?) period of productivity – note the two Birotrons on his left, photo by Barry Plummer

wages (even if they were only 48p an hour). None of the songs which appear on the Expanded & Remastered version of *Tormato* were recorded at Advision apart from 'Money', according to Peter.

At the end of our conversation, we asked Peter whether he thought the project would have gone better with a really good producer involved. He has no hesitation in confirming this. He feels there was too much politics and, "the more people involved meant even more politics." The band wanted Nigel Luby and Geoff Young was actively involved, but really only in order to 'hold Nigel's hand' because he was principally a live sound man. In the end, according to Peter, it's only going to work if you have somebody who knows the board, is in control and says, "This is what we are going to do."

I mentioned to Rick Wakeman that Steve Howe told me *Tormato* was almost impossible to record and Rick agreed:

> "Steve is right ... we all disagreed about the production for a start. I thought and still do that it was the worst mixed Yes album ever which is a shame as there are some good tracks ... but

[it] really needs looking at again!"

Here is Peter's final word on recording Tormato as he looks back from today:

> "It was fun. Working with Rick was hilarious ... he would entertain us for hours ... we would be on the floor in stitches and say, 'Rick, for Christ's sake, let's just do something, get something down so we can go home'. Those days are gone, man. Everything now is on a laptop or in your bedroom. It's all pre-programmed, so I miss those days. And in fact, it was probably one of the reasons I left the industry ... I lost that vibe in the studio ... [that] you can't beat, really."

2

THE TIME DAVE AND HIS BROTHER JOINED YES

Dave Watkinson, author of the book *Yes Perpetual Change*, is also one of our favourite guests on the *Yes Music Podcast*. Back in May 2020, Dave came along to tell us the story of the time he and his brother found themselves in the studio with Yes while they were putting the finishing touches to *Tormato*. It's a great tale.

Dave had seen Yes on the *Going For The One Tour* in 1977 and remembers spotting an article about the band. He wondered why these journalists, who weren't that bothered about Yes, always got to meet the band while the real fans, like him, never did. As a self-confessed cheeky, Northern nineteen-year-old, he decided that he would just make it happen. So, he wrote a letter to Yes' management office in London and was amazed when an envelope dropped through his Lancashire letter box, about ten days later. Opening it up, Dave's amazement grew even further as he had been invited to join the band in their recording studio! Needless to say, he framed that letter and still has it at home, more than four decades later.

Dave and his brother, a keen studio technology enthusiast, set off on the long trip to London turning up early at RAK studios near Regent's Park. They were greeted by iconic producer Mickie Most, who had founded RAK Recording Studio in 1976, not long before Dave's visit. Most was perhaps best known for his work with artists such as the Animals, Herman's Hermits, Donovan (who supported Yes on the *Going For The One Tour*), Lulu, Suzi Quatro, Hot Chocolate and the Jeff Beck Group. Despite this, he made the brothers a cup of tea and then left, saying the band weren't due to arrive for another two and half hours, so Dave and his brother could just hang around the studio and control room.

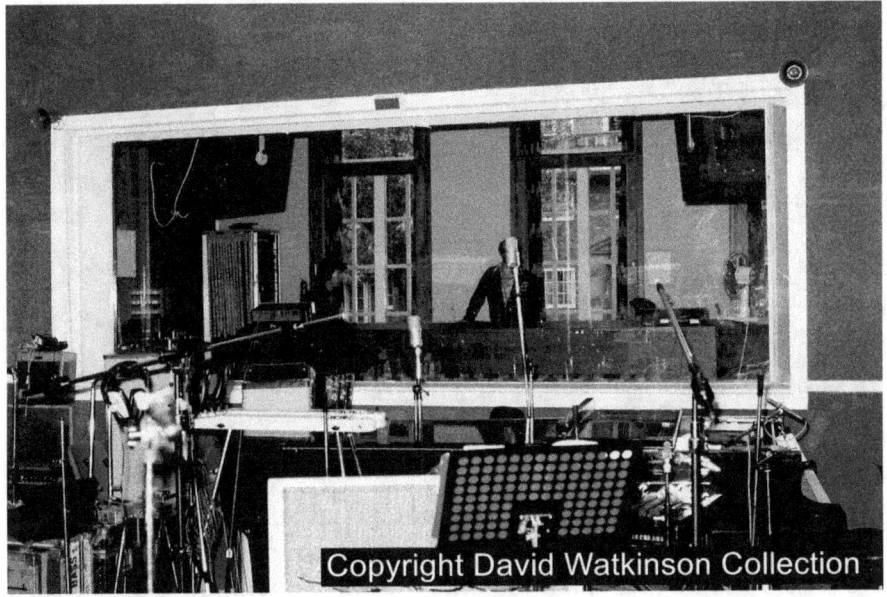

A view of the control room from the studio at RAK, photo courtesy of David Watkinson

This was quite a surprise for Dave. He recalls assuming that they would just get to say hello to the band and be shuffled off home, not be able to walk around unattended. He says he tried out " ... the kettle drums ... strummed a few guitars in the booth ... did a run up and down the keyboards ... [played] a few bass pedals ... and [Alan White's] kit."

"I basically was in Yes for a very short period of time as I wandered around, but I'm just not credited."

After enjoying tinkering with the musical instruments for some time, the band still hadn't arrived, so Dave and his brother ventured into the control room and made themselves at home. They spotted master tapes marked with working titles of *Tormato* songs and literally put their feet up on the control desk (see photographic evidence below).

Dave 'in control', photo courtesy of David Watkinson

Eventually, Claude Johnson-Taylor, guitar roadie and equipment manager for Yes and Steve Howe, arrived with a couple of young men and went into the mixing room. Looking out of the window to see which Yes man would arrive first, Dave spotted a little Honda Civic pulling up outside the studio. Out of it emerged Jon Anderson. Dave describes Jon as, "lovely, gentle and open", as he greeted the brothers, but, despite this, Dave was, "nervous as hell," to meet one of his heroes, someone he had only seen on record covers and in the distance on stage previously.

Chris Squire and Steve Howe arrived almost at the same time, the former in his habitual Rolls Royce and the latter in an exclusive Bristol car. Finally, Alan White turned up and the band was complete as Rick Wakeman was in Switzerland by this time (according to the other band members). In fact, Dave told me later that Rick wasn't there because he had suffered a heart attack and was in Switzerland for treatment. Dave

THE TIME DAVE AND HIS BROTHER JOINED YES

The Yes cars outside RAK, photo courtesy of David Watkinson

describes everyone as 'chilled' and then they got to work.

Jon went into the vocal booth and started to work on the song 'Money', which was only to be released in 1991 on the *YesYears* collection.

> "My brother and I watched Jon singing the song 'Money' in the sound booth. We both recall him moving onto his tip toes for the high notes. Also, the song wasn't released because Abba and Pink Floyd were singing about it too, which was discussed in the studio."

Dave recalls how surreal the whole experience was. At one point, he found himself sitting in the control room next to Chris and Steve dressed, "interestingly and extravagantly, having a cigarette," and they all listened to a number of versions of 'Money'. Next was a run through of 'Don't Kill The Whale' including, according to Dave, a long bass introduction which isn't there on the finished version. He assumes it is languishing on a piece of tape somewhere.

I asked Dave about the photos of the studio and the fact that the instruments look almost crammed in, not in defined areas. He said that

Dave with Jon Anderson at RAK, photo courtesy of David Watkinson

it did indeed seem to be like that. There were about five guitars for Steve in a line, another for Jon in a booth, lots of keyboards and Alan's multicoloured drum kit including the weird fluted North Toms (see chapter 6). It's important to remember, however, that the band had already completed most of the main recording at Advision and had moved to RAK to mix, add additional parts and record songs which weren't included on the record such as 'Abilene' and 'Money'. It seems the band had brought everything including the kitchen sink into the smaller RAK studio, just in case it was needed.

One of the photos shows Alan White playing a huge, triple-tiered (three-manual) keyboard, complete with pedals. This was the relatively new Yamaha GX-1. According to Gerard Bassols in his book *The Musical Instruments of Progressive Rock*, this instrument cost $60,000

Jon Anderson's area at RAK, note the sound baffles which are still in the studio today, photo courtesy of David Watkinson

at the time. Nigel Luby seems to be flicking some switches on the console and it looks like fun, personal experimentation with the new-fangled kit. In fact, this was one of only two GX-1s in the country at the time, the other belonging to Keith Emerson of ELP. He used it to record the band's iconic version of American composer Aaron Copland's 'Fanfare For The Common Man'.

Dave feels that one of the most important aspects of his visit was the opportunity to take photos of Yes in the studio. As he points out, there aren't many visual records of the band working in the studio on *Tormato* at RAK. One of the slightly odd items he spotted in the control room was a photo of the Queen, roughly taped to the wall. Across it, someone had added a newspaper headline, "Good Old Chris," and written, "Never Mind The Bo***cks, Here's Yes," (or something simi-

Chris Squire and Steve Howe taking a break at RAK, photo courtesy of David Watkinson

lar). This was a reference to certain sections of the music press' attitude towards 'old fashioned' rock bands, a few years after Punk had reared its head. Apparently, Yes also had fun with stickers on the seats and walls of the studio.

Finally, I asked Dave about how he thought the band were reacting to the album they were finishing off. He said they seemed pleased with it, and it led to some of the greatest concerts in the band's history, starting very shortly after Dave's trip of a lifetime.

Dave and I visited RAK Studios on *My Own TOURMATO* in January 2023. Dave was astonished how little the building has changed in forty-five years. We walked through the glass double doors, recognising them from the 'On The Silent Wings Of Freedom' video (see chapter 24) and

Dave among the kit at RAK, photo courtesy of David Watkinson

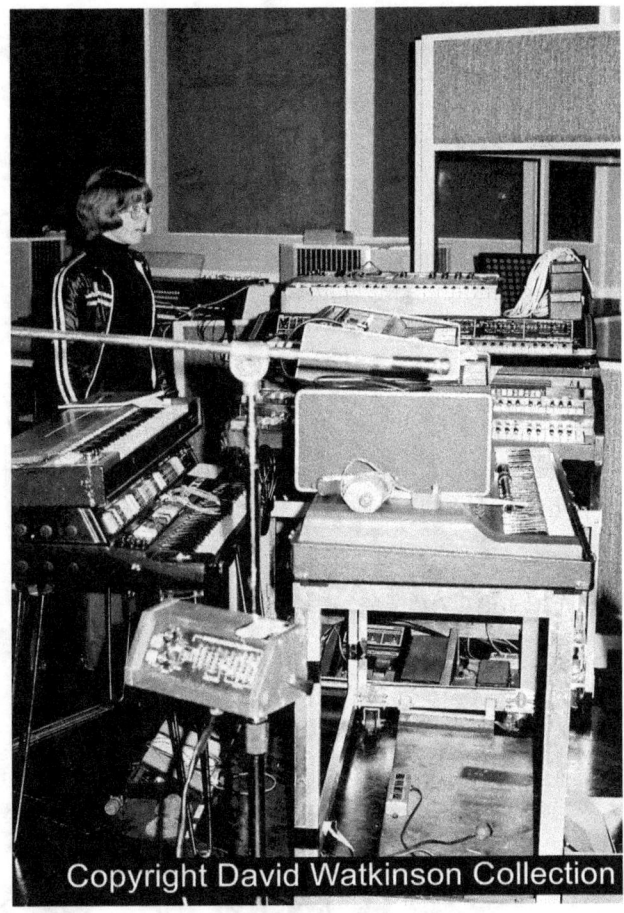

passed numerous recording awards on the walls. After seeing Dave's photos from 1978, the two friendly receptionists confirmed that the same mixing console and the same sound baffles were still in use in the studio where Yes recorded *Tormato*.

Nigel Luby and Alan White playing with the new Yamaha GX-1 at RAK, photo courtesy of David Watkinson

Photograph of the Queen, adorned in comical style by the band, detail from photo courtesy of David Watkinson

Yes: The Tormato Story

Dave returns to the scene forty-five years after he first visited RAK with his brother in 1978, note the window on the right, behind which is the console used by Yes to record Tormato, photo by William Mulryne

PART 2 – THE INSTRUMENTS AND TECHNICALITIES

3

THE RAREST MUSICAL INSTRUMENT IN THE WORLD

One of the most enjoyable aspects of running the *Yes Music Podcast* is being able to ask experts questions to which only they know the answers. One of these remarkable interviews was with Chris Dale. He came along to tell us the story of Yes' involvement with the rarest musical instrument in the world – the fabled Birotron. As we will discover, Rick Wakeman had a vested interest in using the ill-fated synthesizer on *Tormato* and advertising the fact that he did so.

The Prototype Birotron B90, photo courtesy of Streetly Electronics

This keyboard was intended to be a successor to one of the most important of all prog instruments, the Mellotron. That keyboard had been responsible for a lot of the strings, choirs, flutes and other sounds heard in Yes music up to *Tormato* (and was used later as well). No other organ or synthesizer of the time could reproduce quite the same orchestral sounds and add breadth and depth to all kinds of music, especially progressive rock, where grand musical statements were being sought.

The inventor who gave his name, in part, to the new instrument, Dave Biro, set about creating it because he couldn't afford a Mellotron. He built a basic, wooden frame and then used nineteen, independent, 8-Track players, containing four sounds each, connected to a keyboard. It was a very rough instrument, but Dave believed it had potential because it fixed one of the most troublesome aspects of the Mellotron – the tape running out.

The Birotron and the Mellotron both use loops of tape to produce sounds but, as Chris explained, "When you press a key on a Mellotron, a pinch roller grabs the tape and moves it forward, and you're hearing that sound – and then you take your finger off the key and a slinky spring pulls the tape back." The physical length of the tape means that the Mellotron is only capable of playing a particular sound for a maximum of eight seconds, after which it stops. This limitation of the Mellotron can be heard clearly in a lot of popular music of the 60s and 70s. Perhaps the most famous is the flute sound on The Beatles' Strawberry Fields Forever. Take another listen to that song and you'll be able to spot the Mellotron's mechanics creating restrictions in how it could be written. There is even an excellent YouTube demonstration by Marco Hoogland[2] to watch on this topic. This problem was eliminated by the Birotron, through its use of 8-Track tapes.

I have nine *Tormato* 8-Track tapes in my collection and the ones used in the Birotron were almost identical. The hard, plastic casing was the same as standard 8-Track cassettes and the tape inside is a continuous loop which plays round and round indefinitely, if you hold the key down. Incidentally, some of the prototype instruments had an unintended 'feature' which could have supported the '11th Illusion' concept

---

2   https://tormatobook.com/mellotron

the band were trying to develop at the time of *Tormato*. Chris explains:

> "Depending on how the delay controls are set, some of them can do a magic trick by delaying the notes or chords you play. You won't hear these notes or chords as you play though, because they play 'in the future'."

According to the original Birotronics CEO, Peter Robinson, Rick Wakeman used this 'feature' a few times on the *Tourmato* tour. He would play 'silent parts' made up of notes and chords and walk away. The Birotron would then play the parts back in the same sequence with Rick off the stage, to the amazement of the crowd.

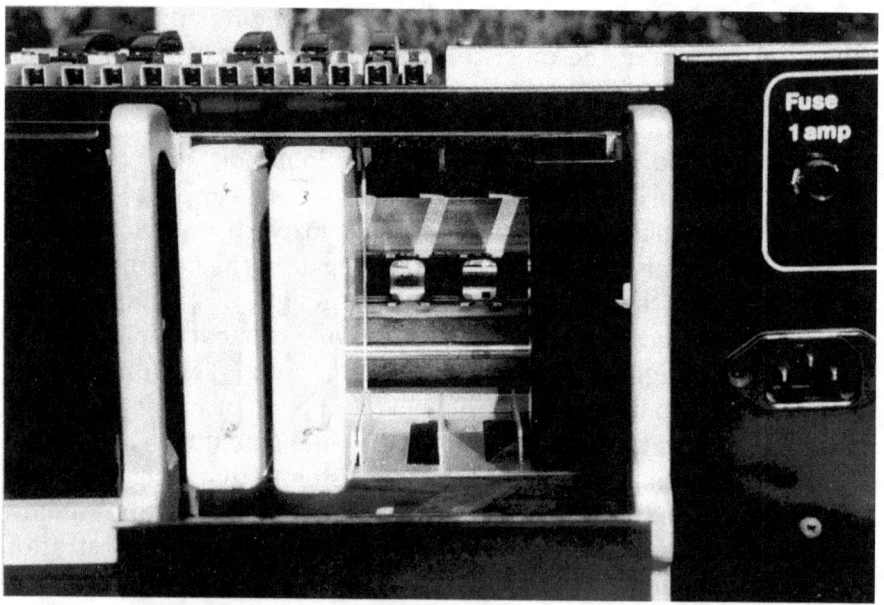

Reverse of Birotron showing two 8-Track cartridges labelled '4' and '3', two tape heads and the cast iron braces, photo courtesy of Streetly Electronics

Another advantage of the Birotron was that, unlike the Mellotron, you didn't need two people to carry it. It was essentially a table-top instrument and photos of Rick Wakeman in concert on the 1978 *Tourmato* show two Birotrons on top of stacks of other equipment, including a baby grand piano. Rick's setup at Advision also included two Birotrons, one on top of the other (see photograph on page 39).

The Mellotron had a specific number of sounds it could produce while the Birotron's use of 8-Track cartridges meant, in theory, that it would be possible to use an unlimited number of different sounds because the tapes could be swapped in and out fairly quickly. This led to an 'incident' during the recording of *Tormato* which Steve Howe retells in his autobiography, *All My Yesterdays*. As the Birotron cartridges were exactly the same as commercially produced 8-Track releases, it seemed like a good idea to Steve to play a prank on Rick Wakeman. Steve's recollections are not quite accurate because he mentions that he messed around with Rick's double-manual Mellotron – which is not possible as it doesn't use 8-Track tapes. Regardless of this error, Steve describes swapping the Birotron 8-Track tapes for albums by Seals and Croft, Frank Zappa and others while Wakeman was in the toilet. This was during an actual recording session, so when Rick returned to play a part for a song, Steve describes the result as a "mashed-up racket". He and the other band members were apparently all in the control room waiting for the fun to happen. Rick was not amused and stormed out of the studio.

According to Chris Dale, there was a plan to produce libraries of 8-Track tapes for Birotrons and sell them via music shops. In addition, during the development phase, there were also bespoke sets created for particular customers. For example, Led Zeppelin ordered a set but, as we shall see, nobody ever received a production version of the Birotron.

Rick Wakeman could see the potential in this new instrument, particularly following his own efforts to create a more usable, reliable live keyboard. Working with Yes' live lighting wizard, Michael Tait, they rebuilt two Mellotrons, putting them together into one, giant cabinet to create a double manual keyboard. Rick can be seen playing this double Mellotron in the film of the *Going For The One* sessions from 1976.[3] However, this unit still suffered from the same problems of differing global voltages and temperatures as the traditional Mellotrons. (As a side note, Chris Dale now owns this instrument and has restored it.) Several refinements were built into the Birotron to try and address these issues, including the use of sealed 8-Track cartridges, meaning that suspect tapes could be swapped out quickly. Also, a speed control allowed the whole instrument to be speeded up or slowed down by ten

---

[3] https://tormatobook.com/goingfortheone

'turns', to help keep it in tune with the rest of the band.

The original concept for the Birotron featured 8-Track cartridges arranged beneath the keyboard as can be seen in the 1976 patent below. Rick Wakeman took over the patent in 1978 by which time the form factor had changed dramatically:

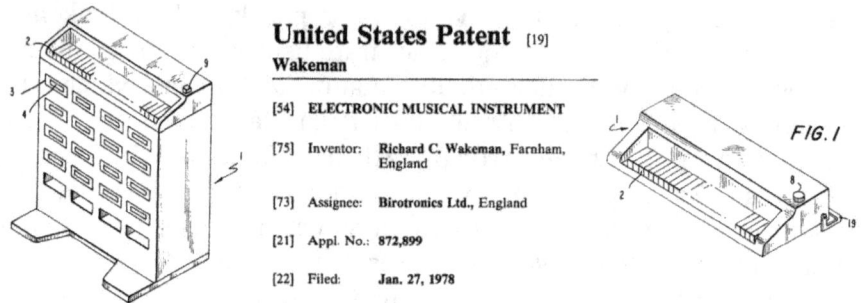

Left – the original concept design patent for the Birotron in 1975 with 8-Track cartridge players below the keyboard, centre and right – Rick Wakeman's patent from 1978

Clearly, a lot of effort was put in to try and ensure the Birotron would be a serious successor to the Mellotron and other similar instruments like the Chamberlin. This included Wakeman taking prototypes on the road with Yes for the *Going For The One* and the *Tourmato* tours. As can be seen in the photo below from the 'On The Silent Wings Of Freedom' video, two different Birotron case shapes existed. The top one in this shot is the older, straight-sided case and the one on the bottom features the later, 'lower at the front' design. Chris told me that the straight-sided models were early prototypes built in 1975–1977 and were so rare that some Birotronics employees never even saw one. The 'lower at the front' machines were made between 1976 and 1978 and were designed to, "make it look a bit more inviting, space age, and futuristic." Chris believes that the model on the bottom in the photo below has small supports built into its top, so that the upper one could be placed securely.

One of the reasons why so few of the prototypes exist today is because they were subjected to what Chris describes as 'durability/torture'

From the 'On The Silent Wings Of Freedom' behind-the-scenes video – note the two different Birotrons stacked one on top of the other on Rick's left

tests, including being dropped out of helicopters or thrown off small buildings – most of them did not survive.

The prototype machines do, in fact, appear on a few studio albums, according to Chris Dale. There's a possibility that *Going For The One* contains a Birotron choir on 'Wonderous Stories' but *Tormato* has several easier-to-confirm instances. It is present at the end of both 'Rejoice' and 'Arriving UFO' and 'On The Silent Wings of Freedom' contains a Birotron string sound.

> " ... the Birotron kind of surfaces and gives you this ... soothing, beautiful sound ... "
> Chris Dale, *Yes Music Podcast*, October 2021

Chris says the instrument is probably in a lot of other places on the record as well, but it's very much buried at the back of the mix. He feels that it was a deliberate intention of Rick's to mix the Birotron into the background of these albums (and his own release, *Criminal Record*), because the sounds themselves were not 'finished' – much like the in-

> **RICK'S STAGE EQUIPMENT**
>
> **KEYBOARDS:** grand piano (with Hempinstall pickup); Mander pipe church organ; Hammond C3 organ; Polyphonic Moog; 4 Mini-Moogs; 4 Birotrones; Fender Rhodes piano; R.M.I. Computer Keyboard; R.M.I. Rock-Si-Chord piano; Baldwin harpsichord; Godwin organ
>
> **EFFECTS AND MISCELLANEOUS EQUIPMENT:** Soundcraft 1612 mixer; 2 Phaselinear amps; Clair Bros. electronic cross-over; Delter digital delay; JBL speakers and horns; assorted effects (phasing, flanging, etc.) by Greg Hockman, Systems Tech Inc., Kalamazoo, Michigan

From the 1977 Going For The One Tour Book – evidence of four Birotrones (sic) in use, author's collection

strument itself – and were being used to test what would work and what would not.

The Birotron was advertised in newspapers and trade magazines as early as 1975 and a huge number of musicians were interested. Over a thousand pre-orders were received with a value of more than one million dollars – on paper. They included household names like Paul McCartney, John Lennon, Led Zeppelin, Vangelis, The Beach Boys, Chicago and many others. The CEO of Birotronics, Peter Robinson, told Chris Dale that instead of checking the order book he would just look at the bands in the charts at the time and that would be the same list.

However, the only musicians ever to receive an actual instrument were Rick Wakeman, Tangerine Dream and the band Earthstar. Part of the problem was the difficulty of manufacturing the components necessary for the Birotron. It was very important to the people involved that everything was done properly, with no corners cut. The instrument had to be durable and reliable to use in a live situation, otherwise what was the point of trying to improve on the Mellotron? Consequently, several parts could only be produced by a handful of small companies, whose specialised techniques couldn't be replicated by others. For example, the cast iron used for the Birotron's back braces came from certain, special junkyards. This material was then sent to another company that could refine the metal and make the braces to the required specifications. Attempting to produce instruments at scale from custom parts that couldn't be mass manufactured in the huge quantities and timescales needed for assembly and sale was a serious problem. Chris has spoken to ex-Birotronics workers about this in detail:

"One gentleman told me that as soon as an instrument was done it was sent out, and that he never saw more than 5 or 6 being worked on in a room at any given time. As one went out another came in. This made it difficult to keep track of how many were being made. So, because of that, today no one knows how many were made."

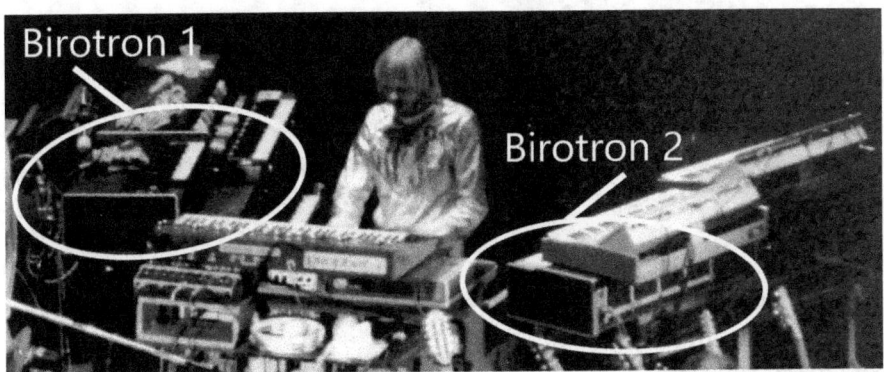

Two Birotrons (presumably the same ones as in the 'Silent Wings' video) in use by Rick Wakeman, Wembley 1978, detail from photo courtesy of Jeremy North

When the Birotron factory moved to new, smaller premises, there was no secretary. Sometimes the workers had to answer the phone to customers wanting to know where their Birotrons were, particularly after a demo tape was made available. Some artists or managers even turned up in person at the Birotronics workshop which was located alongside rehearsal facilities and a recording studio at the company known as Complex 7 (see below). Chris has discovered that big names such as Suzi Quatro, David Bowie/The Spiders From Mars, Steve Winwood, Paul Kosoff, Michael Shrieve and Klaus Schulze were in and out of the studio and rehearsal rooms and, even more importantly for us, Rick and Bill Bruford also jammed in the larger studio there, presumably for their abortive trio with John Wetton.

Surprisingly, I managed to find an issue of International Musician and Recording World (now long defunct) from October 1975 which

Complex 7 advertisement, International Musician and Recording World magazine, October 1975, author's collection

includes a double-page advert for not only the Birotron but also the brand new company, Complex 7, which offered various services to musicians in the UK. These included the Packhorse Case Co. Ltd. who are mentioned for special thanks in both the 1977 *Going For The One* and 1978 *Tourmato* tour programmes.

As pointed out by Chris Dale, the Birotron in the advert above is clearly a mock-up, dummy instrument with nothing inside the case. The other services mentioned are studios, equipment leasing, piano pickups and a flight case company, all under the brand name of Complex 7. This is intriguing information but imagine my surprise when a few pages further on in the magazine I came across the article on the facing page.

From this evidence, Birotronics was only one part of a much larger enterprise which Rick Wakeman established, or was at least involved in, at the same time. I don't know how long the other companies survived but I imagine it might have been longer than the Birotron itself.

Returning to production problems, Chris also talks about the need to miniaturise components which had never been developed in this way before, so tolerances for accuracy became much smaller as well. In those days, there were no computerised systems to help. For ex-

WAKEMAN GOES INTO BUSINESS

A NEW group of companies trading in various aspects of the music industry has been formed in High Wycombe. The company is called Complex 7 and boasts Rick Wakeman as one of its directors.

The company name is indicative of the seven companies that comprise the group. Housed in factory Unit Two, Abercrombey Industrial Estate, Abercromby Avenue, High Wycombe, the organisation is originally a brainchild of Rick Wakeman.

He started looking for factory premises to house his massive amount of equipment, and then decided that if he were to get slightly larger premises, he could also have a service workshop. From there, it was a natural step to an area large enough to house a rehearsal room with studio potential.

BIROTRON

At the same time, Rick had met an American keyboard inventor called Dave Biro and it seemed the ideal opportunity to set up an operation to market Dave's new instrument, the Birotron, in the U.K.

The complex was officially opened last month and it is really a drive-in haven for bands and their road crews. Tired, ragged bands, thrashed to bits by brutal tour schedules and underpaid one-night stands can arrive at the complex and refresh themselves, their music and equipment all under one roof.

The functions that the company operates is expanding continually. At the moment, they include manufacturing and marketing the Birotron, manufacturing and selling flight cases, operating a hire service (based upon Rick's mountain of equipment), marketing Helpinstall piano pick-ups, offering rehearsal rooms, service facilities and general storage facilities.

Since Rick's idea first grew the company has grown away from him somewhat and now has a board that includes several personalities well known in the music business.

Pete Robinson looks after the whole operation of the company. He's responsible for overall development and with the other technical and administrative directors, he is working to make Complex 7 the professional's pull-in.

Storage area

Complex 7 article, International Musician and Recording World magazine, October 1975, author's collection

ample, the motor in the Birotron was made by only one company and included a tachometer to monitor the speed. This drove the cost up immediately. Also, the roller that takes the tape forward, known as the capstan, needed to be very narrow and made from precision steel.

Chris describes the development situation as, "in the beta test phase the whole time." By the late 70s, the computer chip arrived, and digital keyboards had started to appear. Wakeman and Birotronic realised they were never going to make any money from a tape-based instrument. As a result, all plans for releasing the Birotron were shelved. I was keen to know if Rick Wakeman agreed that digital technology had ended the Birotron dream. He told me the reason was:

> "Simply because technology suddenly moved on and anything that ran with tapes was declared obsolete ... great shame."

Chris sent me a clipping (see page 44) from the FAQ section of *Keyboard Magazine* (an American publication) from November 1979 which shows that nobody in the music technology industry was aware of what had happened to the Birotron.

Chris added, "Birotronics had been already falling apart earlier and most likely was out of business by that point. So, there was no way to

When the signal comes out it has to be decoded or expanded, which eliminates noise and increases dynamic range. Shown is a diagram of the Roland Chorus Echo system of tape head placement.

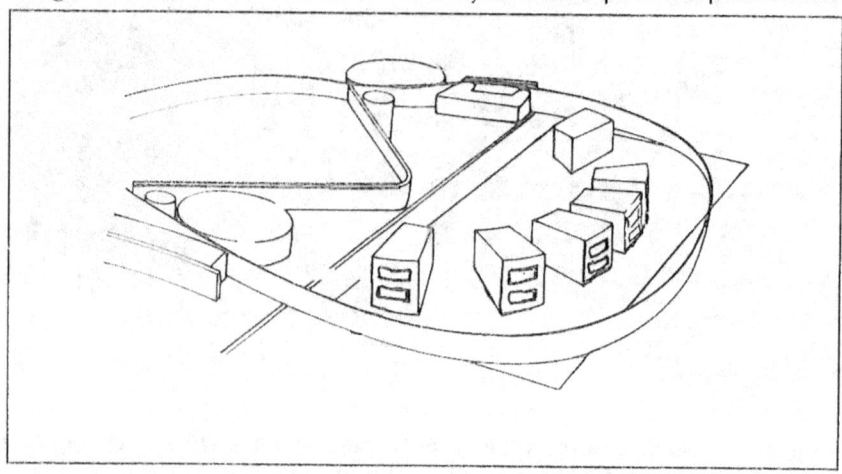

Whatever happened to Rick Wakeman's plans to market the Birotron? This is the question that gets the Most Frequently Asked award of 1979. However, we have no idea, other than that the machine hasn't come out as it was supposed to. Rick hasn't been available for comment either. So sit tight, all you folks who want a Birotron, we'll let you know what's going on as soon as we hear anything from Wakeman.

Illustration courtesy of Chris Dale

answer what was going on. They positioned this question in the layout under a different question about a tape echo unit – which looked cool and emphasised tape technology. Of course, it could be a coincidence!"

In another strange twist, a company called Pepperidge Farm (who owned the Campbell Soup brand amongst other businesses) got involved in the 1980s after Rick Wakeman had been forced to abandon the Birotron. Hank Rudkin and Chet Wiley were interested in producing a version of the keyboard which would solve some of the major manufacturing problems and simplify the design. A remote keyboard would have connected to a separate housing containing the cartridges, which sounds like a development of the original 1975 patent drawing above. They invested some money and produced some sounds, but the 1981 recession finally ended hopes for the instrument in all its potential forms.

Rick Wakeman playing the Birotron at Wembley in 1978, detail from photo courtesy of Jeremy North

The very positive postscript to this tortuous story is what Chris Dale has managed to do to preserve this rarest of all instruments for future generations. As with all great projects, this one appears to have begun accidentally. As mentioned above, Chris owns and has renovated Rick Wakeman's double Mellotron which was used on several Yes albums. During testing, Chris noticed that one of the sounds produced by this instrument didn't feel like a Mellotron voice and he wondered if it had come from somewhere else. It was a sort of odd vibraphone sound. In the course of his Mellotron research, Chris found himself talking to Alan White backstage at a Yes concert. The drummer suggested that someone should also collect Birotron tapes because it was very likely they would otherwise completely disappear.

Excited about this new endeavour, Chris tracked down Dave Biro and asked if he still had any Birotrons. The answer was a predictable 'no'. However, Chris eventually did manage to find a broken-down instrument which he set about restoring. Again predictably, the tapes with the machine didn't work so that was another hurdle to overcome. After much hard work, Chris has managed to get his Birotron working again and points out that the quality of its components, which gave the original team so many headaches, meant that the process was somewhat easier than it could have been. However, it turned out the more difficult problem was the tapes themselves. 8-Track tapes wear out over time, having been designed for only one hundred hours of use. The few musicians who received a prototype machine had to use the same tapes over and over again because there was no way to get replacements. The master tapes were also lost when Birotronic went

Photo courtesy of Chris Dale

out of business, although an online article[4] seems to suggest they were found some years ago and UK company Streetly Electronics are restoring them. As a result, Chris had to repair and preserve all the existing tapes he had, as far as possible. This involved baking them and then recording the sounds from them within twenty-four hours onto a computer, after which the tapes would be completely unplayable. These computerised 'master tapes' could then be used to make new Birotron cartridges from blank 8-Track tapes.

Over the years, Chris has collected wrecked Birotron parts from the prototype machines and has set about repairing them to use as spares for his working instrument. He says, "Most of the parts are just rusted junk now. Some might be salvageable, but because they're impossible to find, there is no other choice." Spare a thought for Chris as he slowly scrapes the rust off the parts – it's horrible, messy, intricate work but essential to the survival of the rarest musical instrument in the world. Some parts Chris has managed to find appear to come from a 'damaged beyond repair' unit that Rick Wakeman used on the *Going For The*

---

4   https://tormatobook.com/streetly

One and *Tourmato* tours, and it may also have been used during the Tormato recording sessions. This is likely because Rick only ever had access to between four and six machines. It was certainly used to play live because the cabinet has two raised, rectangular pieces screwed into its top to support a Minimoog or another keyboard. Chris has managed to get his hands on the most amazing items!

Another example is the photograph on page 46.

Birotron showing rear, controls and internal components, photos courtesy of Streetly Electronics

Here we have a unique item – the last known photograph of more than one Birotron together in the same place. According to Chris, it shows three machines in a garbage bin, one or two of which were probably used by Rick Wakeman and, Chris recalls, referred to by Rick in an interview as 'damaged beyond repair'. Apparently, these are the instruments a Birotronics technician was desperately trying to repair in 1980 before they were abandoned, as can be seen here.

Rick Wakeman is aware of Chris' project and Peter Robinson, original CEO of Birotronic, has given Chris documentation and information to help the restoration process. Chris also now owns the 'Birotron' name as a trademark[5] and Peter is delighted that Chris is doing this painstaking work to preserve an instrument which the company spent upwards of half a million dollars on, never made a penny from and almost bankrupted Mr Wakeman. I certainly hope that one day Rick will be able to take to the stage once again and play 'On The Silent Wings of Freedom' on a newly restored 'Chris Dale' Birotron.

---

5   https://tormatobook.com/birotrontrademark

4
THE OTHER TORMATO KEYBOARDS

In a similar way to guitars, keyboards in a progressive rock band like Yes appear in a huge number of different variations. Steve Howe may have used thirty or more different guitars on Yes records to achieve a variety of sounds and I wonder how many different keyboards have appeared – surely just as many, if not more. This is at least partly due to the advances which have been made in keyboard technology since prog rock began. A Hammond organ works in a rather different way to a Fairlight CMI, and I imagine there is just as much difference between a Fairlight and the Waldorf Iridium.

If Yes have always had a 'revolving door' policy for personnel, the keyboard policy has been jet-propelled. Perpetual Change indeed!

Keyboard listings from the Tormato sleeve notes:

'Future Times':
Birotron, Hammond Organ and Minimoog
'Rejoice':
Birotron, Hammond Organ and Minimoog
'Don't Kill The Whale':
Birotron and polymoog (sic)
'Madrigal':

Harpsichord
'Release Release':
Polymoog, Birotron and Hammond Organ
'Arriving UFO':
Polymoog, Birotron and Piano
'Circus of Heaven':
Polymoog and Birotron
'Onward':
Polymoog
'On The Silent Wings Of Freedom':
RMI, Birotron and Polymoog

Some classic keyboard instruments turn up again and again in Yes music, sometimes where there is an intention to evoke the sounds or feeling of previous eras, but others, like the aforementioned Birotron, only appear once or twice for a variety of reasons. On the *Yes Music Podcast*, we wanted to understand what the other keyboards were on *Tormato*, why they were used and how, so we called on Chris Dale once again.

We started with the Hammond organ. It was invented by Laurence Hammond in 1929 and uses internal tone wheels, combined with the later draw bars that can be moved in and out by the player to alter the sound. The original idea was that the Hammond organ would be marketed as a home instrument, or for churches, to replicate a pipe organ. However, a lot of people were sceptical because of the lack of pipes, so the draw bars were developed to provide a similar experience to pulling stops on a pipe organ.

The Hammond was renowned for its robustness. It was incredibly heavy to transport but it would withstand all kinds of rough treatment, which made it ideal for use in a rock band. This was in stark contrast to a lot of the newer instruments which were comparatively fragile and prone to damage when being carried around in tour trucks. In fact, Chris suggests that part of the reason Mellotrons and other keyboards were often damaged by roadies was that they were used to dealing with Hammonds which would soak up extreme mistreatment (as proved by the deliberate actions of Keith Emerson!).

An essential part of the Hammond sound for rock music comes from its pairing with the Leslie speaker. Hammond had their own speakers, but Don Leslie also developed separate speakers after the Hammond was released. Laurence Hammond was upset because he thought Leslie speakers ruined the sound of the Hammond, but owners, especially in the rock world, appreciated the Leslie's ability to make the sound appear to come from all directions simultaneously. This was partly due to its unique, rotating action.

Chris told us that the most common Hammond setting is achieved by pulling the first three draw bars out. This produces the characteristic rock sound used by many players, especially when combined with chorus or vibrato. However, Rick Wakeman used this instrument in an unusual way on *Tormato*, compared to what he had done previously, in order to achieve a different effect. His unusual settings for the draw bars mean that it sounds almost completely unlike a Hammond. This was to make it blend with and 'separate' the Polymoog and the Birotron. Most bands had traditionally used the Hammond's ability to project its sound to play keyboard solos or to hold chords down to create an atmosphere (as Wakeman had done for the beginning of 'And You And I') but here a different sound was needed.

Another keyboard mentioned on the sleeve notes for *Tormato* was the Polymoog, also a comparatively recent invention. The keyboard was originally planned to be just one part of a much bigger setup from Moog called the Moog Constellation. It was intended to contain three elements – the Polymoog, the Lyra (which eventually appeared as a handheld guitar-type keyboard called the Liberation), and a set of bass pedals which evolved into the Taurus. Instead of selling this as a complete setup, Moog ended up selling them as three discrete instruments. The most successful was the Taurus pedal board that took on an emblematic prog rock persona of its own, featured by bands like Yes and Genesis. The original idea was to have the Polymoog for the high solo parts, the Lyra for the mid-range and the Taurus providing a massive bass element.

Chris also points out that the look and feel of the Polymoog encouraged keyboardists to play quickly – to use it as a synth soloing instrument. Unlike the Mellotron with its short span of thirty-seven keys, the Polymoog looks like it's inviting you to whizz up and down its long keyboard. Despite this, the concept behind the Polymoog, as the name suggests, was that it could play more than one note at a time, unlike its smaller cousin, the Minimoog. In part, the Minimoog was responsible for defining Prog Rock keyboard soloing precisely because of its monophonic nature. If you could only play one note a time, how were you going to play an impressive solo? Well, one answer was to play as many notes as possible in the shortest time possible, hence the style of many keyboard solo spots featuring Wakeman and others. It was technically possible to get three notes at a time out of a Minimoog, according to Chris, but it involved tuning each of the three oscillators to a different note and then triggering the chord by pressing a single key on the keyboard – that's a bit of a cheat and wasn't the intended purpose of the oscillator set up. Keith Emerson did indeed use this technique on records like ELP's *Brain Salad Surgery* to create weird 4ths and 5ths.

However, this wasn't the point of the Polymoog with its new-fangled polyphony making chords, pipe organ and strings effects possible from a synth. The idea was to create a Moog instrument with a lot more flexibility, a lot more scope in terms of sound sculpting. It was a tricky thing to get right, though. You had to be very careful how you constructed rich sounds because of the way the Polymoog was set out.

Over the years the Polymoog has gained a somewhat negative reputation, at least on records like *Tormato*, with its shrill sound which has been blamed for the keyboard parts interfering with or being in competition with the guitar. Chris describes *Tormato* as 'almost its own genre' within Yes music. He sees it as a kind of offshoot of Yes and he does recognise the conflict between what Rick Wakeman was using the Polymoog for and Steve Howe's guitar parts. He thinks the two instruments were in exactly the same register as each other and, when two elements are tonally so close, they seem to cancel each other out. Combine this with the Birotron, also in a similar register and there are three instruments all competing for the same space. Perhaps part of Howe's dissatisfaction with the album was due to the fact that Wakeman had two keyboards to his one guitar in that register, meaning he was immediately at a disadvantage. As Chris says, it's almost as if the two musicians were deliberately trying to annoy each other. Surely not ... In previous albums Howe and Wakeman seemed to be brilliant at finding sounds that complemented each other, but not here. It does make me wonder, again, if Wakeman felt he had to use the Birotron on *Tormato* because of his vested interest in its success. Alternatively, it may have had more to do with the theme of trying to innovate in order to stay relevant in a supposedly post-prog musical landscape.

THE OTHER TORMATO KEYBOARDS

Rick Wakeman's dramatic array of keyboards at Wembley in 1978, detail from photo courtesy of Jeremy North

Like the ill-fated Birotron (see chapter 3), the Polymoog was a commercial failure. Chris attributes this partly to a sense of disappointment from customers. They thought they would be able to produce a rich, big sound from the machine but due to the way the polyphonic technology worked, it wasn't possible – the resulting sound was thinner than the Minimoog. Some players were able to use the instrument effectively, not least Rick Wakeman himself on *Going For The One*, as well as artists like Gary Numan, but these instances seem to have been exceptions.

Studio photographs show Minimoogs in the keyboard setup as well and both 'Future Times' and 'Rejoice' include Minimoog in the instrument credits, but Chris believes these were only used for occasional accents and Wakeman was probably trying to move away from his dependence on that instrument.

Around this time, certain music publications gave the impression that they thought of bands like Yes as 'dinosaur rock', which may have contributed to the pressure on bands to sound more modern. To Chris, rock sounds in the early and late 70s are like two different eras. It's as if the 60s sounds carried over into the start of the new decade followed by disco elements in the mid 70s and by the end of the decade musicians were attempting to find a more sophisticated sound – but not always successfully. Maybe this can be heard in parts of 'On The Silent Wings Of Freedom' where the RMI keyboard was used to add an organ sound here or there.

Like White's North drums (see chapter 6) and Squire's harmonised bass (see chapter 8), the whole band seemed to share a desire to try something new and, for Rick Wakeman, the RMI Music Computer was part of his solution. Rocky Mountain Instruments, to give them their full name, were an innovative US company who produced the RMI piano, which can be heard on early Genesis recordings as well as on *Yessongs*, where Wakeman uses it for his *Six Wives of Henry VIII* solo. This electric piano had advanced features such as the ability to set a simulation of attack and decay, which means that Rick could use the same instrument in a pipe organ manner and then later in the solo more like a harpsichord. From there, the company developed the RMI Keyboard Computer, which used punch cards to control its sounds. Depending on where the holes were in the cards, flute or organ sounds, for example, would be produced by this mid-range instrument. Wakeman took this instrument on tour a couple of times. As so often, there seems to be a bit of confusion about the naming of this keyboard on the *Tormato* sleeve notes. Judging from the live photos of Wakeman's set up on the *Tourmato* tour, I believe the instrument referred to slightly unhelpfully as simply 'RMI' was the RMI Keyboard Computer II. Its characteristic colourful rocker switches can be seen above the keyboard in this photo:

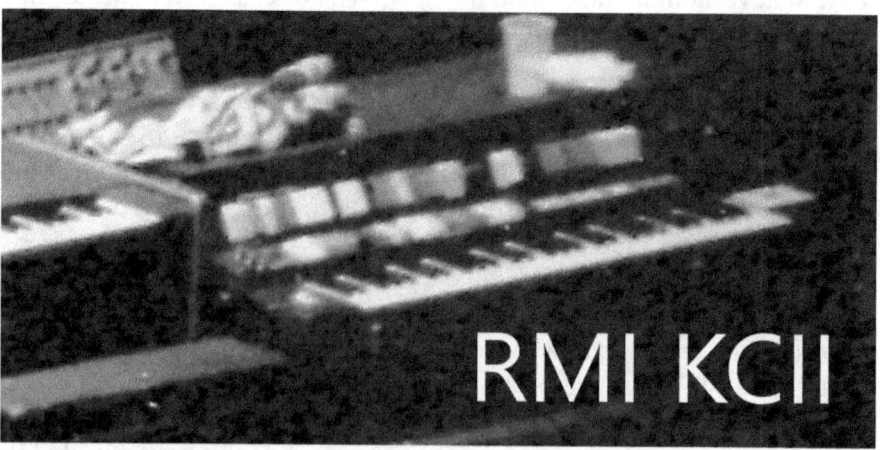

RMI KCII keyboard on the Tourmato, detail from photo courtesy of Jeremy North

Among the most obvious uses of a fairly unusual keyboard instrument was the harpsichord on 'Madrigal'. As a classically trained musician, Rick was often keen to use 'real' instruments to complement his electronic arsenal. Thus, there are real pipe organs on *Close To The Edge* (St. Giles' Cripplegate, London) and *Going For The One* (Eglise réformée de Saint-Martin, Vevey, Switzerland) as well as many instances of acoustic pianos of various types. In fact, when Wakeman had the chance to play the giant pipe organ at Lincoln Cathedral in 2001, he was very keen and recorded the bulk of a solo album of semi-classical pieces in a very short space of time.[6]

Chris points out that electric versions of the harpsichord were available at the time *Tormato* was recorded, such as the Beatles' choice, the Baldwin Electric Harpsichord, but Wakeman explains exactly what the Madrigal instrument is on the *Yes Greatest Video Hits* collection. He and other band members were interviewed at Pensacola Civic Center, on the *Union Tour* in 1992 and he mentions Thomas Goff, the London-based instrument maker who died in tragic circumstances in 1975. Incidentally, Rick confirmed this information to me in a tweet:

In a slightly unusual move for *Tormato*, an acoustic instrument with more to do with the sixteenth/seventeenth century was used, rather

---
6   https://tormatobook.com/lincoln

than brand-new technology. Whether you think it was an effective use of the instrument on this song is up to you.

While researching the instrument, I spotted the following Facebook post regarding Thomas Goff and the harpsichord on 'Siberian Khatru':

> "Rick has a great back story about the harpsichord solo. When Rick was at the Royal College of Music, there was a rule that you weren't allowed to play on the harpsichord unless that was your specialty (Rick's was piano). But he'd sneak into the room and play the harpsichord anyway. One day he got caught by an older gentleman whom Rick assumed was an instructor. He asked Rick what he was doing in there ... Rick told him he was practicing on the harpsichord. When the gentleman asked him why he chose that particular harpsichord to practice on, Rick told him because it was a Goff harpsichord and Goff is the very best. The man handed Rick his card and told him not to play the harpsichords at the Royal College ... instead come to his house. It was Thomas Goff himself. Fast forward to 1972, when Yes were recording Siberian Khatru, and the guys agreed a harpsichord would be idea for the solo in the middle. Rick called Mr Goff and asked to borrow one of his. Goff said OK, but he'd need to be there while they were doing it. Eddy Offord, the engineer, starts to put mics up inside the harpsichord (as you would for a piano) when Goff says, "What are you doing? You can't mic a harpsichord the way you would a piano because the mics will pick up the plucking sound on the strings. Overhead mics only." That's what they did, and the rest is history."
>
> Joel Y Pirard on Facebook

We were keen to find out more about Goff and why Rick chose to use his instruments for all his Yes recordings, so we spoke to renowned keyboard expert and academic, James Gardner.

Born in Liverpool, James performed in rock bands before becoming interested in electronic music and particularly keyboard instruments in the 1990s. After a time programming synthesizers, establishing electronic bands and composing, he eventually moved to New Zealand and now has a thriving academic career. He is currently Adjunct Senior Fellow at the University of Canterbury in Christchurch where his research interests include 'the Technological, historical, and sociocultural study of Electronic Music Studios (London) (EMS)'. This encompasses both the computer music studios of Peter Zinovieff and the famous music synthesizers such as the VCS3 and Synthi 100 which EMS produced.

James also produced a wonderful programme for Radio New Zealand in 2019 called *The Fall and Rise of Harpsichord 6*.[7] It tells the story of a Thomas Goff harpsichord, later nicknamed, 'The Beast', that made its way to the National Orchestra of New Zealand.

We started by asking James to explain how the ancient instrument works. Despite looking quite like a piano, the harpsichord works a bit like a mechanical guitar. Rather than a felt hammer hitting a string as in a piano, when you press a key on a harpsichord, it pivots so the front goes down and the back pushes up a long strip of wood called a jack. This jack holds a plectrum that plucks the string and then, as it comes back down, it moves out of the way to avoid plucking the string again and a little piece of felt stops the sound. This is a little like a guitarist using a plectrum to pluck individual strings but, of course, on a harpsichord each string sounds just one note. The plectrums were traditionally made of quill – a bird feather. Thomas Goff favoured raven feathers and later many manufacturers including Goff himself started using condor feathers. These were procured from live condors at London Zoo, it seems. An alternative was very hard leather and in the past 50 or 60 years a more resilient, plastic material called Delrin has been used. Unlike a piano, there is no sustain pedal on a harpsichord. Also, added complications include the ability, on some instruments, to play more than one string at a time or pluck at a different place on the string, in order to produce a different type of sound, but the mechanism remains the same, in principle.

As to when the instrument was invented, it's a complex picture, but essentially harpsichords began to be produced in Italy around the sixteenth century and then Flemish makers started producing larger, heavier-framed and two-keyboard models in the seventeenth century. These innovations provided more dynamic and sonic variation. Rick Wakeman plays a two-keyboard harpsichord in the Madrigal video

---

[7] https://tormatobook.com/harpsichord

(see below). Further improvements were made in Italy, France and Germany for over two hundred years.

The harpsichord was eventually eclipsed by the piano by the end of the eighteenth century, at which point it had virtually disappeared. Advantages of the piano included its availability and its ability to produce a full range of dynamics. The way the piano came to dominate the music scene was, perhaps, a little like how electric and then electronic instruments took over the world of popular music in the twentieth century. As the name suggests, the pianoforte was capable of playing everything from quiet to loud music because of the way the mechanics of the keyboard works. If you press harder on the key, the sound is louder, completely unlike the harpsichord, with its much more restricted methods of changing dynamics. So, the piano had a massive expressive advantage.

At the end of the nineteenth century, musicians started to become interested in the older instrument again, but it wasn't until the 1930s or 40s that what James describes as 'three strands' came together – the players, the makers and the audience. Early Music champions such as Arnold Dolmetsch, who was also important in popularising the recorder and the lute, began to build harpsichords again in about 1896. Players such as the Polish-French-American, Wanda Landowska and the Briton, Violet Gordon-Woodhouse, began to record on the harpsichord around 1920. A modern harpsichord/piano hybrid instrument was invented by the French company Pleyel et Cie called the 'Grand Modèle de Concert' and was championed by Landowska. A large number of classical composers began to create music specifically for the new harpsichord instruments throughout the 20th Century including Poulenc, Manuel De Falla, Górecki, Elliot Carter, Dutilleux, Iannis Xenakis, Benjamin Britten and John Cage.

As we know, the pop and rock world wasn't immune to the charms of the newly rehabilitated instrument either. The Beatles used a harpsichord on 'Piggies' from *The White Album* in 1968 when stand-in producer Chris Thomas saw there was one set up for a classical recording at Abbey Road. He ended up playing it on the song. Another of my favourite uses is in the Stranglers' 'Golden Brown' from *La folie*, released in 1982. Inevitably, James' knowledge of pop and rock uses of the harpsichord is vastly superior to mine. If this is an area you are interested in, I suggest you take a look at the large number of YouTube videos I embedded into the show notes for James' episode on the *Yes Music Podcast*.[8] It includes music by Frank Zappa, Tonto's Expanding Headband(!), Steve Hillage, John Barry, Jimi Hendrix, Elton John, XTC and Pink Floyd, amongst others.

Going back to the fascinating story of Thomas Goff, James explained that he was originally a barrister (lawyer) from a very high-class family. He was also aide-de-camp, a personal assistant to the Governor General of Canada during the First World War. Goff was given a clavichord (another piano precursor instrument) in 1932 and this appears to have been the catalyst for him to leave the legal profession. This meant he had to rely on his own, independent income, presumably from his family. Goff began to study carpentry and worked with photographer and amateur instrument maker, Hubert Lambert. In the grand tradition of the English gent, Lambert had been making clavichords as well as harpsichords, essentially for his own amusement. Goff then discovered someone called J. C. Cobby and struck up a professional arrangement with this working-class, master cabinet maker.

Goff only ever referred to him as 'Cobby', and together they went on to make just thirteen harpsichords, but many more clavichords. Goff's workshop was in a very tall, narrow house of Dutch-looking design at 46 Pont Street, London, which James thinks he inherited. Today it is worth millions of pounds. He lived there with a butler called Pink and it was rumoured that the pair had more than a simple, master-and-servant relationship. Pink lived in the basement, Goff lived on the ground floor and the two middle floors were let out to tenants including Lord Waldegrave, an influential English politician best known for his ministerial work in the Conservative governments of the 1990s. Finally, rooms in the two attic floors were given over to workshops for himself and Cobby. Quite how they got the instruments up and down the narrow stairs is a bit of a mystery. Goff made all components apart from the exquisitely detailed cabinets that were constructed by Cobby. There were many concessions to modern techniques and materials in Goff's harpsichords, one of the most important being the aluminium internal frames, not something available centuries earlier.

---

8   https://tormatobook.com/jamesymp

46 Pont Street as it appears today from My Own TOURMATO in January 2023, photo by William Mulryne

According to James, Goff was not a driving force behind the movement to popularise clavichords and harpsichords at the time, but he was heavily involved. He had a knack for publicity and established a series of concerts at the Royal Festival Hall in which up to four of his own harpsichords were used to play music principally by J. S. Bach. The concertos for two, three and four harpsichords were heard for the first time in generations played on the specified instruments, rather than pianos as had been the practice. The annual series did much to further the cause of authentic performances of Baroque and early music. In addition, Goff made sure that recordings made with his harpsichords always bore his name but, as he only ever sold a few and preferred to lend them out for use, it wasn't exactly for marketing purposes. Clearly, this didn't happen with *Tormato* because Goff died in 1975. He did sell a lot more clavichords which were comparatively affordable – and portable!

In 'Madrigal', James considers the use of the Goff instrument by Rick to be, " … completely authentic Wakeman," rather than wanting to define exactly how his harpsichord playing compares with modern-day masters of Baroque and Classical technique. This is not a criticism of Wakeman. It is undeniable that he has his own unique figurations, his own ways of ornamenting chords which are characteristic of his playing. It is through these facets that it is possible to recognise a keyboard line played by him in almost every situation. In some ways, Wakeman's technique is close to a harpsichord approach because there is no way of sustaining or adding dynamics to a note. Composers had to use ornaments, such as trills, turns or mordents. The practice became common in the Baroque period in a wide range of instrumental and vocal music. A parallel in prog rock music could be said to be the techniques which evolved around instruments like the Minimoog that is only capable of producing one sound at a time. To cope with this, players like Rick Wakeman developed approaches not dissimilar to some Baroque techniques. As we know, Wakeman was and remains to this day a master of Minimoog technique, even if it is missing from *Tormato*.

James believes that the use of the harpsichord on 'Madrigal' gives the song an archaic quality. It makes sense to use another acoustic instrument in addition to Howe's guitar, but he does wish it had been tuned a little more accurately. He wonders if the take which was eventually used on the album was late in the recording process and the harpsichord had gone out of tune through natural use by that stage. However, James does appreciate what he calls the "busy arpeggios", the ornaments, the "Rococo 32nd note runs" and other stylistic effects, as well as how 'Madrigal' fits into the running order of songs on the album. The song before it, 'Don't Kill The Whale', ends in B Minor then 'Madrigal' begins in D Major – the relative major key. Madrigal also provides a bit of a breather before the "big chunky riff" of 'Release, Release'.

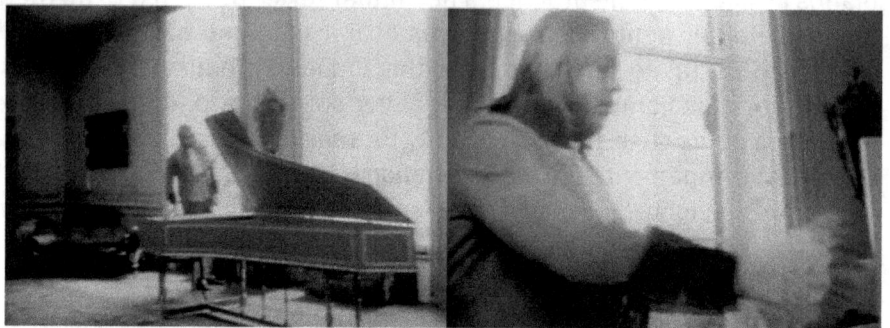

Rick Wakeman and the Robert Goble and Son harpsichord, from the 'Madrigal' video

As for the 'Madrigal' video (see chapter 24), Rick is seen playing a harpsichord so it would be natural to assume this is the Thomas Goff instrument used for the record. Not so, says James. Wakeman is in fact playing a Robert Goble and Son harpsichord made in Oxford. It's another twentieth century model and it is not clear exactly why he didn't use a Goff. Maybe the director liked the look of this one, or maybe it was already in the Classical room which is the setting for the video. The instrument appears to be based on a Dulkan harpsichord from 1745 that is now in the Smithsonian Institution.[9] Goble made other, plainer versions of this model but this one features beautiful, floral painting and an exquisitely carved sound hole, even more elaborate than the original.

While researching Goble, I discovered a tragic set of twists in this instrument-building story. As described in James' radio programme, Thomas Goff was so deeply affected by the retirement or imminent retirement of both his butler and his colleague, Cobby, that, without warning in 1975, he took himself up to the roof of his house in Pont Street and let himself slide off, falling to his death. A desperately sad parallel is that in 2000 Anthony Goble, the 'son' in the Robert Goble and Son partnership, ended his own life at Battersea Bridge in London. He

---

9   https://tormatobook.com/smithsonianharpsichord

Dulcken Double Manual Harpsichord, photo courtesy of Division of Culture and the Arts, National Museum of American History, Smithsonian Institution

had a history of severe mental health problems and had spent time in hospital as a result. Even more upsetting is that Anthony Goble was re-enacting the death of his own mentor and teacher, Richard Nicholson, who died at the same bridge seven years earlier. [10]

By the 1970s, recently made harpsichords and clavichords had fallen out of favour. Classical musicians and audiences had begun to investigate and champion the use of original instruments rather than their new counterparts with all their technologically advanced features. An amusing indication of this move was seen (and then not seen) at Goff's harpsichord concerts as early as the 1950s. His instruments were rather quiet and so, being a pragmatic fellow and definitely no purist, Goff reinforced their volume by adding microphones and speakers. After complaints from the concert-going public about this counter-authentic enhancement, Goff hid the speakers behind flower arrangements and painted the cables the same colour as the stage. The complaints ceased.

---

10   https://tormatobook.com/anthonygoble

Sound hole on the Dulken harpsichord, photo courtesy of Division of Culture and the Arts, National Museum of American History, Smithsonian Institution

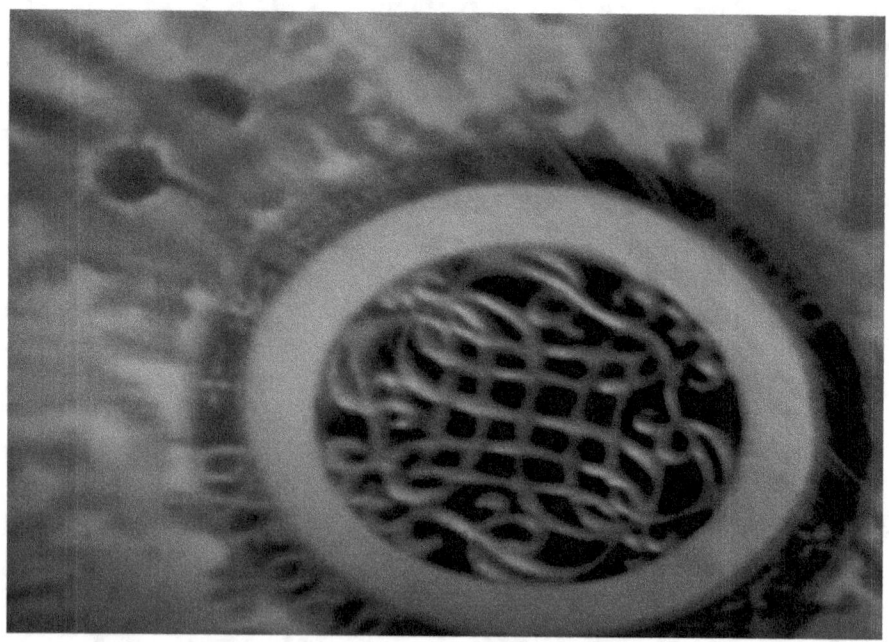

Sound hole from the Goble harpsichord in the Madrigal video

I'll leave the last word on the suitability of harpsichords or clavichords in rock music to James:

" ... [you're] still reliant on speakers, and that's not the same as having non-amplified strings vibrating in a room ... but I don't have a problem. I actually like the sound of anything that even resembles a harpsichord or a clavichord ... I'm a kind of sucker for plinky sounds anyway."

5

STEVE HOWE'S GUITARS (AND A BIT ABOUT JON ANDERSON)

There are few people on the planet as knowledgeable and as demonstrably passionate about the guitarists of Yes than Fernando Perdomo. A great champion of Peter Banks, we managed to tap into his deep well of Steve Howe expertise for our episode of the *Yes Music Podcast* about what guitars and approaches were used on *Tormato*. In addition to Fernando's expertise, I'm indebted to Geoff Bailie who shared his copy of *The Steve Howe Guitar Collection* (Backbeat Books,1993) with me so I could see what Steve thinks of the guitars on *Tormato* as well.

Before moving on to the specifics of equipment, Fernando told us about what makes Steve Howe's guitar sound unique. In a world where everyone else was using distorted Les Paul or Stratocasters, Howe opted for a much cleaner, more compressed sound, looking back to the Chet Atkins approach. He also has a very underrated right hand that provides a percussive element to his playing. This was, perhaps, most evident on 'The Gates Of Delirium' from *Relayer* where Howe turned to the even brighter attack of the Fender Telecaster.

Howe's reliance on a clean tone means that, where other guitarists might be able to hide errors in technique behind a distorted sound,

Steve's playing always has to be precise. Some people even refer to a 'banjo-like' approach with each individual tone ringing out. Fernando puts this down to Howe's influences including Wes Montgomery and Joe Pass. Steve is a huge jazz fan and also a country enthusiast, as can be heard on Yes songs like the Simon and Garfunkel cover, 'America'.

In early bands like Tomorrow, Howe played psychedelic rock but still with his big-bodied Gibson ES175. Fernando points out that if that kind of guitar is plugged into a distortion setup, it will be entirely unmanageable. Other guitarists resorted to stuffing their large-bodied jazz guitars with Styrofoam and other materials to stop the feedback, but Steve has never treated any of his guitars which is part of the reason he has never played with a lot of distortion. The first time Yes ever had a fully saturated guitar sound was in 1983 with Trevor Rabin and 'Owner Of A Lonely Heart'. On joining Asia in the early 80s, Howe reconsidered his whole approach. As Fernando put it, "He had to join the distortion club."

Moving back to *Tormato*, by 1978 Steve had become more of a "Les Paul guy," according to Fernando. Steve explains in his *Guitar Collection* book: "Much later, I came on to Les Pauls when I was collecting guitars, and I began to build up a very useful range of different versions and types." On *Tormato*, "Steve Howe still sounds like Steve Howe," according to Fernando but he does have a little more gain to work with than on the ES175. He used the Les Paul Junior on '*Going For The One*' in the previous year and the Les Paul Signature on 'The Steve Howe Album', released in 1979.

In the Tormato sleeve notes, the guitars on each song are listed as follows:

'Future Times':
Gibson Les Paul Custom
'Rejoice':
Martin 00045 and Gibson Les Paul Custom
'Don't Kill The Whale':
Gibson 'The Les Paul'
'Madrigal':
Spanish guitar
'Release, Release':
Fender Broadcaster
'Arriving UFO':

Gibson 'The Les Paul'
'Circus Of Heaven':
Gibson elec. & Ac. Mandolin
'Onward':
Gibson 'The Les Paul'
'On The Silent Wings of Freedom':
Gibson 175D

I've always found the inclusion of the Gibson Les Paul Custom as well as 'The Les Paul' rather confusing and I did once imagine that there were terminology mistakes on the sleeve. However, Fernando was able to explain the differences between these two similarly named instruments.

Steve Howe playing The Les Paul at the Advision Tormato sessions, photo by Barry Plummer

The Les Paul Custom used on *Tormato* was made around 1956 and it seems that Steve made pretty substantial customisations to it in collaboration with legendary luthier, Sam Li. Li had come to England from the Caribbean as part of the Windrush generation and found a niche for his cabinet-making skills in guitar repair and building. Derek Dearden (see chapter 7) told us that Li had a workshop upstairs in the Yes equipment warehouse in Talbot Road, so he was right in the middle of the Yes community of roadies, technical and live stage developers. He went on to look after many of the most important guitars in rock history, for example the Les Paul belonging to Fleetwood Mac guitarist, Peter Green.

Li added four humbucker pickups to Steve's Les Paul in place of the original two single-coil pickups and converted the two tone controls to make four pickup volume controls instead. To handle the tone, he changed the wiring of the selector switch to act as a control for that. I'm no expert but that sounds like a lot of changes to me. The reasons behind this development appear to have included the short-lived quadraphonic sound experiments going on at the time (see chapter 1). However, Steve managed, almost literally, to receive official sign-off for the modifications when he showed his Les Paul Custom to Les Paul himself in 1975. The legendary guitarist agreed to sign the truss-rod cover. Les appeared to be surprised but not upset by how the instrument looked.

By contrast to the Les Paul Custom, which has been produced non-stop since 1954, 'The Les Paul' was one of only a small number made. It was a very heavy instrument so, as Steve puts it, "It wasn't a guitar to rehearse or record with all day, unless you could sit down." It is possible literally to see inside Steve's The Les Paul because someone on YouTube who calls himself Trogly found the guitar, bought it and filmed it for a video entitled, 'THE Fanciest Les Paul EVER Made | Steve Howe's 1976 Gibson The Les Paul Wine Red | Review + Demo'.[11] It is amazing to see every aspect of the instrument examined and recorded, even if the final assessment of the guitar is that it is rather difficult to play! The craftsmanship, materials used and attention to minute detail are remarkable, and anyone interested in the mechanics of electric guitar making should make a point of watching the video.

---

11 https://tormatobook.com/thelespaul

On 'Arriving UFO', Steve combined The Les Paul with a guitar synthesizer from Korg, called the X911. In these early days when using a standard guitar set up with a synth, latency was an issue (in a similar fashion to Chris Squire's Mu-Tron pedal – see chapter 8) which means that the faster you played, the more the effect lagged behind. This defect or feature, depending on your point of view, can easily be heard from the start of 'Arriving UFO'.

I was also interested to know more about the Fender Broadcaster which Steve plays on 'Release Release', the 'heaviest' of the songs on *Tormato*. Steve describes how he modified his Broadcaster in his guitar collection book:

> "There's a new bridge cut into the body, the tuners are new, and the body's been stripped to natural and bound. I do now regret some of the changes I made but they were all done to get the guitar feeling right."

Rather than using leading-edge technology, here Howe opts for a very old guitar model – in fact, the first commercially produced dual-pickup electric guitar ever made, appearing in 1950. It was only called the Broadcaster for a short time due to a copyright claim on the name from rival instrument manufacturer, Gretsch, and was renamed the Telecaster to tie in with the latest technological trend in the 1950s – the television set. Telecasters continue to be produced today but Howe chose this archaic version for 'Release, Release' in order to achieve more attack than was possible with the Les Paul models. The telecaster-type pickups on the Broadcaster are mounted closer to the origin of the strings than in other models and this produces a much brighter sound, particularly when paired with the Telecaster pickup itself. Incidentally, this pickup is the same as Fender use on their lap steel guitars. Steve was very familiar with this pickup as it is the one on his double-necked steel on its rolling stand, familiar from many Yes concerts. Turning the treble all the way up produces what Fernando tells us is called the 'ice pick' sound, so keep that in mind when you listen to 'Release, Release'!

It is intriguing to note that Steve used the Broadcaster here rather than his usual white pick-guard Telecaster, which provided the main sound for *Relayer* and is the instrument he still uses today in live concerts for songs needing that attack. However, in *The Steve Howe Guitar Collection* book, he says that he actually used a Telecaster on *Tormato*. Perhaps that's a slip of memory or a use of the term interchangeably. He mentions that 'Release, Release' was an important song which he would have preferred to have been first on the album. He describes what he played as having, " ... a nice sort of chordal approach, harking back to that Mick Green influence again." Green was a member of The Wayfaring Strangers, early rivals of The Beatles (still The Quarrymen at that stage) and was an eventual collaborator with Paul McCartney and many other top rock names.

An anomaly on *Tormato* is the absence of Steve's trademark steel guitar but one instrument which does appear, and has become synonymous with him, is the Gibson ES175D. It is perhaps telling that Steve only uses this guitar on one song on *Tormato* though – 'On The Silent Wings Of Freedom'. As he says in his *Guitar Collection* book:

> "There was an incident, very early on, when my 175's jack socket got broken, and while it was being repaired I began to think seriously about the possibility of buying a Les Paul. But then I picked up the repaired 175 and it was like being back in love again."

He also says, "I seem to go to other guitars to be someone else, like putting on a mask ... But the Gibson ES175 is the guitar that I come back to when I want to find my true nature again." Does this mean that for seven out of eight songs on *Tormato* Steve is trying to be someone else? Perhaps that would fit in with the other band members' efforts to do something different on the album.

Most Yes fans are well aware of Steve's self-confessed obsession with the ES175. He bought it in 1964 when he was in The Syndicats and has used it extensively ever since. He admits in his *Guitar Collection* book that he often becomes interested in something if other people don't have it, so the rarity of this guitar in the early 1960s attracted him. His ES175 had to be ordered especially from the U.S., and it was hugely expensive. Just about the only person he's ever let touch the instrument, let alone play it, was Chuck Berry in 1969 at the Royal Albert Hall when Bodast were supporting The Who and Chuck. Berry was impressed with it, but since then Howe states that, "Nobody else touches the guitar, nobody else tunes it, nobody else strings it." Steve even admits sleeping with the guitar on the first US Yes tour in 1971 (although stresses that there was no inappropriate contact).

A diverting sideline is the appearance of this guitar in Chris Hoskins' Advision photos:

Steve Howe at Advision, photo courtesy of Chris Hoskins

It's another Gibson but it has a Les Paul-style headstock and a Firebird-style body. According to Fernando, this is the Gibson RD Artist Custom. This was one of five different variations, including a bass. Gibson added electronics to most of these guitar models in an attempt to counter the perceived threat of electronic keyboards in the musical instrument marketplace. The person responsible for the electronics was none other than Bob Moog whose keyboards were used extensively by Rick Wakeman (see chapter 4) and many others. This came about because Gibson's parent company also owned Moog Music at the time.

Bob's state-of-the-art circuitry included the ability to use a 'switchable bright mode', treble and bass boost, compression and expansion. It was all powered by a 9v battery and the circuit board ran the length of the guitar body, on the back. However, in his *Guitar Collection* book, Steve says that Gibson gave him one of the guitars to try out in the recording of *Tormato* but he, "didn't like the styling," and didn't use it at all. This resulted in less guitar electronics being used on the album than there could have been. Yes fan Sean McCarthy contacted me about this instrument:

> "Interestingly ... Steve took a liking to the ES Artist model later on with Asia. He had 4 Gibson ES Artist models all with the Moog electronics. The guitar finish colors were black, tobacco sunburst, natural and cherry sunburst. He still uses the cherry sunburst guitar when he plays with Asia and actually used it on the latest Yes tour when his Gibson ES345 model was in for repair. I believe he sold the other 3 colors."

Steve often refers to the difficulty he experienced collaborating with Rick Wakeman around the time of *Tormato*. He describes this in his *Guitar Collection*: "I got the distinct feeling that Rick Wakeman and I were groping around for some of the time – Rick for sounds and me for parts." He felt that the keyboards were impinging upon his territory and interfering with his guitar work. However, 'Madrigal' was an exception, partly because Rick Wakeman used a harpsichord (see chapter 4) and Steve used his Sakurai Kohno Spanish guitar. This instrument is another which ties in beautifully with the story of Yes because Steve bought it in Japan on the first Yes tour there in 1973. In his *Guitar Collection* book, he describes how he has used this instrument for all his Spanish guitar recordings since 1973, so you can hear it on 'The Ancient' from *Tales From Topographic Oceans*, 'Birthright' from *ABWH*, 'Aqua Part 1' from Asia's album, *Aqua*, and, of course, 'Madrigal'.

Another acoustic instrument also appears on the record (or at least I think it's just one instrument) referred to as the Gibson elec. & Ac. Mandolin. According to the guitar collection book, this is the Gibson H1 Mandola from around 1918 that is used in the final section of 'Circus Of Heaven' (not 'Circus *From* Heaven' as Steve puts it in the book). He uses it for playing arpeggios and he says it sounds, "something like a [capo adjusted] 12-string." He used it on stage just for this part of 'Circus'. Apparently, it's an experimental instrument, according to Howe, and it was marketed by Gibson at the time as the mandolin equivalent of the tenor banjo or the violin's big sister, the viola. It has a lower sound than a traditional mandolin and this can be heard on 'Circus Of Heaven'. Steve seems to have several Gibson mandolins and mandolas in his collection, including models with both body styles – symmetrical and asymmetrical.

Finally for Steve, we reach a guitar which is not a Gibson. The Martin 000-45 which appears just on 'Rejoice' is best known for its use by Eric Clapton on his iconic *Unplugged* concert and album. Fernando tells us that there are different body styles in this range of acoustic guitars. There is a huge, wide-bodied Dreadnought but Steve prefers the Auditorium models, which are designated by three zeros. The 000-45 produces less volume than the Dreadnought, but it is also less 'boomy' and so more of a finger-picking instrument than a chordal one. The zeros signify the body size, so the triple zero guitars have a 'jumbo' body, according to Fernando. Initially very impressed with the late 1920s 000-45 he bought in the 1970s, Steve says that despite trying he hasn't managed to get it onto many records.

In addition, there is another acoustic guitar on *Tormato*, but it's played by Jon Anderson – mentioned on the sleeve notes as the Alvarez 10 string guitar. More than one instrument is pictured being used by Anderson in the various photographs from Advision but the one referred to as the Alvarez is the instrument which Peter Woolliscroft mentioned in chapter 1. Jon insisted on playing it throughout the *Tormato* sessions and then decided that he wanted it taken out of the mix altogether. It's also the one which appears in the 'On The Silent

Jon Anderson in the 'Silent Wings Of Freedom' video

Wings Of Freedom' behind-the-scenes video where it doesn't seem to have an individual microphone or pickup. Peter described the instrument as looking like a kind of mandolin and you can see why from its multiple strings and odd cutaways at the sides (see facing page).

The Alvarez is credited on 'Future Times' (not 'Rejoice'), 'Arriving UFO' and 'On The Silent Wings Of Freedom'. Fernando says it is a 'partial 12 string' guitar which would mean that four of its strings are doubled, up an octave.

However, this guitar turns out to be mis-credited on the sleeve notes. It is actually a Puerto Rican cuatro. Cuatros are available in about three different shapes but the ten-string 'moderno' version has the distinctive cut-outs top and bottom, as can be seen in the photo above. There are many photographs of Jon playing a cuatro moderno on the *Tourmato* tour (as well as another acoustic guitar).

This cuatro was not made by Alvarez either (who, as far as I can see, have never produced one). The mislabelling on the sleeve notes is perhaps because the real name of the instrument was not known by the musicians at the time. The big difference between a cuatro and other 10-string guitars, is that cuatros have five doubled strings rather than extra bass strings, so presumably the fingering is different to a standard or a ten-string guitar. Maybe Jon tuned it to five out of six strings of a standard guitar setup but it's not clear. In subsequent years, Anderson has played a variety of unusual stringed instruments including the three-string McNally Grand Strumstick Dulcimer.[12]

The error in naming in the sleeve notes is similar to the situation around the famous Steve Howe 'Portuguese vachalia' (Portuguese twelve-string) which was subsequently discovered to be a Spanish laúd. He used it first with Yes on *The Yes Album* and it provided most of the sonic fingerprint of 'Wonderous Stories' from *Going For The One*. As a final note, the Puerto Rican cuatro is quite closely related to the Spanish laúd.

Getting back to Steve Howe's guitars on *Tormato*, or rather his amplifiers, Fernando points out that Steve always used Fender amps. Chris

---

[12] https://tormatobook.com/strumstick

Hoskins' Advision photos show at least five and possibly even more different Fender amps in use by Howe. This, once again, differentiates him from other prog guitarists at the time, very few of whom played Fender amps or even Fender guitars. For example, Steve's predecessor in Yes, Peter Banks, used British-made Marshall and Hiwatt amps. Robert Fripp of King Crimson, Steve Hackett of Genesis and Roger Waters of Pink Floyd all used Hiwatt. According to Fernando, one of the few other guitarists to use Fender amps at the time was Steve Hillage, but even he had a much more Marshall-like distorted sound, unlike the clean tones of Howe.

Steve Howe's setup at Advision – note the five or more Fender amps, The Les Paul on the left and the Gibson RD Artist Custom on the right, photo courtesy of Chris Hoskins

Marshall and Hiwatt amps used big cabinets and low efficiency speakers. This is great when you want that 'compressed' and distorted sound particularly associated with Marshall amps. Guitar chords sound huge but, when you start trying to play lead lines, they don't come through as effectively. The large Marshall cabinets contained four 30-watt speakers whereas the Fender amps contained 60-watt speakers and so produced a lot less distortion and compression of the sound. Fernando refers to the Fender sound as, "punchier, louder and rounder," which is great for jazz. In fact, a lot of jazz guitarists use Fender amps with one hundred watt speakers because they are practically impossible to distort.

It could be argued that, at this time, Steve was bucking the trend of his band mates and staying close to his own signature sound rather than making a full commitment to achieving a different and new sound on *Tormato*. When he reached the next completed Yes album, *Drama*, maybe he decided the time was finally right for a new guitar approach and that process, perhaps, was complete with Asia a few years later. There's even a story of a Gibson amp blowing up after Steve plugged his guitar into it to record the solo for Asia's massive hit, 'Heat Of The Moment'. This led to some weird notes he was unable to re-record. Take a listen to the song and you will probably be able to hear what transpired.

6

THE 'FLARED TROUSERS' OF 70S DRUMS

Chris Kimball established the multi-Guinness World Record winning drumming event, Woodstick, in 2003 in an attempt to raise money to combat polio. Alan White appeared at Woodstick a number of times.

Chris' drumming videos came to my attention when I was hunting around the internet for information on the weird-looking drums Alan used on the *Tourmato* tour as well as at RAK studios (see chapter 6). It turns out that Chris has restored a set of these scoop-bottomed North drums, so I invited him along to the *Yes Music Podcast* to tell us about them.

For almost his whole career, Alan White was associated with Ludwig drums, stretching back to the iconic kit he used with John Lennon's Plastic Ono band in 1969 (the set which was cruelly stolen from him shortly before his death). We asked Chris why the bizarre North drums turned up in Yes shows in the mid to late 1970s. He pointed out how unusual North drums sound, with their unique, dry, loud timbre and the 'ringing' tones they produce appeal to some drummers. Others hate this sound, of course, but Chris loves it and presumably Alan was attracted by it as well. In addition, the drums certainly make a visual statement, something which would have fitted in particularly well with the Yes aesthetic of the 70s. Although the *Tourmato* tour, the *Ten True Summers Tour* and the *Going For The One* tour didn't feature the fabulous fibreglass creations of Roger and Martyn Dean, North drums did appear alongside the extravagant 3D modelling of previous tours, as we shall see below.

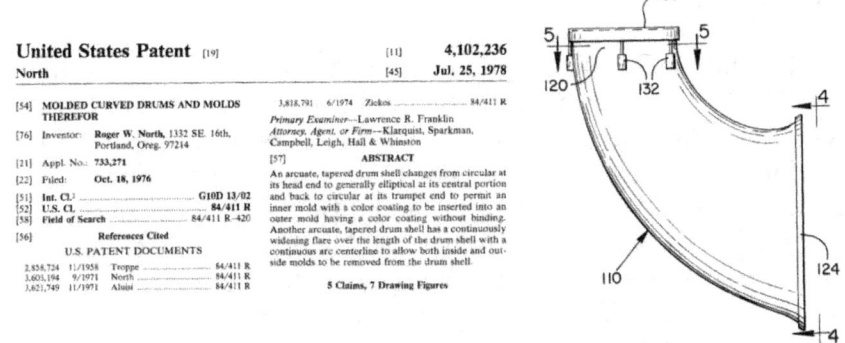

The first part of Roger North's patent (expired) for his 'curved drums and molds therefor', originally filed in 1976

I have managed to identify at least four different North (or hybrid) drum kits which have been used by Alan White from concert photos, videos and anecdotes. The earliest example appears to be in the video for 'Spring – Song of Innocence' from Alan's 1976 solo album, *Ramshackled*.[13] The kit contains both white and red drums so maybe it's a combination of two sets.

As Chris points out, it seems that the first time any North drums appear with Yes is on the *Solo Album Tour* of North America in 1976, so that fits in nicely. On that tour, in true proto-Spinal Tap fashion, Alan used a rotating drum riser. Chris remembers vividly that the conventional drum kit was used throughout the concert apart from one song, during which the entire riser rotated to reveal a "gorgeous, white North drum set". Needless to say, the young high school student thought this was the coolest thing he'd ever seen and wanted to get a North kit for himself. However, funds were short, and he ended up creating his own ver-

---

13 https://tormatobook.com/ramshackled

sion from sewer pipes! Confirmation of the concert setup came from Joseph Cottrell in a comment on the show notes for an episode of the *Yes Music Podcast*:

> "The drum riser definitely did rotate to reveal Alan's North kit, which was almost completely obscured by his main kit, so the reveal was very surprising. It was in the middle of 'Ritual' for the 'drumpocalypse' bit, and that was indeed the only time he played them for the entire concert."

The third kit I found was in photos from the *Going For The One Tour* in 1977. This time, a mustachioed Alan White is seen with a vibrant, dark green North kit but with a mixture of the single-headed North toms and double-headed more standard-looking ones (probably Ludwig). There's no rotating stage this time and this hybrid North kit was used for the whole concert, with timpani taking up the space behind Alan from whence the North kit had emerged on the earlier tour.

Interestingly, Alan spoke about his use of North drums on Yesworld.com. When asked if he had ever used them for recording Yes albums, he replied:

> "Well not in the studio itself, but they were recorded live. We used them in 'Topographic Oceans' for the drum solo in 'Ritual'. We used to have a regular drum kit and also the North drum kit and for the solo I'd spin around, the North kit would come up and I'd play the solo on the North kit and then switch back to a regular kit. It was on a little riser that was motorized so you had one kit and then all of a sudden you turned around and there was another kit. That was a lot of fun."
>
> Alan White, Yesworld.com interview, March 2017

However, I think Alan's memory was playing tricks on him because, as pointed out by knowledgeable Yes fan Jon Dee, he used a hybrid North kit in Montreux for the *Going For The One* recording sessions. Alan can be can seen playing the drum set in a jam with Chris Squire in the behind-the-scenes video recorded by Clive Richardson (see chapter 24). In addition, the kit set up at RAK studios when Dave and his brother visited (see chapter 2) was also a hybrid North set. I did wonder whether it was brought in just for those last-minute overdubs and additional recording at RAK but, if you watch the fascinating video of the recording of 'On The Silent Wings Of Freedom' at Advision studios, almost right at the end there is a momentary shot of those classic North scooped toms. It is clear that it is the same kit as Dave played around with later at RAK, a fact and confirmed by Advision Tape-Op, Peter Woolliscroft. Chris Hoskins' photos from Advision also provide evidence of North drums being recorded for *Tormato*. Incidentally, Alan uses a cut-down kit including the North toms for the video of 'Don't Kill The Whale' as well (see below).

Alan with the hybrid North kit – top left courtesy of Chris Hoskins, top right by Barry Plummer, bottom left On The Silent Wings Of Freedom video, bottom right RAK Studios, courtesy of Dave Watkinson

The Advision kit is, once again, not a full North kit, but a hybrid of North toms and double-headed toms like the green kit on the *Going For The One* tour. This time, however, it has a somewhat mind-altering combination of blue/green, red and yellow. It is also the same kit that was used on the 1978 *Tourmato* tour, as evidenced by Jeremy North's Wembley photos. By the time the band toured the US in 1979, the North drums had been replaced by Ludwig ones, but we will learn more about that a little later.

Left – Alan White's kit including red and blue North toms at Wembley, photo courtesy of Jeremy North, right – from the Don't Kill The Whale video

We asked Chris about the origins of these crazy looking drums. Roger North gave his name to the instruments and the company that produced them. He was a Boston-based drummer whose band, Quill, were first on the bill on the second day of Woodstock in 1969. Sadly, there were some audio recording problems at that event and there isn't a proper video record of their performance. However, there is some home video, a photo or two and a YouTube video[14] with still images. These contain evidence of Roger's flange-bottomed drums in use.[15] Before becoming a musician, North went to the Massachusetts Institute of Technology and started creating fibreglass drum prototypes in his apartment. Everyone who saw them wanted their own. Chris recalled a story of Roger attending a Billy Cobham concert and setting his drums up on a speaker cabinet or a box. Cobham saw the kit and liked it, so, via various connections, North started building drums for famous drummers including Cobham, Alan White, Joe English (Wings), Doug Clifford (Creedence Clearwater Revival) and Russ Kunkel (as pictured with North drums on the cover and sleeve notes of Jackson Browne's album, *Running on Empty*).

The development of the drums continued in the early 70s and the original patent (see above) was issued in 1971, leading to commercial manufacturing in 1973, despite Roger North admitting later that he wasn't particularly interested in making drums and he'd rather play them! Roger experimented with the design of his instruments and the earliest examples have a longer tube. Eventually, in 1976, the patent

---

14 https://tormatobook.com/quill
15 https://tormatobook.com/quillphot

was sold by North to MTI (Music Technology Incorporated) and they began to manufacture kits, ending up in Italy with an injection-moulded polystyrene process rather than a fibreglass technique.

North drums were designed specifically with projection in mind as the technical diagram in the original North Drum catalogue shows:

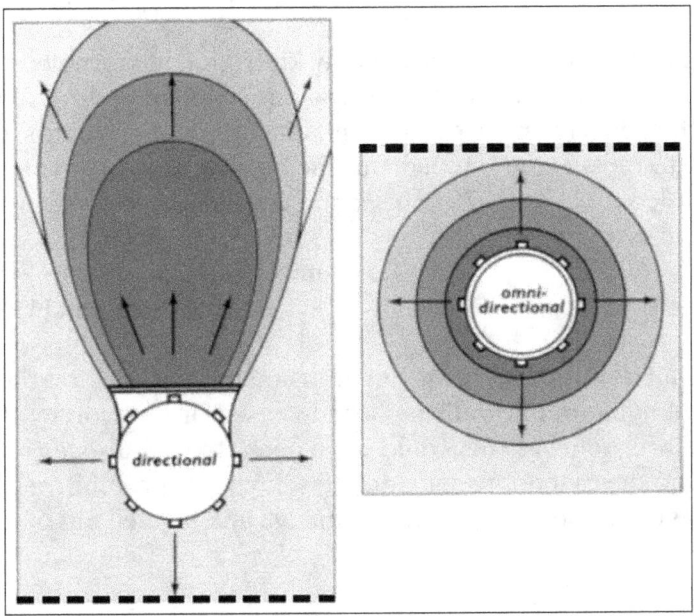

Illustration from North Drums catalogue[1]

---
1 https://tormatobook.com/northcatalogue

I'm no acoustic engineer but this is clearly a simplification of the sound properties of the drums, but at least it makes the point. Chris explains that the dry sound of these drums comes both from the fact that they have no second 'resonant' drumhead like traditional drums and they use fibreglass or plastic construction, rather than wood.

Overall, Chris believes Alan White's attention was drawn towards North drums because Yes were known as a band whose approach and sound were different. Therefore, it's no surprise to see that Alan White would want to experiment with different and unusual sounds. This is exactly what you get with North drums and perhaps also accounts for the mixing of North toms with more 'traditional' double-headed ones. As Chris says, "You don't use a China cymbal all the time but when you need a different type of sound it's nice to have one."

By the time of the 1979 *Ten True Summers Tour* of the US, the North drums had disappeared from the setup and Alan had returned to using Ludwig drums. As described in a forum post:

> "By 1979, Alan had received a new kit from Ludwig, now in a natural dark wood finish. Ludwig enticed Alan to drop the North drums from his setup by making him various odd-sized toms to replace the North drums he had been using. If you have the video from Phili (79), this is the kit Alan is seen playing the "Ritual" solo on."
>
> Google Groups post attributed to Vince S
or quoted by him (1998)[16]

Sadly, Alan's shift away from North drums was echoed by the general drum-buying public and the brand ceased production by the early 1980s. Chris believes this could have been due to sub-standard marketing and the cost of the instruments which was prohibitive for many. Also, maybe the sound was too distinctive and just fell out of favour.

---

[16] https://tormatobook.com/endofnorth

7

THE OTHER DRUMS

Another of my investigations was triggered by seeing the Alan White instrument list for 'Arriving UFO'. We know that Alan was using North drums and the appearance of gongs isn't much of a surprise in this strange aural concoction, but I was intrigued by the inclusion of 'drum synthesizer' in the list. Alan used electronic percussion elements alongside his acoustic kit for the vast majority of the time he was in the band, but there is no mention of the brand or type of drum synthesizer he was using in the *Tormato* sleeve notes. The *Tourmato* and *Ten True Summers* programmes also have no instrument lists at all. As we shall see, the company responsible for Alan's synthesizer does appear in both programmes but I didn't realise that until later in the story.

Several older programmes do include lists of instruments, so I went back to the tour book for *Going For The One* and took a look. Under Alan's 'MISCELLANEOUS INSTRUMENTS AND EQUIPMENT' section I found Musser vibes, four octaves of crotales and Premier 550C sticks, which was all predictable, and then 'drum synthesiser (custom-built by Survival Projects)'. The 1978 and 1979 programmes both include special thanks to Survival Projects Ltd., so I thought it was safe to assume that this was the drum synthesizer used on the *Tormato* recording as well. A little more research unearthed references to electronic percussion in an answer Alan gave to a Yesworld.com question from a fan:

Jonathan Silk:
"When did you start adding electronic percussion to your studio/live kit?"

Alan White:
"I started adding electronic percussion to my kit at a very early stage when other drummers were starting to add them. In fact I built my own, investing a lot of money in a small company that built a drum synthesizer that worked off of microphones. Nowadays it would be considered a steam-driven electronic music centre because it was very slow in reaction, and to get any great sounds, the rack was huge; it was like one of the really old Moog synthesizers from the past."[17]

Unsurprisingly, this piqued my interest. It seems that Alan also had financial interests in new instruments, just like Rick Wakeman did in the Birotron (see chapter 3).

Searching online for Survival Projects Ltd. brought no further clues, so I decided to go through the patent route. Technology companies often file for patents to protect their intellectual property as both Birotronics and North Drums did, and perhaps Survival Projects had as well. It took only a moment to locate a patent from 1979 for a sawtooth waveform generator. To my untrained eye, it looked like it could be something to do with electronic drums, but the important point is that the patent had the details of the company and the name of the inventor.

The applicant was Survival Projects Limited and the inventor was Derek Paul Dearden. A great discovery! Next was to search for references to Derek Dearden which returned the Anatronics Audio website.[18] I discovered on the About Us page that the name of this organisation is derived from the Anatron, a device designed by Derek Dearden and renowned record producer, Paul Northfield. This device morphed into the MegaFilter which is still available today from the company. It turns out that Paul Northfield and Derek Dearden both worked

---

17 https://tormatobook.com/alanquote
18 https://tormatobook.com/anatronics

at Advision in the mid-70s. Paul went on to engineer or produce more than 247 albums from the likes of Gentle Giant, Rush, Asia, Queensrÿche, Suicidal Tendencies, Infectious Grooves, Porcupine Tree and Dream Theater and now continues this work in Canada. Derek left Advision in 1976 so wasn't there when Yes arrived to record *Tormato*, but he did maintain a significant Yes connection because he founded Survival Projects and set up workshops within Yes' own equipment warehouse in Talbot Road, Notting Hill, alongside luthier, Sam Li (see chapter 5). Derek went on to develop audio effects for the band, including the drum synthesizer for Alan White and subsequently worked with bands of a similarly high profile such as Queen, Pink Floyd, AC/DC and ELP. Clearly, we needed to speak to Derek, so we invited him onto the *Yes Music Podcast*.

Derek joined Advision in 1974 and first met Steve Howe and Alan White when they came in to work on their solo albums. Although he had already left Advision, Derek also came into contact with Eddy Offord when he came into the studios from time to time and he visited him at his home in Bearsville, near Woodstock, New York. Derek recalls Eddy being, "pretty eccentric" and did meet his crow (see chapter 1) when Eddy was recording the backing tracks for *Drama*.

Paul Northfield was responsible for Derek starting at Advision after tipping him off that a job was going there in the maintenance workshop, alongside two other employees. They were to be responsible for ensuring that all the studio gear was working properly. Derek managed to secure the job because he was able to say he had been working as a test engineer in a digital electronics factory, which was at the cutting edge of music technology at the time. In fact, Derek had only worked there for about a month, but the Advision staff were suitably impressed. On the perceived strength of his credentials, Derek became responsible for repairing the Eventide and other equipment that Advision's sister company, Feldon Audio, were importing into the UK and selling to various other studios. As Derek explained:

> "The digital delay line from Eventide was one of the few digital pieces of equipment around and of course the average audio engineer would open up the lid expecting to find half a dozen op-amps [operational amplifier integrated circuits], and a few transistors, and see two huge boards covered with small-scale

integrated digital ICs [integrated circuits]. I was one of the few people in the country who could actually repair Eventide delay units."

As mentioned in chapter 8, Eventide equipment supplied by Feldon Audio made a major contribution to Chris Squire's bass sound on *Tormato*.

We asked Derek about the formation of Survival Projects, and he explained that the company came about as a result of work he did for Alan White. Alan had come into Advision with his drum tech, Nu Nu Whiting, to do the mixdown for his solo album, *Ramshackled*. Derek spent a lot of time chatting with Nu Nu, discussing what kind of electronic device could be added to Alan's North drum kit. Nu Nu was after something novel and unique. There were a few conversations with Alan to discuss Derek's ideas and he liked what he heard. Alan offered to pay Derek a retainer and give him workshop space in Yes' equipment warehouse to develop some prototypes. Survival Projects was the company, which was set up to exploit the design commercially, if it was ever developed as far as a saleable product.

Derek was, therefore, right in the middle of the activity at Yes' legendary equipment warehouse in Notting Hill. All the Yes band members would pop in from time to time and Derek described it as, "a social club for the roadies for all of the main rock bands of that era." Derek's workshop was initially very small and tucked into a downstairs corner, but he later moved upstairs into a much grander space which had a window onto the main area beneath. This workshop had been vacated by the legendary luthier Sam Li (see chapter 5) who simply disappeared one day and was never seen again at the warehouse. Here's how Derek described the location:

> " ... it was a funny place because in that little side street, about a couple of hundred yards from Portobello Road, in between a pub and an Indian grocery shop, there was a steel roller shuttered door that looked just like the entrance to a single car garage."

Apparently, behind this car-sized entry, it opened up into a huge space described by some as 'like a bus garage'. It was in this area that Clive

Richardson, Martyn Dean and others constructed the amazing fibreglass stage sets such as the Crab Nebula for the 1976 *Solo Album Tour*. I visited the business which now occupies the building on *My Own TOURMATO* in January 2023. There is a new mezzanine floor in the same location as the one removed when Yes left and the roof trusses are still exposed, exactly as they were in 1978.

Left – the site of the Yes warehouse at 99C Talbot Road as it appears today – note the small opening which was covered by a steel roller shuttered door in 1978, right – interior with original roof trusses, photos by William Mulryne

Derek explained that the aim for the drum device he had discussed with Alan and Nu Nu was to produce something which didn't rely on any kind of fake drum pads. Instead, it would be triggered from real drums and produce sound which was musically coherent – it would actually sound like it was producing musical chords. There was a Moog Drum Controller system[19] available at the time but it didn't have any real musical character, according to Derek. Alan White's predecessor Bill Bruford was to follow a similar path in the 1980s with his Simmons electronic drums.

What Derek decided to create was based on individual microphones for each drum on Alan's kit. These would react to the timbre of sound

---
[19] https://tormatobook.com/moogdrum

when the drum was hit to select and play back 1 of 4 notes in a chord. There would be five drums, all playing different notes of the same chord but in different registers to produce polyphonic music in recognisable, harmonic ways. It would also be possible to feed in a chord sequence using a keyboard and progress through the sequence using the drums. Derek likens this remarkable process to holding a chord on a guitar and picking around it, then changing the chord and continuing. This would be combined with the five inputs at different pitches and using different voices, generated using circuitry from electronic organs. There was also the ability to control other effects.

For me this is mind-boggling. Derek was forging ahead into highly rarefied areas of musical technology. There were some issues with spill from one microphone to another, but Derek recalls some highly successful demos, not only with Alan, but also with other notable figures of the rock world such as Arthur Brown, who performed as a guest on Yes' *Royal Affair Tour* in 2019 and is still active today. He came along with his drummer and seemed suitably impressed, laughing loudly and slapping his thighs.

Unfortunately, Alan White himself was so busy that it was difficult to catch him for evaluation work but, when he did have the time to use the equipment, he was highly impressed and took it with him to Switzerland for the *Going For The One* sessions. On *Tormato*, the drum synthesizer is obvious on 'Arriving UFO', particularly around 2 mins 30 secs and 4 mins 30 secs. The 1979 Philadelphia video of Alan using the drum synthesizer in his solo gives us a good demonstration of the equipment in a live setting (Derek hadn't seen this so I shared the YouTube clip with him. [20])

The drum synthesizer was by no means the only device Derek worked on. This was important because Alan was paying the retainer and needed to see some return on his investment. There was custom work for individuals such as Ray Shulman of Gentle Giant, who wanted to play his violin through a delay unit with quadraphonic output. The sound would be repeated from one side of the auditorium and Ray would play along with that. Then those two parts would move round to the speakers at the back of the stage and the process would go on.

---

20 https://tormatobook.com/alansolo

THE OTHER DRUMS

Alan White during his solo with the Survival Projects Drum Synthesiser from the Yes Live in Philadelphia 1979 DVD

Very groovy. There was also a unit that allowed Brian May to do something similar (although not in quadraphonic sound) in Queen concerts. Brian wanted to be able to control his Eventide pitch shifter from a single foot pedal to produce eight specific intervals, enabling him to create arpeggios from what he was playing so he could accompany himself. The device created by Derek for him became the basis of the famous solos Brian played so many times with the band and I experienced myself at Knebworth in 1986. Brian came back after using the unit on tour and bought another one – he was impressed!

The remarkable list goes on – Derek made an even more elaborate version of Brian's unit, iterations of which were snapped up by Steve Howe, Nigel Luby and David Gilmour. A couple of items were also developed for sale, such as the Survival Projects Stereo Panner which was bought by a lot of independent audio engineers because of its unique functionality.

On the Yes side, Derek made a version of the harmoniser control unit for Jon Anderson, which connected to a string synthesizer and enabled it to be transposed up or down by a series of intervals. Derek remembers playing around with the unit, holding down chords and changing them via the pedal to the amazement of various roadies who passed by. They hadn't realised Derek was such a proficient keyboardist! They soon noticed, however, that he wasn't moving his fingers on the keyboard at all.

Rick Wakeman also benefited from Derek's work through a much improved way of installing microphones in a grand piano and even transforming its tones into something more like the sounds a synthesizer would produce.

The most impressive improvement, perhaps, was to Rick's chamber organ, which he took on the road for passages such as the iconic organ moment in *'Close To The Edge'*. For transport, there were three elements – the pipes had their own giant flight case, there was one for the compressor and bellows(!), and a third for the console. Even more cumbersome, though, was the gigantic one hundred and twenty-eight way multi-core cable for connecting the console to the rest of the organ.

Presumably at the end of their tether, one of Rick's roadies approached Derek to ask if he could do anything to reduce the size and more especially the weight of this cable. Derek responded that it should be possible to send all the signals down a single piece of coaxial cable – and that's what they did. When the signals reached the other end, the relays which opened the pipes would be triggered using a technique which was a precursor to the forthcoming 1980s MIDI control techniques. This, however, was around 1977–78 and there was no way of sending serial data from a keyboard to a tone generator until Derek stepped in.

After all this amazing technological musical wizardry, Derek also brought his skills to stage lighting and produced one of the very first computerised lighting controllers. The resulting system was used on Michael Jackson's world tour and also at *Live Aid*, on both sides of the Atlantic.

Yes: The Tormato Story

Chris Squire playing his trusty Rickenbacker 4001S at the Advision Tormato sessions – note the black Eventide 1745A Digital Delay (see below) behind his right arm, photo by Barry Plummer

8

CHRIS SQUIRE'S TECHNICAL SETUP

Bear in mind that the first progressive Yes music I ever heard was *Tormato* so, as you can imagine, Chris Squire's 'harmonised' bass sound was a revelation. I had never heard anything like it and so I was determined to find out exactly how it had been created.

Enter Miguel Falcão, creator of MiguelBass.com and one of the few people on the planet who has intimate knowledge of Chris Squire's technical setup and bass technique. Miguel has recorded dozens of Squire bass covers and provided his audience with unique insights into the master's work. He is also the originator of the amazing *Play For Chris* project, an annual video tribute to the world's greatest bassist.

Miguel kindly agreed to explain the origins of Chris Squire's iconic Rickenbacker which he used to record the whole of *Tormato* apart from 'Madrigal' which only features bass pedals and 'Release, Release', on which Squire uses the Gibson Thunderbird bass.

> "The Rickenbacker International Corporation (RIC) was founded in 1931 by Adolph Rickenbacker and George D. Beauchamp and developed from a company named Electro String Instrument Corporation, that created and manufactured

electric musical instruments and amplifiers. One of their inventions was the development in 1930 of the 'magnetic horseshoe' pickup to translate string vibration into an electric, amplifiable signal. This was the first ever electric guitar, also known as the 'frying pan'. Hawaiian guitars were the main products to take advantage of the 'frying pan' electrification system, which was then extended through the decades to several kinds of string instruments including guitars, mandolins, violins, cellos, violas and even harps. Right up to the present day, Rickenbacker is regarded as one of the most high-quality and distinctive instrument manufacturers in popular music. The Rickenbacker 4001 bass guitar was the first bass manufactured by RIC with two pickups and came out in 1961 as the follow-up to the single pickup model 4000. The 4001 was the model that cemented Rickenbacker basses' success in a market dominated by Fender and was soon to be the instrument of choice for Paul McCartney, John Entwistle, Pete Quaife and Roger Waters.

Just like its six- and twelve-stringed siblings, the 4001 and later the 4003 basses are often said to have a distinctive sound, sometimes described as a 'twang' (Definition from Oxford Languages: a strong ringing sound such as that made by the plucked string of a musical instrument or a released bowstring). Of course, other factors can significantly change the timbre of a stringed instrument such as the type of strings or amplifiers, but the tone of a Rickenbacker bass is immediately recognisable. Owing to the specificity of the 4001's sonority, it is not considered an all-purpose bass for standard applications where, once again, Fender and sound-alike brands continue to be pervasive and dominant.

Influenced by Paul McCartney and especially John Entwistle, Chris Squire acquired the third Rickenbacker 4001S model to be imported into the UK in 1965 (John Entwistle and Pete Quaife had the other two). Chris' bass was manufactured in 1964 and the model's name was RM1999, the designation for the importer Rose Morris, where Chris was working and thus able to get a good discount. The RM1999/4001S differed from the standard 4001 model, sporting a more simplified look (regarding binding and neck inlays) and no stereo output. However, Chris Squire ended up routing the bass to stereo some years later.

Chris never stated specifically why he kept the Rickenbacker as his main instrument. As we know, he was able to add his own sonic fingerprint to whichever bass he was playing at the time, but he became one of the world's most acclaimed bass players and arguably the one with the most distinctive sound in rock with that very same instrument. Perhaps one sign of how irreplaceable the 4001S was for him, was that for some periods he toured it with serious issues such as neck cracks, one of which was fixed by luthier Mike Tobias. Also, when the limited-edition Chris Squire signature bass was made (a 1000 unit signature series), Chris declared on several occasions that it didn't sound anything like his own bass."

Miguel Falcão, 2022

Speaking to Miguel on the *Yes Music Podcast* specifically about Squire's *Tormato* bass playing, he pointed out that, although several of the songs on the album are credited to a 'harmonised' Rickenbacker bass, this is only one small part of the sound Chris achieves on the record. The Eventide H910 Harmonizer (not the black unit which can be seen in the photograph above and below, behind Squire) was apparently tested in its prototype stage back in 1974, by Jon Anderson who used it on his *Olias Of Sunhillow* solo album. By 1976 it was also being used by Squire.

It was one of the first devices which was capable of changing the pitch of the sound being played through it via early digital processing. It also included a feedback function which could send the processed signal back into the chain, thus creating some of the wild and crazy effects on 'Arriving UFO' where the repeating bass notes seem to get higher with each repetition. The H910 was also a digital delay unit, so the range of effects possible was even wider as the delay could be combined with pitch shifting. In chapter 1, Peter Woolliscroft suggests the unit actually used at Advision was the Eventide 1745M Digital Delay rather than the H910. Maybe more than one piece of equipment was used at different stages or locations in the studio. The black box behind Chris Squire in Barry Plummer's Advision photo at the beginning of this chapter is definitely an Eventide 1745A Digital Delay, as can be confirmed on the Eventide website.[21]

---

21 https://tormatobook.com/eventide

Detail from photo of Chris Squire at Advision showing the black Eventide 1745A Digital Delay in use, photo by Barry Plummer

Videos available on YouTube of the 1977 *Going For The One* sessions show Chris Squire using the Eventide H910 to great effect in a jam with Alan White. My co-host, Mark Anthony K, also pointed out that legendary producer Tony Visconti showed the device to David Bowie, and it inspired him to create new music based on what was possible with "this unit that could mess with the fabric of time". Mark also noted that the harmonizer was notorious for being unreliable. In fact, its tendency to shift randomly from the selected settings has become an actual signature sound, copied by modern electronic simulators, called a 'micro shift' sound, often applied to vocals by Mutt Lange when working with bands like Def Leppard in later years.

In the image on the facing page, taken by David Watkinson on his 1978 visit to RAK Studios (see chapter 2), we can see what Miguel describes as, " ... a modified set of Taurus pedals, which could be the predecessor

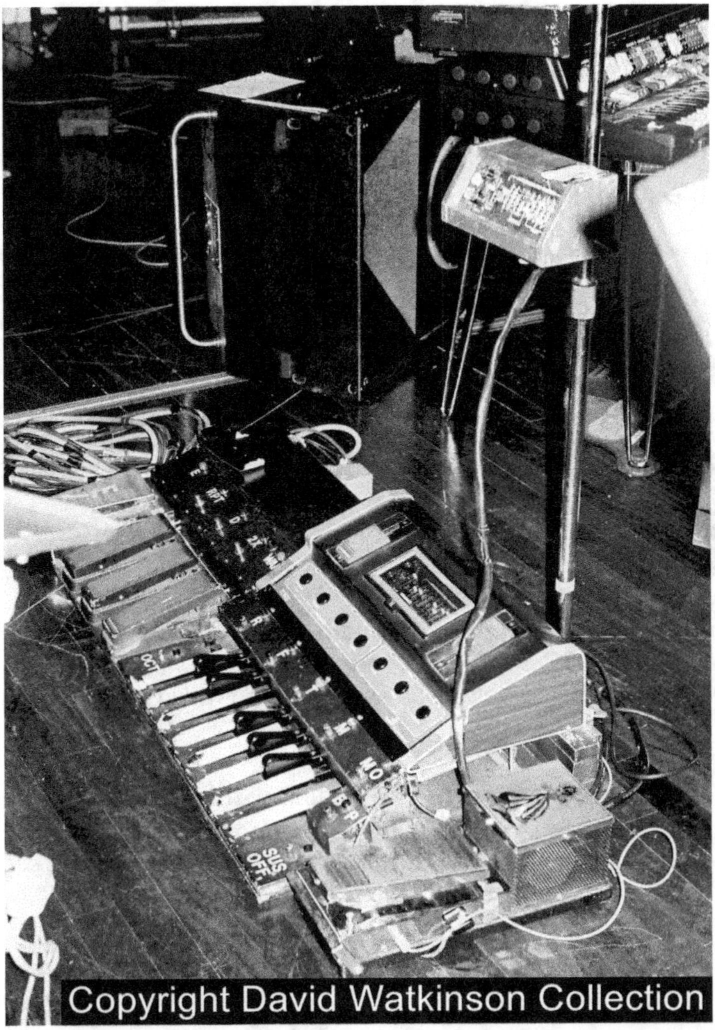

CHRIS SQUIRE'S TECHNICAL SETUP

Chris Squiare's bass pedal setup at RAK Studios, photo courtesy of David Watkinson

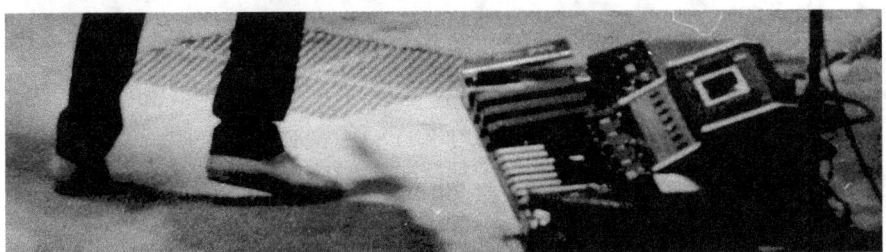

The same unit (apparently minus the external controller) in use at Wembley in 1978, detail from photo courtesy of Jeremy North

of Chris' model shown on the Starlicks video."[22]

This seems to be a previously unseen glimpse into the development of Squire's bass pedal setup. Switches can be seen that have been added to the Taurus bass pedal synthesizer partly to control the effects stored at the rear of the stage in Chris' sound rig.

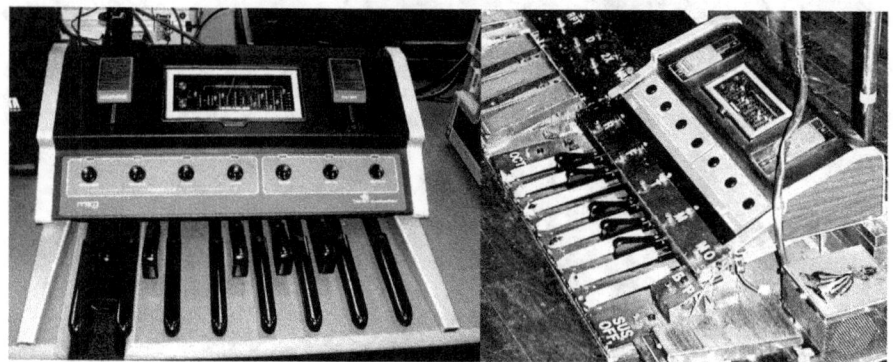

Left – Moog Taurus in its original configuration, photo by glacial23 uploaded by clusternote (CC BY-SA 2.0),[1] right – Chris Squire's modified version, detail from photo courtesy of David Watkinson

---

1 https://tormatobook.com/taurus-photo

We can see that Squire has painted the pedals white, presumably to make them easier to see when playing live (see Wembley photo above) and Miguel guesses that the letter labels that can be seen on close scrutiny might stand for:

R – reverb
F – fuzz
T – tremolo
M – Mu-Tron
MO – the combination of Mu-Tron with the harmonizer for Arriving UFO
OCT – Octave pitch-shifter
BP – (bass pedals) probably on/off
SUS OFF – silences any bass pedal note (equivalent to midi note off)
OCT – selects octave range of bass pedals
RPT, D and 2X – possibly different delay (repeat) settings

---

22 https://tormatobook.com/starlicks

WAH – the indicator for the Crybaby wah pedal (Crybaby)

This is, of course, conjecture but seems plausible to me, particularly when later versions of Squire's setup did indeed use letters in a similar fashion. The unit on the left of the Taurus pedals seems to be a set of 'volume-wah-expression' pedals including, perhaps, a Morley Pro Phaser as used by Squire on songs like 'Safe (Canon Song)' on his solo masterpiece, *Fish Out Of Water*.

The large pedal on the right is a Morley EVO. It sports a cartoon logo of the 'Morley Man', an iconic image of 1970s music technology. The mechanism in this ground breaking pedal is fascinating. The large box with the cartoon contains an 'oil can' with an anodised metal disk that rotates with the help of a motor. There are rubber heads on this disc that act like a tape recorder. The first one 'reads' the guitar signal played into the unit, the next one plays back this signal and the third erases it. The erasing is only partial so, the next time the disc rotates, the signal is played back again in its partially erased state which creates an echo effect. An amazing video on YouTube shows the pedal being taken apart and renovated.[23] Incidentally, the name of the company is a joke at the expense of Donald Leslie, the inventor of the rotating Hammond organ speaker used by many rock keyboardists. Leslie = 'less – lee' while Morley = 'more – lee'.

Finally, the unit on the stand above the Taurus pedals looks like a prototype console that exactly replicates the controls on the pedals. Miguel is sure this will have been custom-made for Chris by Moog and was perhaps a forerunner of the device included with the later Taurus 2 set (incidentally, a commercial failure). This idea is backed up by the following detail from a Chris Hoskins Advision photo of Chris Squire. The rear of the unit can be seen sporting a Moog sticker (see page 102).

Miguel goes on to tell us that there is also another effect which is important to Squire's sound on this album – a kind of automatic wah-wah. The 'wobbling' effect in 'Future Times – Rejoice' and 'On The Silent Wings Of Freedom' is actually produced by a Mu-Tron III pedal, which is controlled not by a foot pedal like the original 1950s wah-wah effects but according to the dynamics of the instrument. When

---
23   https://tormatobook.com/evo1

Detail from photo of Chris Squire's Rickenbacker and Moog effects control unit, photo courtesy of Chris Hoskins

the strings are hit harder, the envelope filter opens and creates the effect. The Mu-Tron device has additional settings which affect how the guitar sounds and Squire ran everything through a stereo setup which also contributed to the overall sound. Miguel believes that the Rickenbacker bridge pickup would go to the Mu-tron effect and the neck pickup would go to the harmonizer, although this has not been confirmed.

These settings combined to produce a kind of chorus effect – the harmonizer added a slightly de-tuned copy of the original signal, and the stereo wiring added a spatial effect. This provided a lot of 'presence' in his sound which was ideal for songs like 'On The Silent Wings Of Freedom'.

Squire used one or other of the above effects on other songs on *Tormato*, but not in combination. For example, 'Don't Kill The Whale' uses the Mu-Tron but not the harmonizer, as does 'Circus Of Heaven' and 'Onward', but here Squire is not using a pick so the effect is much quieter and more subtle. 'Madrigal' clearly isn't a rock song and only the Taurus bass pedals are used, which are practically inaudible except on the video version of the song. If you want to hear and see exactly what the bass pedals are doing on 'Madrigal', Miguel has produced a video which shows it all beautifully.[24]

It is interesting that Squire didn't ever return to this type of sound approach after *Tormato*. The setup was different on the previous album, *Going For The One*, although Squire was using the Mu-Tron pedal live by then, and by the time we get to *Drama* he had moved on to different techniques. Maybe the *Tormato* bass sound was too extreme, too different. Personally, I love the character of the bass on these songs so perhaps it's another example of what makes this album unique, and we should be grateful that Squire didn't attempt to replicate it later. *Tormato* can be seen as a time capsule in a number of different ways.

The final bass variation of the album is on 'Release, Release', which features the Gibson Thunderbird bass rather than Squire's trademark Rickenbacker. There seem to be no effects at all in use on the bass, presumably to produce a more straight-ahead, rocking sound to complement the song. Mark Anthony K points out that the Thunderbird is a very distinctive-looking bass used by artists like Nikki Sixx of Mötley Crüe and the late Pete Way of UFO. It is also extremely heavy, so rarely finds its way onto the live stage. Like on 'Release, Release', however, its thunderous tonal qualities make it ideal for certain types of studio use. If you haven't heard the interplay between Squire and White on 'Release, Release' recently, do check it out – it's remarkable.

Miguel ends with a note of disappointment that the bass pedals are so low in the mix in several of the songs on the album. Perhaps when someone takes the time to remix what we have, we will finally be able to hear Squire's true vision for the *Tormato* bass.

---

[24] https://tormatobook.com/madrigalbass

Chris Squire at Advision – note the Rickenbacker on the left and the Gibson Thunderbird on the right, photo courtesy of Chris Hoskins

9
WHERE ARE THE MASTER TAPES?

This is perhaps the question asked about *Tormato* more often than any other. Many fans love the album, and many fans hate it, but almost everyone agrees that the best way to make what we do have (even) better is to remix it. Many of us would also love to see Steven Wilson have a go, like he did so successfully with *The Yes Album, Fragile, Close To The Edge, Tales From Topographic Oceans* and *Relayer*. It might also give Roger Dean the chance to create a new cover, which I'm sure many fans would love to see. Personally, I would be sad to see the existing artwork disappear.

While attempting to discover where the *Tormato* master tapes are, or indeed whether they still exist, it has emerged that I've been thinking about the issue in an unhelpful way. I've been using the term 'master tapes' when I actually mean 'multi-track tapes'. Advision 'Tape Op', Peter Woolliscroft's job was to wrangle all the reels produced from each recording session. In Yes' case, this was over the span of three months of recording. You may remember him mentioning in chapter 1 the sheer amount of physical tape that was produced. Recording thirty-two takes of 'On The Silent Wings Of Freedom', for example, meant he was 'drowning in tape' and had to devise elaborate cataloguing systems so that he could locate the reel required. These were multi-track tapes and not master tapes. According to my research, a master tape can be regarded as the 'first final' stereo mix of the songs intended to appear on the album. In the days of analogue recording, it was common practice to copy this master tape immediately and place the first tape (called first-generation) in storage to keep it safe. It was Universal Music Group's massive archive of these first-generation master tapes which was destroyed in the 2008 fire at Universal Studios in California including, according to UMG, works by Peter Frampton, Elton John, Nirvana, Les Paul and R.E.M. amongst several others. (Reports that hundreds of other artists were also affected are denied by UMG.) Clearly, the value of these original masters is very high indeed.

As mentioned above, it is important to remember (note to self), that these master tapes are the first generation of stereo mixes. Although certain tweaks can be made with digital technology, there is no way to remix an album fundamentally from the master (mix) tapes. As pointed out by Yes fan Jon Dee, however, the technology developed for Peter Jackson's *Get Back* documentary is now capable of making much more extensive changes to existing, mixed sources. Perhaps we will see all sorts of albums given this kind of treatment in the future. For the moment, Mixbutton.com sets out a handy explanation of a typical remastering process:

> "When remastering music, the mastering engineers get the digital copies of the track or album using a digital audio workstation (DAW), listen to it and make necessary adjustments in the following order:
> - Firstly, the tracks are ordered to ensure a musical flow, such that each song balances with those that come before and after it.
> - Secondly, noise reduction is used to eliminate or subdue sounds such as hisses, hums, clicks, dropouts, bad edits, whistling, microphone pops, and lisping sounds due to poor microphone placement or old recording techniques.
> - Thirdly, compressing and peak limiting is used to improve loudness, eliminate muffled effects, and enrich the overall sound by sweetening the treble and the bass.
> - Fourthly, the equalizer is used to emphasize or reduce audio frequencies in order to achieve tonal balance and ensure that

beats and harmonies come out clearer, changes are then finalized and presented for final approval."[25]

Steven Wilson worked with the multi-track tapes from the five Yes albums he tackled so that he could restore aspects which were mixed out of the original albums or enhance other parts. He had access to the individual parts recorded by Squire, Anderson, Howe, Wakeman, Moraz, White, Bruford and Kaye and he could reconstruct the songs from scratch, even using different takes when he wanted to. One of the most obvious examples of this is the extended version of 'A Venture' from *The Yes Album*, which was recorded at Advision eight years before *Tormato*. Originally, the song faded out after 3 mins 16 secs, but Wilson restored the ending so that his additional version is 4 mins 47 secs long. He could only do this because he had access to the multi-track tapes, as it states in the sleeve notes:

> Definitive Edition CD
> Mixed and produced from the original
> multi-track tapes by Steven Wilson
> except where noted

When announcing the vinyl box set of the Yes Steven Wilson Remixes, Wilson himself posted on Facebook, "Just to pre-empt the question, I'm afraid there are no plans for any further Yes albums to be remixed, either in stereo or 5.1, so this set is definitive in terms of the remixes."[26] This has inevitably led to speculation as to why there will be no more remixes and it has been suggested that Wilson only works on albums which are personal favourites. He also has rather a lot of other musical activities in his life, as you probably know.

Perhaps he has indeed exhausted his personal list of Yes albums to re-imagine. The five records he has worked on (*The Yes Album, Fragile, Close To The Edge, Tales From Topographic Oceans* and *Relayer*) are arguably the most important for Yes fans and for the general progressive rock buying public. I love *Tormato*, but I wouldn't say it should take its place alongside these five. *Going For The One, Drama, 90125* and perhaps some others could stake their claims but *Tormato*, despite being fascinating and a delight to listen to, certainly cannot be said to

---

25 https://tormatobook.com/mixbutton
26 https://tormatobook.com/stevenwilson

be influential in the same way. There also needs to be a commercial incentive to working on and releasing new versions of Yes albums. These five Yes works are renowned in the progressive rock world and so there is little financial risk in releasing newly spruced-up versions. They are bound to sell, particularly with Steven Wilson's name attached and new artwork by Roger Dean (apart from *The Yes Album*). If you are reading this book, it's possible that you share my infatuation with *Tormato*, but the hard fact is that many fewer people would fancy paying quite a bit of money for a remixed version of *Tormato*. I could be wrong but it's not a risk I'd take without a lot of market research. Maybe the huge sales(!) of this book will persuade the band's management that it would be well worth it ... we shall see.

Despite all this, I have still been on a mission to find out whether the original multi-track tapes of *Tormato* are still out there, ready to be dusted off in the unlikely event of Mr Wilson proclaiming a desire to get back into Yes remix mode. My fear has always been that those multi-tracks have indeed been lost due to nobody realising how important they could be in the future. When we spoke to Peter Woolliscroft, he described the attitude to original multi-track tapes while he was working in studios in the late 70s and 80s:

> "It's always the case with tapes. When you've done the album ... the multi-tracks are almost forgotten because nobody ever thought ... that they were ever going to be needed again. And I used to work with a producer called Tony Visconti and his [store] was full of David Bowie and Mark Bolan out-take multi-tracks that were just going to be thrown away because [no one] ever really thought that they would be of any use. And, of course, now, with hindsight ... they're gold."

I knew from the cover of the *Remastered & Expanded Tormato* that Brian Kehew was credited with 'mixing and tape review' and while searching the internet for information, I came across this quotation on the Tape Op website:

> **"Brian Kehew (bonus): Digging in the Vaults**
> **BY LARRY CRANE**
> **Have you had any crazy technical issues?**

WHERE ARE THE MASTER TAPES?

We were going through Yes' *Tormato* tapes. Producer/engineer Eddie Offord had started the album -he had done most of the Yes records and I know from working on his tracks that he used Dolby A a lot. These tapes don't say Dolby A, but *Tormato* is a famously bad-sounding record. They parted ways with him mid-course and somebody else finished the record. So I'm looking at the tapes and it doesn't say Dolby A anywhere on them — it's typical that they note that when encoded — but I said, "Hold on a second, let me put Dolby on this." And everything — except for some of the later overdubs — sounded amazing. I went, "Aha!" I think we realized what happened. They went to somebody else and the other person didn't see Dolby on the tapes.

Because that record did sound kind of murky...
Thin, flat and terrible. I accidentally discovered the bad secret of it: that it could have sounded a whole lot better."

Tape Op website interview, 2013[27]

This passage seemed to include clues to the questions around not only whether the multi-tracks still exist but also how the resulting record turned out to be sonically disappointing (to some). Here is how my thinking developed: Brian says that they were going through *Tormato* tapes – but he doesn't say if they were the master tapes or the multi-track tapes. However, he does mention overdubs, which would suggest he was working with individual tracks rather than stereo master tapes which had already been mixed. Clearly, the master tapes themselves do exist because we have the expanded and *remastered* CD of *Tormato* for which Brian provided the additional tracks. In a rather puzzling manner, we also know from Peter Woolliscroft *categorically* that no Dolby was used on the sessions at Advision because that would have been inappropriate in the process they were using (see Chapter 1).

In addition, you may remember Peter saying that Eddy Offord was not involved in any of the recording at Advision. Peter maintains that the most Eddy could have done was some recording at the rehearsal sessions for the album. Could Dolby have been added later in the process,

---
27 https://tormatobook.com/kehewinterview

for example at RAK Studios? Peter doesn't say it's impossible, but he gives the impression that he would be very surprised because both Nigel Luby and Geoff Young went to RAK with the band and had been fully involved with all the Advision recording as well. It seems highly unlikely they would have made a mistake which would degrade the quality of the end product, although it is certainly possible.

It was high time Mark Anthony K and I spoke to Brian on the *Yes Music Podcast* to try and clear up some of the questions we had. Brian is responsible for some very important Yes releases of (comparatively) recent years. He is credited on the Remastered & Expanded versions of both *Tormato* and *Drama* as well as the epic undertaking which is the *Progeny* set – *Seven Shows From Seventy-Two*, which has recently been re-issued on vinyl. There isn't enough space in this book to go into detail about how Brian approached the remarkable feat of making *Progeny* available to fans, so I recommend you listen to the *Yes Music Podcast* episode where Mark and I speak to him at length about what he did.[28]

On the topic of *Tormato*, we were keen to know what 'tape review' means. In fact, Brian said that it isn't a particularly effective expression to describe the process. Basically, his role was to take all the tapes from the storage vault which were from the same year as the album recording. He listened to all the tapes and identified anything which wasn't used on the album – complete songs or just elements of songs. As he puts it, " … sometimes it includes the original master track [that] might have a different vocal or a different guitar on it and we try to make a version of that that's releasable and listenable so that people can have … those bonus tracks on the extra bits of a disc."

In this case, the additional tracks were:

'**Abilene**' (B-side of the single, 'Don't Kill The Whale', on most releases)
'**Money**' (previously released on the *YesYears* box set in 1991)
'**Picasso**' (previously unreleased)*
'**Some Are Born**' (previously unreleased)*
'**You Can Be Saved**' (previously unreleased)*
'**High**' (previously unreleased)*

---

28 https://tormatobook.com/kehewymp

'Days' (previously unreleased)*
'Countryside' (previously unreleased)*
'Everybody's Song' (previously unreleased)*
Hidden Track – **'Onward'** (Orchestral Version)

There is some disagreement around which of these songs were recorded at the *Tormato* sessions, with some sources claiming that the ones marked with an asterisk above actually came from the ill-fated Paris sessions of 1979. When we asked Peter Woolliscroft about these tracks, he didn't recall any of them being worked on at Advision, so perhaps some of the confusion comes from the change of studios to RAK, where the band certainly did record overdubs and additional songs.

These previously unreleased pieces were presumably some of the songs rehearsed before the *Tormato* sessions and could have made up part of the theoretical *Tormato II* album. As pointed out by Brian in our conversation, it wasn't his role to work on the songs included on the album itself – the remastering (but not remixing) was done by Dan Hersch and Bill Inglot at DigiPrep. Perhaps the comments from Brian concerning the Dolby issue relate to just the tracks he mixed from RAK. This would make sense as Peter Woolliscroft is sure Dolby was not used at Advision. Brian's working practice is to put the tape on, listen to what's there and, if it's the same as the originally released version, he moves on – it's a two or three minute process.

Still confused, as you can imagine, I contacted Brian again and his swift and kind response goes into a lot more detail. On the terminology he says:

> "There is a confusion about the terms. Multitrack tapes can also be a master tape; Master tape is any original tape used in the recording, which can be a multitrack or a mixtape. Multitrack is the separate elements like bass, drums, vocal, backing vocal etc. Those are Master tapes if they are the originals, and they are dubs or copy tapes if they are a duplication of the original Master tape."

He then goes on to explain that he was working in the Warner Bros. vault where the *Tormato* tapes are stored and, even though he was only concerned with outtakes, it's his belief that, "all the original tapes are kept together, even any safety or copy tapes." Brian confirms that they did use the multi-track tapes of the unreleased material and says it's inconceivable that Warner would store the multi-tracks of the outtakes but not the multi-tracks of the songs which made it onto the album. In fact, Brian says:

> "In some cases, I do remember seeing the original multitrack masters for songs we did not need, the release material already on the record. That would be of no use to us for outtakes, but it was still there, not missing."

This, for me, is pretty conclusive. I think it's clear that the original multi-tracks of *Tormato* are in the Warner Bros. vault.

On the Dolby point and remixing, Brian says:

> "Our new mixes were made in the spirit of the old ones, and sort of to match the original record, but as we felt we had a good new sound we didn't try to copy the thinner sound of the original."

He explains that Dolby has to be used from the outset of a recording and can't be added later. From listening to the multi-track tapes, he thought it sounded like they had been created using Dolby and, when he switched it on, the songs sounded, "...normal and natural again." Brian had no way of telling where the individual tapes were recorded but it seems plausible that the ones he is referring to were recorded at RAK, with Dolby.

PART 3 – THE SONGS

10

SONG REVIEWS

All I could have done when I heard *Tormato* for the first time (see Introduction) and all I can do now is give you my honest opinion of the songs as they sound to me. It's what I have done since the beginning of the *Yes Music Podcast* in 2011 and what follows is an amalgamation of my thoughts from over the years in various episodes of the show, combined with what I've learned while researching this book.

'FUTURE TIMES – REJOICE'

Side one starts with 'Future Times', which segues into 'Rejoice'. Howe and Wakeman play the same theme in unison – then repeat it with Wakeman up an octave, really pushing the mood on. Immediately, it's obvious something is going on between Howe and Wakeman: they are in unison, but guitar and keyboards are occupying the same sonic position. It is, if nothing else, a very unusual opening to an album. The elaborate riff drives and assaults the listener. It certainly makes you sit up. Squire blasts in with the weirdest sounding bass imaginable, phasing and running amok in areas of the aural landscape no bass player has the right to visit. He demands attention from the first note. Alan White's drums are higher in the mix than usual when he comes in and the rhythm section adds to the urgent texture and mood. After a few seconds, the music becomes slightly more laid back and White starts to play a military-inspired pattern on the snare drum to introduce the lyrics.

When the vocals begin, there is great interplay between Anderson and Howe, who plays a strong counter-melodic part to the vocal line. It makes for a very interesting atmosphere. I certainly can't hear any problems with production on the opening track. I like the way the keyboards swirl from right to left in the stereo and the general sound is great. Wakeman and Howe combine well in instrumental passages and there's a bit of that traditional sparring and doubling, supporting the vocals in a high-energy and memorable song. In proper Yes style, a contrasting section takes us away into the stratosphere. You could argue the move back to the original material is a bit rough, ham-fisted even, but I can't help being pulled along. Even Howe's odd backing vocals don't put me off as he whispers sweet and bizarre nonsense in my left ear.

The construction of the track is also satisfying with good use of light and shade between sections. I particularly like the way the backing vocals and Anderson interact in the section around 3 mins 10 secs where the numbered list is declared and then elaborated – "One, the word will enter all our hearts, two, the jewel will alter them", and so on. It is an effective break from the momentum of other sections and highlights the fantastic (in the sense of fantasy) language Anderson has come up with.

The band employ a common technique in many forms of music – the chorus (by which I mean group of singers or actors rather than structural element of a song) have a conversation with, or comment on, the text of the lead singer or actor. This practice stretches all the way back to Greek drama. Perhaps one of the most extreme examples of this in rock music is Queen's 'Bohemian Rhapsody', which deliberately borrows the style from opera to create one of the most memorable effects of all time. Here, it is also very effective. The strange, weird counting section is filled to the brim with some kind of astral significance. This is what I came to crave from Yes records as I found out more.

The whole feel of the song is upbeat. It is joyful and segues straight into 'Rejoice' which preserves the mood and introduces a fantastic Howe theme. Positivity reigns and is reinforced by the way the melodic and harmonic treatments are supported by the rhythm section. Those vocal harmonies fit in perfectly again and the song builds and builds to a climactic finish.

The themes seem perfectly realised to me – Howe leads at times but Wakeman and Squire flit in and out with astonishing lines and the recapitulations of melodies are remarkable. The interplay of bass with the vocals and everything else that is going on is staggering. It is such a treat to hear some wonderful Wakeman soloing over the top of an unusual bed of lines. I still can't hear production issues here – it sounds unusual, fresh and brilliant to me.

'Future Times – Rejoice' gives us over six and a half minutes of classic Yes in scale, in mood, in sound and in construction. It has breadth and touches of the epic nature of the best of previous records. A great start to the album.

'DON'T KILL THE WHALE'

Proudly proclaimed on the hype sticker that came with the Record Store Day picture disc of *Tormato*, 'Don't Kill the Whale' was the only single from the album in the UK (see chapter 14), reaching number 36 in the chart.

Clearly, this was an attempt to follow up 'Wonderous Stories' from *Going for the One* and achieve some single success. However, I think this is more effective than the previous song. It's obviously more up-tempo and showcases the musicianship and virtuosity of all members of the band. Someone new to Yes hearing this single and subsequently investigating the rest of *Tormato* and then the back catalogue would surely find what they were looking for. From the catchy Howe guitar figure which opens the song, I'm hooked, or maybe harpooned like those unfortunate whales.

In Tim Morse's book *Yesstories*, Rick Wakeman describes the origins of the song being a Chris Squire Bo Diddley type rhythm and Chris himself says he wrote different lyrics to it that were then replaced by Jon Anderson. It was Anderson who came up with the whale topic, it seems, but the whole band were feeling quite passionate about the plight of our last heaven beasts. Steve Howe points out that he usually improvised his fills for songs, presumably in the studio and there are some very unusual ones in this song which work alongside the vocal line. Also unusually, Rick Wakeman says he tried to create sounds on his Polymoog to imitate whale noises. Look out for that.

It is, like 'Wonderous Stories', very short in comparison with the classic tracks of recent albums, but where 'Don't Kill the Whale' succeeds is in the way it includes most of the archetypal Yes elements along with more 'commercial' ones in a succinct and satisfying way. Rather than a glimpse of what could be, it is an expertly packaged mini epic.

What do I mean by this? We start with an intriguing Howe solo supported by the rest of the instruments. It starts low, as we have seen before, and then climbs, building the tension and leading the ear of the listener to ask, "What comes next?" The solo has a wonderful lilt to it and it is constructed rather like a vocal line, which climbs up high while Chris Squire's incredible harmonised bass notes intertwine to create an amazing texture. Wakeman provides an unusual, sort of watery keyboard sound.

It reminds me of a great painting where the eye is drawn along a line suggested by the composition of visual elements. When Howe introduces the verse with Anderson singing a line that is memorable not only for the melody but also for the lyrical content. It is a hook in several senses of the word. The Anderson vocals with their harmonies are catchy and singalong – great for a single. The introduction is finely crafted to end in the Anderson proclamation of the importance of not "killing our last heaven beast" – the sentiment is clear even if the grammar isn't.

Also, listen to how Wakeman creates the irresistible groove here. He sets up a keyboard vamp in an off-beat pattern that combines with Howe and the rest of the band to produce a toe-tapping, catchy feel, perfect for a single but also maintaining the critical Yes aesthetic. There's no way this could be any other rock and roll band, or any other combination of musicians.

Howe piles in again with a great solo passage supported by a fascinating mix of piano, bass, keys and drums. The lyrics veer towards the banal with the title line that jars a little, but, overall, the song has great motion, provided by the rhythm section. Wakeman's jangly piano and

Steve Howe's fills are unusual sounding and complement the melody. Rick also gets to blast away on a fleet-fingered solo that is strident and, I suggest, evokes a sense of protest. It is like a rousing call to action – an attractive and memorable section.

Other essential elements of Yes are also present – extended, intricate guitar solo spots, great vocal harmonies, a typical Wakeman keyboard solo, as well as dramatic, warping synthesized sounds, fantastic roaming bass line, rock solid, creative drumming and even a mini climactic ending. There is plenty of punch to the vocals and the accompaniment and the band sounds entirely committed to the song and the cause.

It is an interesting and complex structure. I suppose there are those who would say you can hear the production problems here with the instruments all struggling for supremacy, but I believe it all combines to produce a highly immersive and satisfying experience. Howe brings back that opening guitar refrain and elaborates it in another solo, until Wakeman takes over, and I can see now what he meant about trying to achieve the whale sound. The rather raucous synth voice plays a contrapuntal dance with another keyboard line as it bends its pitch.

All this is wrapped up in a protest song – capturing the mood of the day, or maybe foreshadowing the mood that was to come (see chapter 14).

'MADRIGAL'
I wonder if this is one of the songs which puts people off the album. I can see why it might be viewed as at best quirky and at worst contrived. You won't be surprised to hear that I really like it. It's particularly effective in its proper context on the album, coming as it does after the maelstrom of 'Don't Kill the Whale'.

I'm sure the use of harpsichord by Rick Wakeman irritates those who already view Yes music with suspicion and use words like 'pretentious,' 'pompous' or 'overblown'. However, I'd argue that it is refreshing to hear the classically trained musician integrating another traditional instrument into a progressive rock song. After the grandiose success of the church organ on *Going for the One*, here we have a more intimate sound, with the harpsichord joined by Howe's acoustic guitar, a lovely vocal line from Anderson, wordless backing chorus and some highly effective string arrangement. It is no surprise to learn that the orchestral arrangement like later on in 'Onward', are down to Chris Squire collaborator and childhood friend, the late Andrew Pryce Jackman. Squire and Jackman were both in early bands The Selfs and The Syn and Jackman also provided his inspirational touch on *Fish out of Water*, 'Run with the Fox', *The Steve Howe Album* and many more prog records. While writing this book, I contacted Andrew's son, Henry Jackman (now a prolific and successful Hollywood film composer himself) to see if he had any information or artefacts concerning *Tormato*, but sadly everything is lost in the mists of time. The only thing Henry could recall is that his father worked on the arrangements for 'Madrigal' and 'Onward' at Chris Squire's house, *New Pipers* in Virginia Water.

Rick Wakeman plays the harpsichord properly, as far as I can tell. Unlike the often chugging, uninspired and uninspiring efforts of the Baroque Pop brigade (and that's a real genre, I understand from my son), Wakeman transfers the poise and flowing patterns of his solo piano playing into something unique in this song and the interplay between harpsichord and Howe's classical guitar is beautiful.

The subject matter also fits the general mood. We have a return to a concoction of fantasy. Anderson's melody floats and bobs above with astral images – sacred ships sailing the seventh age, celestial travellers, dancing with the spirit of the age.

However, it's one of the shortest Yes songs for a long time at less than three minutes and the end is somewhat abrupt. Also, the title is misleading, as a madrigal is actually an unaccompanied (mainly) English renaissance part song featuring pastoral lyrics. Some of the most well-known examples are 'Now is the Month of Maying', 'Fair Phyllis' and the 'The Silver Swan'. Being unaccompanied, there would certainly be no harpsichord, but at least the origins of the main instrument lie in approximately the right historical period.

Overall, the brilliance of this song is the way in which it is elevated to something really special, through the musicianship and careful arrangement of these master craftsmen. It could so easily have been banal, cloying or just plain daft.

Yes: The Tormato Story

'RELEASE, RELEASE'

After that little interlude, we are straight into 'Release, Release', one of my favourite songs on the album. As pointed out by Yes fan John Holden, the song's working title was 'Anti Campaign' and maybe that gives us a clue as to the band's intentions.

It starts with a typical Howe riff at different octaves, then moves into a rocky section, but, being Yes, this is initially in an unusual time signature. I've always liked this rhythmical ambiguity. It's a rocker in a way, but the beat shifts in the drums and the bass across the guitar part. Musical forces are pitted seemingly in contradictory fashion with bass and drum parts against Howe's rocky soloing. I am instantly transported back to my teenage bedroom. Doubled bass and keyboard patterns lead us to an instrumental hiatus that always makes me smile. I remember being fascinated by what Alan White is doing here – deliberately playing with the stresses of the music to create an unsettling feel, despite the overall rock sense. The main mood swings back in and it is all huge fun. Chris Squire is clearly enjoying himself bumping along at the bottom and then running up and down with the keyboards. There is complexity and intelligent contrast in this music.

Alan White talks about this song in *Yesstories* by Tim Morse and points out that he wrote it with Jon Anderson. It was one of Jon's favourite songs, apparently. Unfortunately, Alan said it was too much of a powerhouse to play live – they tried but gave up after a few outings. The drum part is interesting and, of course, there is the famous drum solo, but we'll come to that later.

When the vocals enter, their offbeat notes play off the vamping, pumping bass line and drums to continue the odd, unsettling impression. Keyboard and bass doubling and the use of more hiatus moments keeps me smiling, while Howe plays with embellished rock rhythm guitar work. The vocal line itself is another of those unsettling ones which seems to phase across the accompaniment, producing a dazzling rhythmical texture. There are points where the vocals are left on their own, great doubling of the riffs by the instruments and White's drumming is insistent, driving the band onward. It's wonderful, urgent stuff. Like the greatest Yes music, 'Release, Release' has the power to fill you up with positive vibes.

Once again, we have the appearance of the vocal chorus – this time it sounds like Squire and Howe on their own, supplying a commentary on the action before Anderson takes over the reins again. I love the sound and the sentiment of the refrain – "Release release – or abandon your hope for your brother," and then repeated with 'sister'. Wakeman provides an elaborate and intricate exploration of the tonality in his rushing up and down the keys, heightening the mood.

If you're looking for classic Yes features like several different sections, then look no further. Following Rick playing some of his freest runs, we arrive at the fake crowd and drum solo section, which I absolutely love in all its phoney fun. White is joined by Howe a little later with one of the best and fastest riffs he has ever used. All this is to the accompaniment of recorded crowd noise that gives the music an added sense of excitement. The crowd disappears and a new section takes over with a return to the previous sense of impetus, then yet another change as Wakeman takes over the solo duties. You could criticise the Wakeman sounds and especially the way they appear only in the left of the stereo, but I actually like the timbre he produces here.

There's a great electric guitar solo and the music builds up and up towards a backwards cymbal introducing the denouement. Yes, you can criticise the keyboard sounds and it is all a bit uneven, but I can't get enough of it. It feels like a proper Yes prog song, with its twists and turns, its spacey idiocy and spritely synth runs. It is as complex as many of the epics on previous albums – a tour-de-force (of course) of progressive rock, despite being concentrated into less than six minutes.

'ARRIVING UFO'

The next song is another of the controversial ones. Like the celestial travellers of 'Madrigal', the subject matter concerns UFOs – and there's the first problem. Maybe, at the time, it was acceptable to compose a song about UFOs, before *The X-Files* and the widespread ridicule of the serious folk who still believe. However, Anderson sings, "I could not take it so seriously really when you called and said you'd seen a UFO." Well, can we take this song seriously?

Like a lot of *Tormato*, the opening contains a whole host of creative and imaginative effects. Sound phases across the stereo in an attractive manner and then the vocals come in. I can fully understand why a lot of people find these lyrics so irksome. They are at the very least silly, but I still prefer their playfulness to some of the banalities of other, more recent, Yes songs.

Apart from the subject matter, the music is effective with several great hooks in the guitar and the keyboard lines. The feel of other-worldliness is maintained by use of percussion and some fairly science-fiction sounding tones from Wakeman. Howe is trying to create an unusual feel with his oscillating runs and the astral effects on the vocals are effective. I also like Wakeman's dramatic keyboard passage and, throughout, Chris Squire keeps the music pumping with an immense bass line. As always in the best Yes music, directly contrasting sections aren't far away. The combination of fast bass line, some heavily effect-altered lead guitar lines and lots of synth gives the sonic impression of alien visitation.

Again, I can see why some might take against the lightning strike effect and the 1978 electronic drum effects (see chapter 7), but what flows through this song and the whole album is a great sense of energy and commitment, which is somewhat surprising given the way it was produced and the dissatisfaction of the band itself later on.

It is possible to imagine the song as a theme or instrumental music to a 1970s science-fiction film, but maybe a rather low-budget one. Perhaps *Space 1999* rather than *Star Wars*. Listening to it with a critical ear, I can appreciate the view that it is contrived. It has none of the grandeur or poise of previous large-scale pieces, despite some great playing. Maybe it goes too far in trying to sound spacey. However, there are great Squire moments – driving bass lines contrasting with the more experimental ones – and Wakeman and Howe are definitely on form in solos and interplay. The vocal line is also strong, but maybe most listeners can't ignore the lyrics and the more obvious attempts to create a science-fiction feel. Those of us who can get past these elements, though, enjoy it for what it is – maybe a bit daft but good fun all the same.

'CIRCUS OF HEAVEN'
'Circus of Heaven' starts with triangle (or is it crotale?), bass guitar rising patterns and lead guitar. Immediately, these sound either touch-

ingly naive or unbearably twee, depending on your point of view. Anderson begins to sing and, once again, we are walking on thin ice because of the subject matter and how it is described in the lyrics.

This time it's all about a fantastical circus with descriptions of the players, beasts and so on. The music grows with bass drum eventually creeping in and the momentum increasing with keyboard runs and great vocal backing. If you can ignore the actual content of the lyrics, what you get is a beautiful tapestry of different musical elements, all combining perfectly to create a mystical mood. I find it all great fun as it adds layers and more extreme lyrics. Even Alexander the Great gets a look in.

I like the way the song grows, adding careful harmony vocals and Steve Howe's increasingly rapid and spiky electric guitar. I understand how this could be annoying with its tons of reverb, but for me it is an interesting effect. I suppose it may be when Wakeman brings in his fairground-esque, spindly synth that a lot of people have had enough of this preposterous confection. As with other songs, I think the instrumental and vocal arrangements are clever, with more than a splash of Howe backing vocals transplanting 1960s 'oh la la la' interjections into this 1978, end of prog piece. It has none of the awe and wonder of 'Awaken' but it is definitely an effective song.

Around 2 mins 15 secs, the mood changes and Wakeman duets elaborately with tuned percussion, creating a remarkable texture to introduce Anderson singing about, "great animals as tame as the trees". It's a passage guaranteed to induce distaste from a good number of Yes fans. Quite what 'emerald snow' might be, I'm not sure.

The inclusion of young master Anderson is perhaps the final straw for many. Damion is mildly disappointed with the raggedy old circus which was, in his opinion, simply, "OK", despite his father's wide-eyed rapture. How can you really have a proper circus, land-based or cloud-based, without clowns? He's got a point.

Here's a tip. If you have friends who are a bit sceptical about Yes music, don't play 'Circus of Heaven' to them as an introduction to the band. They might possibly get the idea that it's all a bit silly. I have no problem at all with the lyrics or subject matter, but then I must have listened to this track hundreds of times. I grew up with it and I think I understand what Anderson is trying to do. He is always serious about the themes of the songs, and I'm sure this is no exception.

The fast patterns in the instrumentation continue, suggesting circus music and a Wakeman pattern leads to the close of the song. It sounds like Wakeman, Howe and the percussion of White are trying to console the youngster with a bit more of the fairground frippery and then the music fades away.

Insult to brand Yes or not? You decide.

'ONWARD'

It is now impossible for me to separate this song from the sight of Chris Squire's Rickenbacker bass guitar centre stage in a single spotlight at the beginning of multiple Yes shows from August 2015 onward. Yes' touching tribute to their late band mate is unforgettable and I'm very grateful I managed to experience it in Birmingham myself.

'Onward' is a beautiful song, simple but deeply affecting with the remarkable ostinato-like, quasi ground bass parts (the technique used in Baroque music such as Pachelbel's Canon) and a wonderful, layered bass choir fashioned by the master himself. I do remember being very puzzled as to why Steve Howe's staccato picking appears to be transferred from 'Circus of Heaven' directly into the opening of 'Onward' and I still feel the same about it. An odd choice.

Anderson sings the love song perfectly. "Contained in everything I do there's a love I feel for you." It grows to the deeply moving chorus, "Onward through the night of my life." It's beautifully crafted music with archetypal Yes contrasts in the texture – slow bass and lyrical vocal line with a fast-moving guitar part between. There's an arc to the structure of the melody and the French horn solo is one of the most deeply affecting moments of all Yes music. I remember listening to it late at night when I was a teenager. It helped me through some dark times. Little hooks abound here with Steve Howe's aforementioned guitar part flitting about above the texture, providing a perfect contrast to the long lines of the sumptuous vocal melody. The second verse adds vocal harmonies which are again subtle and finely crafted.

The orchestral arrangement adds a polish to the sound. It is muted and gives an impression of culture and elegance compared with the less refined feel of some of the other songs on *Tormato*. When we consider the use of classical instruments in Yes music it is easy to forget the superb Andrew Pryce Jackman orchestration of 'Onward' and 'Madrigal'. 'Onward' doesn't just contain the achingly beautiful French Horn solo, there are also strings in there. Interestingly, Rick Wakeman recently told me that his view of the orchestrations by Jackman are rather different to mine:

> "I was not happy with them. I wanted to do them myself but somehow got rowed out! ... water under the bridge."

Despite Rick's misgivings, 'Onward' is the kind of Yes song I close my eyes to and experience for its deep, enveloping spirit – such a treasure.

'ON THE SILENT WINGS OF FREEDOM'

Finally, we reach the last song and one which many Yes fans consider to be the best on the album. Moments after 'Onward' fades away to nothing, Yes, the masters of contrast, hit us straight between the ears with the opening salvo of 'On the Silent Wings Of Freedom'. I well remember being stunned by what Chris Squire was up to at the start of this song. He's doing things I had never heard any other bass player do before. It's an actual bass solo at the beginning of a song. Crikey!

'On The Silent Wings Of Freedom' includes some of the best drums and bass interplay in all Yes music. It has all the improvised-sounding excess of *Relayer* blended with the imperious feel of 'The Fish'. Jazzy drums, well-placed keyboards and lead guitar that fade in and out enhance the elaborate and mesmerising Squire-fest and it's not clear where this explorative passage is taking us. How many bass guitarists have there been with so much freedom, confidence and brilliance in their playing? This opening is a masterclass in the bass guitarist's art. It is, of course, lead bass playing. Squire is brilliantly supported by the other instrumentalists and the whole piece grows in intensity until Anderson comes in with the strident vocal line. The song has enormous forward momentum with really effective breaks that swing back into the tempo and move onwards.

Eventually, everything ramps up via a guitar progression to the first vocals. An unusual and very high line, the lyrics are once again impenetrable, but seem to fit together. The chorus rocks your socks off with crazily fast guitar work. In the next verse, the accompaniment is fragmented in a rock style and Howe plays some of his most blistering licks ever. He sounds like he's trying to knock down a brick wall with his guitar.

Whatever your preconceptions of this album, do listen to this song carefully as I'm sure you will discover aspects you have forgotten – the interplay between Squire's bass and Howe's lead guitar is astonishing and that effect Squire is using just adds to the tonal mayhem. Not content with the instruments rocking the house down, a set of harmony vocals are added, and Alan White's drumming is amongst the most creative and hard-hitting of his long Yes tenure.

At about 4 mins 38 secs the mood changes, as you would expect from Yes, and Squire plays a meditative exploration of the theme that leads to a church bell. This provides word painting for Anderson to sing, "On the darkest nights," perhaps echoing lyrical themes in 'Onward'.

As he continues, you can sense the tempo beginning to re-establish itself and we are back to the original feel with a complex combination of Howe and Wakeman solos and chorus-type vocals. It is great to hear a bit of that Howe/Wakeman sparring again with one of the fastest and most progtastic Rick Wakeman solos ever. He complained that Steve Howe was trying to play more notes than anyone had ever attempted on a record, but then he himself could be accused of the same thing here and I love it all.

The whole feel is upbeat and positive as it hurtles towards the end of the song and the album. The finish is properly excessive with Squire jumping in to make sure we all remember that he is also capable of adding complex, fast-moving and energetic lines. The ending is abrupt but perfectly coordinated to the millisecond amongst the musicians.

'TORMATO' OUTTAKES by Geoff Bailie

Prog Report stalwart and *Yes Music Podcast* patron, Geoff Bailie, kindly offered his opinions on the other songs which were recorded around the time of the *Tormato* sessions.

"Pink Floyd fans created the term ROIO (Recording Of Indeterminate Origin) to describe musical recordings whose origin or copyright status were hard to determine. Others will call these items 'bootlegs'. While the world of Yes has an abundance of live recordings of an 'indeterminate' nature, studio outtakes have only very occasionally appeared. The *Yes Years* box set, followed by the *In A Word* box set started to yield some interesting off cuts, and with the subsequent Rhino and Panegyric reissues, more bits and pieces have been given official release status.

So, what's out there officially from the Tormato era, apart from the album?

'Abilene'
Well covered elsewhere in this book, and first released as the b-side to the 'Don't Kill The Whale' single.

'Money'
Appeared in 1991 on the *Yes Years* box set. This rollicking rock and roll track has some fabulous Wakeman piano and keyboard soloing. Wakeman's Denis Healey impersonation monologue is certainly something that belonged firmly in the era it was recorded. (Healy was the much parodied British Chancellor of the Exchequer at the time of recording.)

'Richard'
Appeared in 2002 on the *In A Word* box set. To me this is a very strong track. The bass track in particular is extremely inventive and the Anderson/Squire/Howe harmonies are excellent.

'Picasso'
An Anderson composition from the Rhino reissue in 2004. In the 1991 *Yes Years* documentary, there is fly-on-the-wall footage of White and Anderson chatting to Rabin and they refer to the ill-fated Paris recording sessions with Roy Thomas-Baker. White says that Jon was separated from the rest of the band who were set up in a pit area, while Jon sat in a vocal booth painting! Anderson then starts to sing the 'Picasso' song, while gesturing as if playing a guitar and painting – he is possibly mixing up the eras, albeit the line up was the same. The song itself is something beautiful, and certainly better than anything that came from the later Paris sessions. It apparently found its way into

Jon's song suite / musical about fellow painter, Marc Chagall, in much the same form as the demo.

'Some Are Born'
Another Anderson song, from the Rhino release, which was re-worked for his *Song Of Seven* solo album. Most of the elements that later appeared are here in this version.

'You Can Be Saved'
A Squire track also from the Rhino edition. This is another song that clearly progressed beyond just being a sketch, with Anderson and Squire duetting over a lush keyboard backing from Rick, joined by Chris' bass, as the piece moves into loosely arranged multi-part vocals. The absence of White and Howe may suggest it wasn't something that everyone in the studio was into, and so it ended up lost in the mists of time.

'High'
A Rhino-released Howe track that contains part of the instrumental that became 'Sketches In The Sun', performed with Asia and eventually recorded on the *GTR* album. While the GTR version sounds like it was recorded on a 12-string acoustic guitar, this one starts with the same riff on an electric guitar. Howe is joined by bass and drums with some wordless vocals from Jon leading to an actual song section. The backing track does have a certain jam-like quality, like they are working their way through it, but a finished version was not to be.

'Days'
Like 'Some Are Born', this Anderson song appeared on *Song Of Seven*. The Rhino bonus track is an a cappella version which was worked up into a full song for Jon's solo album. It's a lovely experience to hear him singing through this melody, and the version that appeared on *Song Of Seven* is a strong realisation of this original seed.

'Countryside'
This one is credited to Anderson, Howe, Squire and White (no Wakeman although, one would assume, he's playing keyboards on it!). However, it does appear as a Howe solo demo in a similar arrangement on one of Steve's *Homebrew* collections, and eventually gets a main album release as an instrumental song called 'Corkscrew' on Howe's 1991 album *Turbulence*.

'Everybody's Song'
With similar (lack of?) credits to 'Countryside', this instrumental was clearly the origin of the *Drama* song 'Does It Really Happen?' It's intriguing that Jon certainly sings the main line but presumably he didn't write it, otherwise you'd think he'd deserve a credit on that album. My guess is that the words derive from Squire – in particular the, "to you," of the lyrics seems very Chris-like to these ears.

Despite appearing as a bonus track on the Rhino Records reissue of *Tormato*, there is some debate about this track's origins. While very down in the mix, the keyboard parts and particular parts in the guitar/keyboard trade off towards the end of the song are more reminiscent of Patrick Moraz's usual sounds than Rick Wakeman's. So perhaps this actually dates from early sessions for the *Going For The One* album or other studio sessions involving Moraz, but is placed on this disc so as to keep the *Drama* disc an album of music by that line up.

With official releases covered, the question is, what else is there out there of ROIO status from the studio? Well, the answer is that there is more. An internet or YouTube search will turn up the bootleg set called, *Digital Reels and Master Reels (Demos from 1978–1978)*. This appeared on a single CD and contains nineteen tracks. The final seven are the previously mentioned Paris sessions, which mostly appeared on Rhino's reissue of *Drama*. However, the remaining twelve are *Tormato*-era recordings, I believe.

The set starts with two versions of the aforementioned 'Picasso', entitled 'Picasso 1' and 'Picasso 2'. 'Picasso 1' breaks down after around 30 seconds, with 'Picasso 2' being a much longer pass at the song. This is an entirely different version than the Rhino bonus track on account of being almost double the length and featuring some very prominent Wakeman piano which doesn't appear at all on the official release.

Some hard panning of instruments in the mix would suggest the original source here is a rough or reference mix of the sessions – which would also explain the presence of some duplicate songs on this set. As an almost fully acoustic and piano heavy song, I can see why it may have been felt that it occupies similar space to the album's Madrigal, perhaps leading to its elimination.

Next up are two versions of Squire's solo recording of 'Amazing Grace'. Their presence here is interesting and raises the Indeterminate Origins questions that many ROIOs tend to. A similar version appears on the *Yes Years* box set, but is credited to the *Going For The One* sessions of 1976 – a credit which is repeated in the Rhino *Going For The One* reissue. If the *Going For The One* version didn't make the cut, maybe it was tried again for the next album? Perhaps though, it's more likely that this piece was something Squire used when setting up/testing his bass guitar and bass pedals, and someone just happened to hit record during these sessions. There isn't much variation in any of the versions and it's a nice piece, recently remade by Billy Sherwood when Squire passed away.

This is followed by two more versions of 'Money' and ... well things aren't getting any better! The first one, entitled 'Money 5', doesn't have the vocal overdubs (singing and 'Healeying') of the *Yes Years* version, and sounds much more like the band having a loose run through the tune in the studio. There is some nice guitar and keyboard interplay, and several occasions where the two instruments are battling each other for space ... who wins? Well, 'Yes Music' was definitely the loser in this case! The second version, 'Money 6', may well be connected to the version on *Yes Years*. This time Jon's vocal is double tracked (sometimes badly) and it has clear Squire – and perhaps Howe – vocal overdubs. The Healey impersonation is present, more clearly than on *Yes Years*, and this is not a good thing, especially as some of Rick's 'of their time' comments would be considered offensive today. Certainly, this version hasn't been properly mixed but there are great additions which it would have been good to hear pulled out and the fader with the Denis impersonation could have been switched to zero.

'Celestial Seasons' is a very Yes-sounding title for what is a version of 'On The Silent Wings of Freedom'. Listening to it, it could be that this is a work in progress version of the finished track. The bass and drum track along with some guitar parts sound very much like the final version – but Jon's vocal, or at least not all of it, is the finished take. There seem to be multiple, not aligned, vocal tracks present and several guitar ideas being tried out which didn't make the final cut. Again, it has the feel of a compiled, rough, reference mix which Howe, Wakeman and Anderson were experimenting with.

The track, 'Richard', appears in two versions after this. 'Richard 1' sounds very much like the same take used on the *In A Word* box, but this version is a full minute longer – the ending section in particular seems to have been pared back for the *In A Word* release, sadly losing a nice, "He set us free," three-part vocal line. 'Richard 2' doesn't have the overdubs and is two and a half minutes long on account of an early fade.

Two 'Richards' are followed by two versions of 'Days', both a capella renditions of the song very similar to the Rhino versions. I expect one of them is the same version but they're so similar it's hard to pinpoint. 'Some Are Born' which follows sounds very much like the Rhino released track in a less polished form.

The final *Tormato* era song on that release is entitled 'Railway 14 (Arriving UFO)' and, no surprise, this is the track from which the bracketed song was derived. The track itself is an almost eight minute long jam around the bass riff and the repeated keyboard pattern that open the track. It sounds like at least part of this is on some kind of loop or sequencer, repeating the section, while the three instrumentalists extemporise. There are no key changes, so, essentially, it's Howe riffing in the key of G. White starts to add some rhythm patterns almost halfway through, and, around four minutes in, Squire shifts up the neck to play the phrase in a higher register for a few seconds before dropping back down again. While Howe's burst of ideas is interesting, it's a tough enough listen after a few minutes – a brief insight into the band searching for some ideas but really nothing more of merit.

I know that fans of various bands, including Yes, have differing views on ROIOs. Some are in the, "If they weren't good enough first time around ... " camp and have little interest. Others enjoy the exploration process/revelations that a demo or alternate version can produce. In the context of a detailed examination of everything *Tormato*-related, I believe these tracks lead us to a number of conclusions:

1. There was certainly no shortage of viable material for this album, beyond the 42 minutes of officially released tracks.
2. Much of what didn't make the final album was deemed of sufficient quality, at least as ideas, by the band members to take them forward on future projects, including solo albums, in some cases

twelve or thirteen years later.
3. From the future ROIOs that we do have, none any of the extra ideas from the *Tormato* sessions were picked up and used when the band reconvened to create the next album at the ill-fated Paris sessions. Instead, the focus was on creating new music that, mostly, never reached fruition."

Geoff's final comment was backed up by Rick Wakeman when I asked him about which songs were worked on in the Paris sessions. He said, "These were all new and mainly compositions I wrote with Jon during the American tour."

11

THE LYRICS[29]

"I think it's easy to overlook that Anderson actually believes in celestial travellers and UFOs. I think his *Tormato* lyrics are actually moving towards greater literalism, it's just that his wacky ideas are hard to identify in those terms."

Henry Potts, 2023

Writing credits:

'Future Times / Rejoice':
Anderson, Howe, Squire, Wakeman, White
'Don't Kill The Whale':
Anderson, Squire
'Madrigal':
Anderson, Wakeman
'Release Release':
Anderson, Squire, White
'Arriving UFO':
Anderson, Howe, Wakeman
'Circus of Heaven':
Anderson

---

[29] All songs published by Topographic Music, Inc., ASCAP administered by WB Music Corp.

'Onward':
Squire
'On The Silent Wings Of Freedom':
Anderson, Squire

Yes lyrics have long been a topic of fascination for many. Jon Anderson's compositions in particular have featured what for some have appeared to be the most confusing, opaque and frankly weird words in all of popular music. This may have had more or less to do with the consumption of mind-expanding substances, I don't know.

I have certainly always loved the fairly random-seeming combination of religions, belief systems, mystical imagery and astral projections in a lot of Yes lyrics from the 1970s. At times, Anderson has used literary works as inspiration for Yes music, notably 'Gates Of Delirium' from *Relayer* based on Leo Tolstoy's *War and Peace*, *Tales From Topographic Oceans* conceived from a footnote found in *Autobiography of a Yogi* by Paramahansa Yogananda and *Close To The Edge* leaning on *Siddhartha* by Hermann Hesse for theme and lyrics ideas.

According to Yes author Thomas J. Mosbø in his book *Yes But what Does It Mean?*, Anderson turned to science fiction writer Ray Bradbury and his story *Something Wicked This Way Comes* for the inspiration behind 'Circus Of Heaven'. There is a supernatural carnival in that story but, as Mosbø points out, neither the lyrics nor the theme of the *Tormato* song have any direct connection to Bradbury's tale.

Although it is difficult to know exactly which band member is responsible for which lyrics, I would suggest three different approaches to lyric writing. It may be helpful to consider these in the context of the band's reported attempts to appeal to a changing audience. Movements such as punk were clearly more interested in shock value and aggression in their writing than the old timers of the Progressive music world, but are there clues to an accommodation of different styles in *Tormato*?

Style One – Direct
An easy place to start is with the one song on the album which is rather different to the rest – 'Onward'. A comparatively simple love song by Chris Squire, its lyrics are poem-like and pastoral. They are easy to understand and direct, but this does not make them of lesser value

than others on the album. There are only two short verses and a set of repeated chorus phrases which leave plenty of room for the sublime orchestral arrangement from Andrew Pryce Jackman. The beauty of the song is matched by the beauty of the lyrics and, as mentioned above, it cannot now be separated from the Chris Squire tributes in 2015 and 2016.

> "Contained in everything I do
> There's a love, I feel for you …
> … Onward through the night of my life"

'Don't Kill The Whale' has a clear message and, as a charity protest single (see chapter 14), one might expect it to be in this literal style category so that listeners couldn't miss the meaning. Immediately obvious is how few words there are in this song, rather like the other song in this style category, 'Onward'. Both songs contain seventeen lines (as set out in the lyrics sheet), compared to forty-six in 'Release, Release' and thirty-nine in 'Circus Of Heaven'. In its short span, 'Don't Kill The Whale' makes effective use of straightforward rhymes:

> "First" and "thirst"
> "Much" and "touch"
> "Space" and "grace"
> "Frail" and "whale"

These are not arranged in a simple end-of-the-line fashion but, nevertheless, they make the message of the song clearer and, perhaps, the lyrics easier to remember. The meaning, and therefore the effect of the last word used, 'Cetacei' (see chapter 21) was probably lost on audiences in 1978 as well as today, but I do appreciate its inclusion, not least because it sounds appropriate in the song, whatever your understanding of its literal meaning.

Style Two – Fantasy/Science-Fiction Storytelling or Description

The two songs at the beginning of the second side of the album also both use a fairly direct style, but also tell stories or describe events. 'Arriving UFO' clearly has a science fiction theme and 'Circus of Heaven' a fantasy/science-fiction basis. The lyrics of the first part of 'Arriving UFO' and the whole of 'Circus of Heaven' can be read as informal po-ems or stream of consciousness prose, with the rest of the former song veering towards my third style, as explained below.

'Arriving UFO' references someone claiming to have seen a spaceship, but his friend (the narrator) is initially sceptical. Then comes an epiphany as the narrator realises just how important and amazing such an arrival would be, in either literal or metaphorical (spiritual) terms. He seems to become an advocate for the idea of visitation and, "The coming of outer space." 'Circus Of Heaven' describes a scene where performers of an amazing variety parade into town and set up their tent in the traditional fashion of the occupational travellers.

There are points in the text of 'Arriving UFO' where the meter of the words does not evenly match that of the music, as usually is required in popular music, though not in operatic arias, for example. Slightly displaced vocal phrasing is required in order to make the two elements of the music fit together.

> "Strange and startling
> Was this voice just saying
> There's got to be a linking of everyone
> Got to be a centre
> It all comes flooding back"

Some lines may appear to some readers to have too many syllables and some too few. "It all comes flooding back", for example, could have included another syllable towards and the end of the line, "Was this voice just saying," seems to collide with the beginning of the next. This is also the case at the end of the final two lines in the example above. The last line of the song (repeated from earlier), "The coming of outer space," places the stress on "-ter" of "outer" due to what is happening in the music.

Another variation can be seen later on in the line, "With the force as it has been known to be seen." This sentence seems to have been artificially extended to fit the music better. If this was prose, the statement could have ended after 'been known', perhaps, and the rest of the line could be viewed as redundant – depending how one understands the relationship between 'knowing' and 'seeing'.

While the song is broadly accessible, I think the way some of the words are squeezed into the structure makes it fit somewhere between style two and style three.

Additionally, in 'Circus Of Heaven' there are several examples of repetition.

> "The day the Circus of Heaven came [in]to town
> Local folks lined the streets in a Midwestern town
> Waiting anxiously for the parade to begin all [a]round
> On the very last day"

The lyrics on the inner bag of the album are incorrect. Anderson actually sings, "into town," and, "begin all around." The latter phrase makes the syllables fit but the repeated 'town' sounds odd, and I'm not convinced that this is a necessary elaboration for the logic of the line. "Bright fairies," also seems squashed in. As the music builds from this point, there are several more examples of what could be viewed as either remarkable feats of Anderson lyrical manipulation (to fit the melody and accompaniment) or, as some might argue, unnecessarily complicated syntax and word choice. For me, the images conjured up by Anderson are entirely in keeping with the theme of the song. The quirky lyrics fit the splendour of the scene and the more fantastical elements are added, the more the picture appears in my mind. After all, who wouldn't want to witness, "The gigantic dreams of Alexander the Great," or, "a thousand golden angels at play"?

Concerning the appearance of Damion Anderson on 'Circus Of Heaven', Yes author and aficionado Dave Watkinson sent me this interesting Jon Anderson conversation with legendary US DJ, Ed Sciaky, from a 1990s YesFest event, as reported in a fanzine:

> Jon: "I remember he was 5-years-old, and I sat him on a chair and I said, 'Right, you're going to say this.' And he was kind of looking at me and said, 'What do you want me to say?' And I said, 'You're going to say, there's no bears, no clowns, no tigers, no bears, oh my!' And he wouldn't do it. He'd get halfway through and just stop. I kept saying, 'No, keep going.'"

Ed: "And did you dangle the royalties in front of him?"

Jon: "Yeah, yeah, I gave him a couple of pound notes."

As is often noted, never work with children or (circus) animals.

'Madrigal' contains features of the second category, as well as some relating to style three in its brief span. The general feel of the lyrics is close to those of 'Circus of Heaven' and to a lesser extent 'Arriving UFO'. It includes 'sacred ships' sailing the 'seventh age' and 'celestial travellers' who, this time, have always been here, rather than us having to await their arrival. There is also some compound imagery:

"Drifting within the glow and the after-glow of the eve ... "

This line seems constructed to fit the meter of the music again, but it is more direct than some of the more fanciful constructions in style three.

'Future Times' also includes fantasy content. The mythical demon Dantalion makes an appearance, as does his supposed master, Solomon, and I have always enjoyed the numbered list:

"One the word will enter all our hearts
Two the duel will alter them
Three jewels countenance divine away delight away
Four the fight to free the land
Five the islands of Arabia
Six the tears that separate ... "

Style Three – lyrics for musical effect

As I mentioned above, it could be argued that 'Circus Of Heaven' comes near to being included in my third category when it contracts or expands words into the music. Other Yes albums where Anderson opts for a significant amount of 'word painting' for musical effect include *Close To The Edge*, *Tales From Topographic Oceans* and *Relayer*. One of my favourite moments is the repeated, short, syllabic utterances of 'Siberian Khatru' from *Close To The Edge*:

"Outboard, river.
Bluetail, tailfly,

Luther, in time,
Suntower, asking,"

These are not nonsense connections between words of different types and contexts. Rather, they seem to have been deliberately chosen for their musical character as much as for any meaning that could be imputed to them. On *Tormato*, in 'Rejoice', we have lyrics such as these:

"Rejoice forward out this feeling
Ten true summers long
We go round and round and round and round
Until we pick it up again ... "

While not conventional in construction, the sentences in this passage do convey meaning. When combined with the music, they give the impression of the singer being thankful for and rejoicing in a sustained period of good fortune. They may conjure up entirely different concepts for each listener, but there are several moments within the various songs on *Tormato* when I feel the same kind of flow of Yes emotion that I experience from their earlier albums.

'Release, Release' has often been cited by critics and fans as the song on the album that tries to borrow the most from, or appeal to, fans of more recent popular music trends (to 1978) such as Punk. It also, perhaps, is the song on *Tormato* which most obviously points the way towards what was to come on *Drama*. Certainly, the music is highly energetic. It kicks into gear after the introduction with lyrics which help to create an air of urgency. The opening phrases are fragmented with stresses on almost every syllable. Against the rocking accompaniment, the bridge section plays with an offbeat rhythm deliberately to unsettle the feel:

"We've heard before, but we just don't seem to move
The pressure's on is there lack of concentration ... "

Some lyrics are used to emphasise the feel, with short phrases like sharp hits in groups of three on a snare drum, to reinforce the energy: "Lift us up," "show us how," "show us now," as well as in the chorus, "Release all, release all ... " This is all in keeping with my third style but elements of the uncomfortable squeezing in of words are also present, as noted before. The meaning is comprehensible, once again, but the structure and use of language is unusual and does not fit with the melody structure at all:

> "Power at first to the needs of each others days
> Simple to lose in the void sounds of anarchy's calling ways …"

The second line above is a good example of Anderson fitting his written concepts into the song, despite the existing construction, rather than creating words to enhance the music. Clearly, the styles I am suggesting are at play here are fluid, and Yes, as always, tend to defy neat categorisation.

The final song on the album, 'On The Silent Wings Of Freedom', is perhaps the most difficult to categorise. The lyrics almost all infer direct meaning, though in poetic clothing. They fit the music well, without needing creative word-play from Anderson in his vocal delivery. There is plenty of unusual imagery, of course, such as:

> "On the back of your forty-second screamdown
> Do you choose to be lost midst the challenge of being one"

The choice of words fits the sound of the song with its breathless and exciting moments, so 'Silent Wings' could fit into my second or third category. The name of the song itself sets the mood for the feel of the music and perhaps a better title for the album is contained within the lyrics – "Celestial Seasons".

I enjoy all the lyrics on *Tormato* and I am delighted that they contain plenty of the unique character contained within other 1970s Yes songs. There are, perhaps, hints of a shift towards more literal construction which is continued in *Drama*, but I suggest that *Tormato* lyrics are overall closer to earlier albums than what was to come.

Before we leave this examination of *Tormato* lyrics, here are the thoughts of Jaime Martin (used with his kind permission) specifically on numbers in *Tormato*, from the Facebook group *I think of music, therefore I exist (1948–1979)*:[30]

---

30 https://tormatobook.com/lyrics

THE LYRICS

"For me there are strong connections between *TFTO*, *Tormato* and *Drama* lyrics

Going For The One was released on July 7, 1977 (7/7/77). *Tormato*, one year later, manages a numerology based in numbers from 1 to 7, complemented, secondarily, with the 8 (number of album themes), 9 (number of locations in the topographic map, number of album tracks) and 10 (number of locations in the schematic map). The last appearing number is one thousand.

1 as a number is quoted, as 2 to 6, in 1A 'Future times': "One the word will enter all our hearts". Secondarily other songs speak of, "being one".

2 also in 'Future times': "Two the duel will alter them" (our hearts)

"3 jewels, countenance divine".

from Blake, "the countenance divine shine upon our clouded hills"

"4 the fight to free the land"

"5 the islands of Arabia" (Bahrein)

"6 the tears that separate"

Number 7 appears seven times:

In 3. 'Madrigal': "Sacred ships do sail the seventh age" (it is quoted two times)

In 6. 'Circus of heaven':

"Seven solemn flying silvered regal horses rode by
Seven golden chariots in tow, a wonder to behold
The seven lords of the mountains of time
There then arose where nothing really stood there before
A giant tent rising one thousand feet high from the floor
Townspeople flocked inside with their eyes all amazed
To greet the seventh lord of the seventh age"

Number 10 appears only once (in 'Rejoice'): "Rejoice forward out this feeling / Ten true summers long"

One thousand:

Surrounded by what seemed a thousand golden angels at play ('Circus of Heaven')

"A giant tent rising one thousand feet high from the floor" (COF)

With all the data, we have to guess the correspondence between numbers, topographical locations (Tors and other), tracks / songs, and concepts. To help, we must use the key ideas, words, correspondences of cardinal points/seasons/times of the day, and many other associations, including those derived from Hindu philosophy. And of course the connections between W. Blake "Jerusalem", this album and 'Machine Messiah' among others."

While this kind of reading offers plenty of food for imaginative thought, it may also be in danger of 'overreading'. The conscious mysticism of many (particularly 1970s) Yes lyrics seems to invite a smorgasbord of interpretation and possible meaning. Make of it what you will. Jon Anderson has on several occasions said that he is interested in the meanings people discover or impute to his words.

PART 4 – ALBUMS AND SINGLES

12

TORMATO ARTWORK

The late Storm Thorgerson and Aubrey Powell ('Po') founded the design company Hipgnosis and produced their first ever album cover for Pink Floyd in 1968, the same year that Yes was established. Storm and Po established a studio in a seventeenth century terraced house in 'Tin Pan Alley' (6 Denmark Street), the heart of the London music scene of the 1970s. The newly formed Sex Pistols used an outbuilding at the

Tormato cover printing proof, author's collection

back of the property in the mid-70s as offices, a recording studio and living accommodation. John Lydon's graffiti can still be seen today, and the Pistols rehearsed there in their earliest days. The Rolling Stones recorded their first album next door at Regent Sound Studios and Advision Studios is less than a mile away.

Yes' collaboration with Roger Dean (apart from the use of his Yes logo) had ended temporarily when Hipgnosis were engaged to produce something rather different for *Going For The One* in 1977. The band continued to use the company in 1978 for *Tormato*. It is interesting to note that Jon Anderson's 1976 solo masterpiece *Olias Of Sunhillow* had art direction by Hipgnosis. Steve Howe, however, has maintained his preference for Dean, his great friend and long-time collaborator. After Anderson and Wakeman had left the band in 1980, the next album, *Drama*, reverted to Dean. When Anderson returned but Howe left for *90125* (1983) and *Big Generator* (1987), Dean's artwork was absent again, as it was for *Talk* (1994). These facts may be unconnected, and Anderson was in the band for *Union* (1991) and *Keys To Ascension* (1996/7), not to mention *ABWH* (1989), all of which have Dean covers – and Steve Howe on guitar.

Hipgnosis cover for Tormato, author's collection

Yes: The Tormato Story

As *Going For The One* was recorded in Montreux, Switzerland, Po visited the band there to pitch the artwork concept to them and then took the photos for the inner gatefold (with assistance from photographer Rob Brimson). For *Tormato* however, Yes were recording in London and the concept for the album cover was somewhat different. There was no requirement this time for trips to sunny Los Angeles to photograph skyscrapers like on *Going For the One*, or even Switzerland, but rather to the windswept, rocky terrain of Devon. In my recent email communications with Po, he mentioned that he took the photograph of *Yes Tor*, which is in the background of the front and back covers of *Tormato*. However, when we interviewed Rob Brimson on the *Yes Music Podcast*, there was a different version of the story, as we shall see.

Rob says his life was changed when he saw Hipgnosis' cover for Pink Floyd's album *Ummagumma*, as well as a couple of exhibitions. That cover is one of the most memorable images in all of Rock and I'm sure you can picture it in your mind's eye. It's the one with the members of the band pictured inside or outside a door to a garden. There's a mirror on the wall and in this we can see different versions of the main photograph, with the reflection repeating off into infinity and the musicians swapping positions each time. It's like a Surrealist painting in a hall of mirrors and the result (known in art as the Droste effect) is extraordinary.

Rob decided to become a photographer and follow the narrative style of Hipgnosis, but it was another example of coincidence and happenstance that led to him working directly with the art design group – Storm came to his college to give a lecture. It wasn't universally well-received, but Rob felt he had 'a bit of rapport' and managed to arrange a week's work release in Hipgnosis' studio. This eventually led to him being based there between 1975 and 1979, which obviously covers *Tormato* in 1978. While he only spent a short time creating record covers, he continued to work in a similar, narrative style, particularly in black and white and using hand-coloured images, as he started to migrate towards advertising photography. The surreal aspects of his work, derived partly from Hipgnosis' style, fitted in well with the general direction of advertising and design at the time and for many years into the future.

Rob believes that Storm was one of the most extraordinary people he has ever met and as close to being a genius as is possible. Rob described him as, "very gregarious, very loquacious, very talkative, very persuasive and with a love of film-making."

After some early, faltering steps, Storm and Po came across Pink Floyd and then bands started to find them because of their unique and special style of photography. Rob knows of no instances of Po and Storm actively pursuing a band to work with them and he remembers Storm saying that the only musician he would be prepared to 'leave lunch for' would be Bob Dylan. It could have been seen as arrogance, but Rob maintains it was based on self-awareness. He knew that coming up with ideas like putting a cow with no other information on the cover of a record would support the artist's own integrity and intent.

This was truly revolutionary in the record business. Previously, if you wanted an album by Cliff Richard and The Shadows, you'd walk into a record store, ask for what you wanted and walk out with it. It wasn't actively *sold* to you. By the time large record 'superstores' appeared like HMV, Tower Records and Virgin Megastores, there were hundreds of record sleeves to flip through, as you looked for your Cliff record. You would be, "assaulted or arrested by these really fascinating abstract images ... the temptation is to pick them up, have a look what that's about." This was Hipgnosis' unique selling point. Their ability to create covers which made you stop in your tracks. Not all bands understood this, but those who did beat a path to Storm and Po's door to collaborate and promote their records. Whether you think this worked for *Tormato* or even *Going For The One* is up to you.

We were interested in knowing more about the Hipgnosis process and Rob said that the shoots were always demanding, with high standards, because they were always trying to do what appeared to be impossible. Storm, in particular, could be very hardline. Once a band had been 'sold' the image, there was no going back. Rob remembers doing a poster where he slightly altered the layout and Storm went mad. Rob tried to say that he thought it would look better with less clutter, but Storm said, "You're not paid to think." As Rob pointed out to us, though, that was highly ironic because, if you were with Hipgnosis, that's precisely what you *were* paid to do.

The building where the Hipgnosis studios were located in 1978 in Soho's Denmark Street, known as Tin Pan Alley, photo by William Mulryne

TORMATO ARTWORK

Asking Rob about *Tormato* specifically, he told us that he was shown a sketch, possibly by Colin Elgie (see below), of a man standing by a Tor with divining sticks, "looking like an amateur palaeontologist or ... someone involved in some mystic activity." Unfortunately, no one knew what Yes Tor in Devon looked like, so the mock-up drawing was fairly vague. Storm said that Rob could do the location shoot for the cover because he and Po didn't want to drive for a day to Devon, stay in a hotel overnight, wander around probably in the rain and then drive back to London, all just to, "take a black and white photograph of a rock." Rob was happy about this delegation and packed himself up with an Ordnance Survey map. He stayed overnight in the closest town, Okehampton.

Owing to the amount of equipment Rob needed to bring with him, he took the decision to drive his very ordinary car across the moor towards Yes Tor. This wasn't strictly legal, and the car wasn't made for cross-country travel (it certainly wasn't a Land Rover!) Rob and his car ended up falling into a hole that was very difficult to reverse out of and resulted in damage to the steering. Despite this mishap, he got the shot, lining it up more or less like the sketch, bearing in mind none of them had ever seen the Tor before Rob's trip. He used some filters and as many effects as he could in order to achieve a slightly surreal effect.

Back in the studio the next day, he showed the resulting contact sheet to Storm and Po. Suggesting that they should add the cost of repairing his car onto the bill for Yes was met with a sharp intake of breath and then a laugh from Po. There followed an explanation of the economics of record sleeves. According to Po, it was essentially a charity and they worked for nothing.

As Rob was to find out (and be reminded of by his former room-mate Colin Elgie's episode on the *Yes Music Podcast*), this sometimes extended to unpaid modelling for photo shoots. If you've ever wondered who the guy in the suit is on the cover of *Tormato*, it's Rob and he's still a bit cheesed off he didn't get a penny for doing it. At the time, he had no idea it was for this cover! However, Rob has recently been in contact with Po about the *Tormato* work and, I'm pleased to say, he has apologised for not paying for the car. Also, as mentioned above, Rob was able to remind him that it was him who went to Yes Tor. It turns out that Po had confused the trip with one he had done for an Al Stewart shoot around the same time.

I wanted to know what Rob thinks of the cover now and he said that *Tormato*, "seems to be a slightly unsatisfactory album on lots of levels." He believes there is quite a bit of really interesting music on the record, but he thinks the squashed tomato on the cover is wasted. It's a clever pun, but he's sure it was not included in the original design which was only to be *Yes Tor* and the figure in front. This supports the idea that the name of the album changed after the artwork was finalised. Rob prefers the cover without the tomato and believes it was a surprising decision for a band like Yes, whose covers had previously been sophisticated.

There have always been differences of opinion over how and when the album name changed from *Yes Tor* to *Tormato* (not to mention the working title, *The 11th Illusion*). In his autobiography, *All My Yesterdays*, Steve Howe says that Storm and Po threw the finished artwork onto the ground and, "trod some delicious tomatoes onto it." This is at odds with Rick Wakeman's account, in which he claims to have been the one who threw a tomato at the cover. Here's what he recently said to tour manager, Jim Halley, who very kindly contacted Rick after I asked if he knew the definitive story:

> "Yes, it was indeed me who threw a squashy tomato at the painting ... The album was originally going to be called *Yes Tor* but Brian Lane suggested we then change it to *Yes Tormato*!"

Rick certainly sounds sure that he remembers what happened and maybe this is the answer. The band were unhappy with the cover, so Rick threw the tomato at it. Brian Lane suggested, as a joke, that they could change the name to *Tormato* on seeing the fruit squashed onto the artwork – a pun! Aubrey Powell said to me that it was probably Rob Brimson and him who re-photographed the artwork with the tomatoes, as Rob was an expert with 10x8 cameras. Perhaps it's fitting that the name of the album appears to have been suggested as a joke. *Yes Music Podcast* patron, Geoff Bailie, spotted an interesting passage in Aubrey Powell's book, *Vinyl Album Cover Art – The Complete Hipgnosis Catalogue* which backs up the joke cover and title idea:

> "How very brave of a progressive rock band like Yes-who had had a huge career by the time we came to designing this album- to have a tomato thrown at their cover image. They also took

themselves quite seriously, so it was to our surprise that they took to this piece of self-mockery.

However, that said, they nearly didn't buy it. Steve Howe, the band's guitarist, came up with the title of '*Yes Tor*', named after a hill top on Dartmoor in Devon. When Hipgnosis presented the idea of a man with a divining rod at the base of the Tor, joker and keyboardist Rick Wakeman claims he threw a tomato at the picture out of dissatisfaction with the outcome. I remember it differently – I think I threw the tomato at the offending photo. However, claim and counter-claim will never put it right. Whoever did it, there was definitely a general air of unhappiness present."

Incidentally, in the same book, Po mentions that Hipgnosis were to return to work with Yes five years later, albeit not to create an album cover and with a rather different band configuration. *Yes Music Podcast* patron, Hogne Bø Pettersen, contacted me to say that he interviewed John Balance from the electronica/noise band Coil, many years ago. John worked for Hipgnosis and, when he noticed that Hogne was wearing a Yes t-shirt, he said, "I made a music video for Yes with Po." As Hogne says, it's strange how worlds collide. Here is the passage from Po's book:

"Despite this potential hiccup with the group, Hipgnosis were welcomed back in 1983 in our new guise of GreenBack Films and made the video for the single Owner Of A Lonely Heart, which became the first Yes record to reach No 1 in the US charts and I say – tormaaatooo."

When I interviewed Steve Howe for the *Yes Music Podcast* in October 2022, I took the opportunity to ask him to explain more about his view of the name change. He said that he couldn't remember anything very accurately after all these years, but he doesn't believe the name *Tormato* had anything to do with Brian Lane. Steve said that he had been very happy with the name of the album being *Yes Tor*. He said the tors have great historical connections, as they are mounds in the middle of nowhere and, "people used to stand on top of them so that they could look out if the enemy were coming or if a deer was worth catching, you know? So, these were like points of reference." The name *Yes Tor* itself also seems to have a mysterious origin. Over the years, as noted by Jaime Martin,[31] scholars have suggested that the name was derived from the Anglo-Saxon word 'earn' which means eagle (giving us 'Ernestorre' and 'Yernestorr') or perhaps 'eyst' which means storm. In another theory, the tor is named 'Eastor' which seems to be 'Highest Tor' and in the local dialect could have been pronounced more like 'Yes Tor'.

Yes fan Paul Laue from Illinois visited Yes Tor with friends and family in 2014, photo by Michael Dubuque, courtesy of Paul Laue – left to right – MaryAnne Dubuque, Mike Dubuque, Paul Laue, David Palmer

Steve said he thought *Yes Tor* would have been a fascinating direction for the band to go in but then it was, "completely messed up, totally destroyed," by the addition of the band photo, superimposed in front of the tor. The next thing he remembers is being sent a version with, "bloody tomatoes all over it." He assured me that he could take a joke but this was, "disgusting". After this, he can't remember who it was, but someone suggested changing the name to *Tormato*. Steve's view was, and still is, this: "That's about as dumb arse as I can say." Clearly, he's not a fan of the cover idea. The only way they could go forward with it,

---

31 https://tormatobook.com/yestormeaning

Steve told me, was to treat it as a kind of in-joke album sleeve.

When I asked Rick Wakeman recently if he was happy with the name *Tormato*, he said, "Why not? ... after all, I threw the tomato!" However, his view of the artwork is still somewhat negative:

> "It's awful ... for whatever reason we went down a different path .... and, as far as I was concerned, one that was a dead end."

Po, centre, arranges the band for a promotional shot at 'Blow-Up Bridge', photo by Jim Halley

The band shots which appear on the back cover of the album were taken by Aubrey Powell at Macclesfield Bridge in Regent's Park, near RAK Studios. The Bridge is nicknamed 'Blow-Up Bridge' due to an incident in Victorian times[32] when Regent's Canal, which runs beneath the bridge, was used to transport goods by barge. One day in 1874 a barge named *The Tilbury* was travelling under Macclesfield Bridge with a cargo of coffee and nuts, as well as, "the perilous combination of two or three barrels of petroleum and about five tons of gunpow-

---

32 https://tormatobook.com/blowupbridge

der," according to *The Spectator* newspaper. Suddenly, the barge exploded, the three men on board were killed and Macclesfield Bridge was destroyed, apart from its cast iron columns. These columns had incidentally been made in Coalbrookdale, where the world's first iron bridge had been created. Apparently, the animal occupants of the nearby Regent's Park Zoo were highly agitated by the noise, while dead fish that were catapulted into the air by the blast 'rained down' in the West End of London.

Fortunately, no such disasters transpired as Yes undertook their photo shoot, and the resulting shots adorned not only the back cover of the album but were also used in other places such as the official press kit for *Tormato*. Photos taken by Jim Halley at the shoot are fascinating and feature Blow-Up Bridge in the background:

Promotional photo shoot underway in Regent's Park, with Macclesfield Bridge in the background, photo by Jim Halley

On *My Own TOURMATO* in January 2023, I visited the location of the photo shoot along with several other important places in London. Yes author, Dave Watkinson, and I attempted to recreate the *Tormato* photograph above, and we found the exact place the band used, just five minutes' walk from RAK studios. Here is my son, William Mulryne's, photograph of Dave and me on a day which was much colder than when Po took the Yes publicity photos:

Author and Dave Watkinson in front of Macclesfield Bridge pretending to be in the band shoot, photo by William Mulryne

A well-known story about the *Tormato* shoot is that when the band donned their *Going For The One* Yesshows tour jackets and sunglasses for the back cover photo, it transpired that Chris Squire had forgotten to bring his. Fortunately, tour manager Jim Halley had his jacket with him and was able to lend it to Chris. However, each jacket had the name of the owner printed on the right-hand side so 'Jim' had to be altered to 'Chris' on the resulting image, presumably by hand in those pre-Photoshop days. To be fair, none of the names are particularly visible on the back cover of the album and Rick's name seems to be completely obscured by some of the tomato debris or perhaps a fold in the material, but you can see them if you look carefully.

The front and back covers are not the only parts of the *Tormato* packaging worthy of note. There are also front and back designs on the 'inner bag' as well as the record labels, that are based on the inner material (at least in the majority of pressings). I was able to track down the artist responsible for these elements.

Yes: The Tormato Story

Right – detail showing the rear of Rick Wakeman's tour jacket with the Roger Dean Yesshows logo printed on it (and some passing joggers in the background), photo by Jim Halley, left – a 2023 jogger on Blow Up Bridge, photo by William Mulryne

In 1978, Colin Elgie was living in London, working as a freelance illustrator. When studying at his local technical college around 1971, he discovered that some of his lecturers were alumni of The Royal College of Art. They knew some people who worked for Hipgnosis and gave Colin a phone number to get in touch, which he did. Although never employed by Hipgnosis, Colin ended up receiving commissions from them from time to time over the next ten years when they wanted, in Colin's words, "something a little bit more decorative," or something they couldn't put together using their usual photographic montage techniques.

Common practice would be that someone from Hipgnosis would call Colin and ask him to come in to discuss a project. For *Tormato*, however, Colin says the situation was rather different. He would normally be involved in the whole concept for the album cover, perhaps contributing bespoke lettering for the front, but this time his input was restricted to the 'inner bag' and he was unaware of how the main cover was being developed. As far as Colin can remember, the brief was to create something for the inner sleeve consisting of Yes Tor and paths, in a kind of map design, to run underneath the text. The paths look like ley lines that are supposed to link together places with 'earth energies' where ancient peoples built structures. Jon Anderson certainly believes in this idea.

Colin's design used on the label of the Friday Music Tormato re-release, author's collection

I mentioned to Colin that a completely different version of his artwork exists on the inside front cover of the first *Tourmato* tour live programme. It looks like a prototype version with a different lettering style. Other elements seem to have been copied directly from a real, published map. Colin was unaware of this use of his design and agreed that this was probably done because his artwork wasn't ready for the printing of the programme. As you can see below, the two versions are quite different:

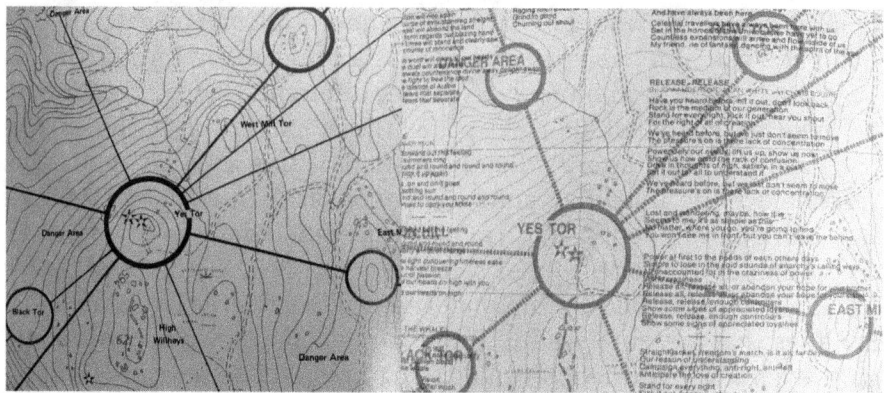

Left – Colin Elgie's design from the 1978 tour programme, right – from the album inner bag, author's collection

The back of the inner bag is treated in a slightly different way with symbols, lines and numbers. Colin describes it as a 'graphic device' and the intention was probably to create something with, "sci-fi spookiness – X-Files before X-Files". I'm not sure if it is intentional or not but there also appears to be the outline of *Yes Tor*, shaded with stripes of orange.

Science-Fiction was certainly a current trend in 1978, with both *Star Wars* and *Close Encounters of the Third Kind* in cinemas the year before *Tormato* was released. Yes used the John Williams theme from the latter film as the orchestral introduction to their concerts on the *Tourmato* tour. Also, 'Arriving UFO' was clearly heavily influenced by the general popular interest in otherworldly contact.

Since Colin was the key figure in the look of the inside of the album, I asked him what he thinks of the front cover. He said that he appreciates the verbal pun of the title but feels that the photo montage is a little too literal. Colin was also involved in other *Tormato* artwork. Find out more about those revelations in chapter 14.

Another puzzle contained in the sleeve notes is the inclusion of, "Special thanks to: ... all the Garys from South Shields who have been with us through 'ten true summers long.'" Yes fan Julian Butler contacted me to say the following on this topic:

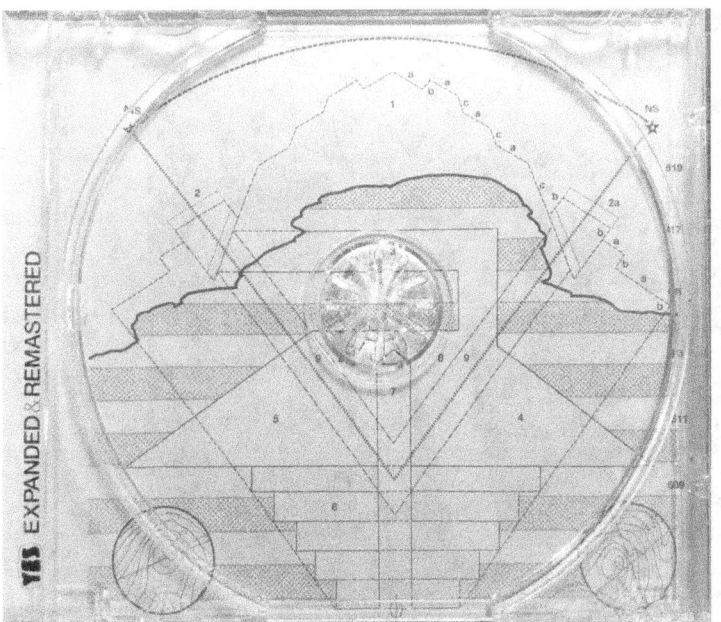

Inner bag back design, as reproduced without the overlay text in the packaging of the Expanded & Remastered CD, author's collection

"I was 7 years old when the album came out and it has always been a favourite. My father told me that 'Gary from South Shields' (we can't remember his name, but he was a very distant friend of a friend, we live in Washington ... near South Shields [in the North East of the UK]) had found out that Yes were recording the album at Advision, so by chance he rang them up and asked to speak to Mr Anderson. Luckily, he was there and after a chat he asked for a credit on the album ... however, Jon couldn't remember his surname."

After a further conversation with his father, Paul, Julian added:

"[My father] recalled from his school teaching days back in Washington that a girl he taught called Laura Linney (he thinks) was the girlfriend of this Gary ... hence where the tale came from."

Yes: The Tormato Story

Paul Butler is convinced that the man turning his head to the right in this photo from the Drama Tour in 1980 is Gary from South Shields, photo courtesy of Paul and Julian Butler

I turned for help to Dave Watkinson, hoping to rely on his encyclopaedic knowledge of Yes fandom. He did not disappoint. Dave met 'Gary from South Shields' at Yes conventions and trips to hunt down Yes landmarks in London. He even has a photo of them together. In his recent book with Stephen Lambe, *Yes in the 1980s*, Dave included two letters, one from Steve Howe and the other from Alan White. They were written in May 1980, in response to Gary Lilley, whose address was in South Shields. This was 'the Gary'. (Perhaps Julian's father's recollection is faulty and it was not Laura *Linney*, but actually Laura *Lilley* he taught, a sister or relative of Gary?) Gary had written to the band in 1980 as he had often done in the 1970s, but this time he was bemoaning the loss of Rick Wakeman and Jon Anderson. Gary was well known to the band from written communication and occasional visits to the

TORMATO ARTWORK

Confirmation that Gary Lilley was mentioned on the sleeve notes for Tormato, photo courtesy of David Watkinson

management offices in London. Dave tells me he bought, " ... about five boxes of material," including, "30 plus posters and about 15 cuttings books, having thousands of items from the whole of the 70s" from Gary's family after he died a few years ago. Dave also told me about the most remarkable item in Gary's collection:

> "Gary owned one of the rarest collectables which I bought from him maybe twenty-five years ago, when he sold some items. These were the days of trading by handwritten letters. This was the *Olias of Sunhillow* 1/5 silver pendants made by Jon Anderson for his family and friends and can be seen in many a photo of Jon up to about 1980."

Jon is almost certainly wearing one of the pendants in Dave's photo of them both at RAK Studios (see chapter 2). Unfortunately, Gary couldn't handle the end of the 70s version of the band and his collecting and Yes following days ended in 1980.

On reflection, I believe the expression, "all the Garys," could be the band using 'Gary' as a kind of collective term for all Yes fans. In the *Tormato* sleeve notes, they were thanking all the fans who had been with them for their first ten years.

Whatever the artists and fans think of the cover, it seems the band themselves have never been keen on it. *Yes Music Podcast* patron and former DJ, Doug Curran, sent me a transcript of part of an interview he conducted with Yes backstage on 19th September 1978 at Richfield Coliseum, near Cleveland, Ohio, broadcast on the legendary WMMS Cleveland radio station.

Doug: So tell me about the album cover

Chris: Do we have to! (laughter by all).

Rick: We're not very happy with it.

Doug: So why use it?

Chris: We had spent a shedload of money having Hipgnosis work on it, taking our photo. Po liked it.

Steve: They didn't like my idea for a photo of *Yes Tor* in Devon, in my area. I quite liked calling it *Yes Tor*.

Doug: I agree. Were there any other ideas discussed by the band or by Hipgnosis? I heard that the working title was 'Eleventh Illusion'?

Jon: Yes, some of us are into magic tricks and illusions. We wanted to magically appear on stage for these in the round shows. It was harder than we had hoped.[33]

Alan: Hipgnosis showed us a cover mockup of all black with white text covering the entire thing, saying This is an album cover, on and on. We thought well, that's different! (laughter).

Chris: But it's not Yes. We prefer artwork to complement our music. Photos of us are OK but not our first choice for covers, for the inside OK if need be.

Alan: We've been told that XTC is using that idea for their new album coming out soon. So, we won't have that one foisted on us again! (much laughter from us all).

```
This is a RECORD COVER. This writing is the DESIGN upon the
record cover. The DESIGN is to help SELL the record. We hope
to draw your attention to it and encourage you to pick it up.
When you have done that maybe you'll be persuaded to listen to
the music - in this case XTC's Go 2 album. Then we want you
to BUY it. The idea being that the more of you that buy this
record the more money Virgin Records, the manager Ian Reid and
XTC themselves will make. To the aforementioned this is known
as PLEASURE. A good cover DESIGN is one that attracts more
buyers and gives more pleasure. This writing is trying to pull
you in much like an eye-catching picture. It is designed to get
you to READ IT. This is called luring the VICTIM, and you are
the VICTIM. But if you have a free mind you should STOP READING
NOW! because all we are attempting to do is to get you to read
on. Yet this is a DOUBLE BIND because if you indeed stop you'll
be doing what we tell you, and if you read on you'll be doing what
we've wanted all along. And the more you read on the more you're
falling for this simple device of telling you exactly how a good
commercial design works. They're TRICKS and this is the worst
TRICK of all since it's describing the TRICK whilst trying to
TRICK you, and if you've read this far then you're TRICKED but
you wouldn't have known this unless you'd read this far. At
least we're telling you directly instead of seducing you with
a beautiful or haunting visual that may never tell you. We're
letting you know that you ought to buy this record because in
essence it's a PRODUCT and PRODUCTS are to be consumed and you
are a consumer and this is a good PRODUCT. We could have
written the band's name in special lettering so that it stood
out and you'd see it before you'd read any of this writing and
possibly have bought it anyway. What we are really suggesting
is that you are FOOLISH to buy or not buy an album merely as a
consequence of the design on its cover. This is a con because
if you agree then you'll probably like this writing - which is
the cover design - and hence the album inside. But we've just
warned you against that. The con is a con. A good cover design
could be considered as one that gets you to buy the record, but
that never actually happens to YOU because YOU know it's just a
design for the cover. And this is the RECORD COVER.
```

*Go 2 by XTC
1978, designed
by Hipgnosis*

33 See chapter 31

Yes: The Tormato Story

The image on page 163 is the album cover concept Alan was referring to which was indeed used by XTC after having been rejected by Yes, 10cc, Pink Floyd and others.[34]

---

[34] https://tormatobook.com/reject

13

PROMOTIONAL ALBUM COPIES

Nowadays, most promotional copies of new albums are distributed to reviewers via secure online systems, in digital format. This means that physical promo copies have almost completely died out. I have been fortunate enough to receive relatively recent promo copies of albums from artists such as the Downes Braide Association and The Anderson Ponty Band. Back in 2017, I was sent a pre-release CD version of the live double album, *Topographic Drama, Live Across America*, but Yes promotional copies seem now to be exclusively transferred via the internet.

Back in 1978, things were rather different. Every radio station and journalist needed to have a physical copy of the new vinyl record to play on their turntable, either to broadcast or to critique. This means that promotional copies of *Tormato* are not particularly difficult to find. They can be easy to spot as well, with "Promotional Copy NOT FOR SALE" stamped onto the cover, often in gold lettering. Similar messages are often printed on the record label as well. Atlantic Records usually added a sticker to the cover with the track listing and even tick boxes (check boxes) to indicate what they referred to as 'Suggested Cuts'. The US promo album I have draws the DJ's attention to 'Release, Release', 'Arriving UFO' and 'Circus Of Heaven', interestingly. It's not clear whether these are official Atlantic choices or someone else's, because they have been added in ballpoint pen. Promotional copies usually came with a cover letter, similar to a press release, giving details of the record.

US promotional vinyl, author's collection

I also have an Argentinian promo vinyl copy of *Tormato* that not only has an unusual label without the Colin Elgie maps, but is also overprinted with, "PROHIBIDA SU VENTA – DISCO PARA DEMOSTRACION," in black towards the top and, "PROHIBIDA SU VENTA," in large, red lettering at the bottom. A sizeable sticker gives a similar message on the back cover.

Argentinian promotional vinyl labels, author's collection

Perhaps the most interesting promotional copy I have is from 2004. It's a CD-R of the expanded and remastered *Tormato* from Rhino and

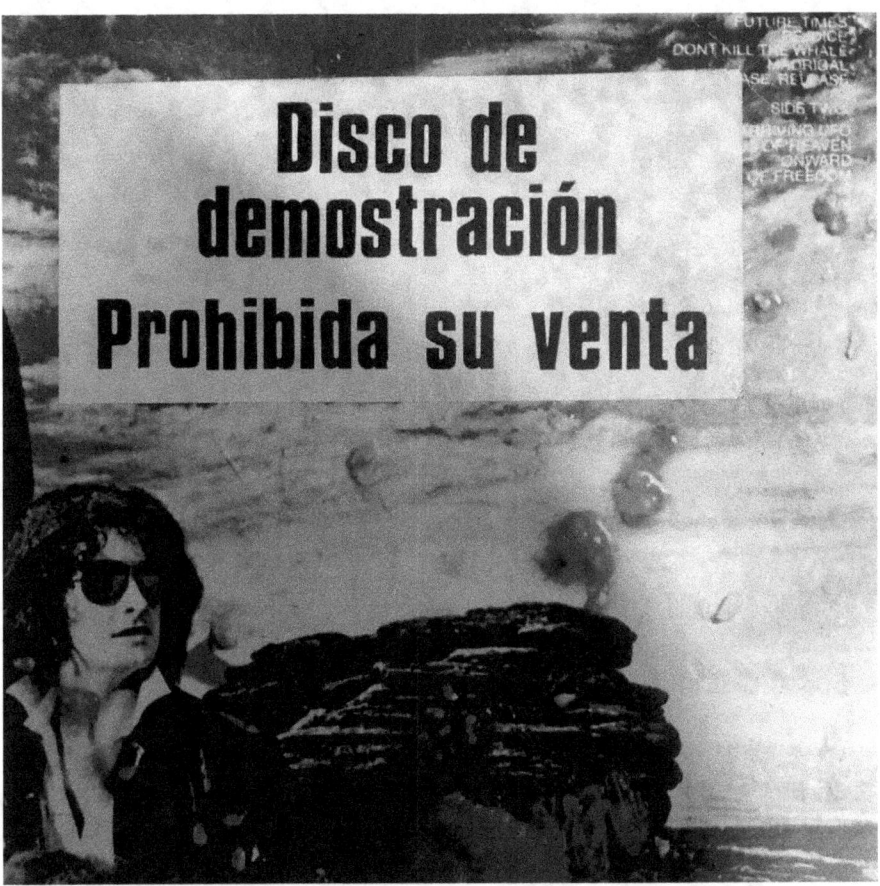

Argentinian promotional copy, back cover, author's collection

it was duplicated by the Imperial Tape Company in Santa Monica, California. The company, now called Imperial Media, is still in business and was the first to offer the duplication of thirty-two CD-Rs at a time in the early 1990s. The *Tormato* promo CD-R has no cover and no sleeve notes at all, but the bonus tracks are clearly noted on the back. You may be wondering whether the 'hidden' instrumental version of 'Onward' is included – it is. Just like the production version, only seventeen tracks are listed on the back of the CD-R but there are eighteen in reality.

Yes: The Tormato Story

Expanded & Remastered CD-R, author's collection

14

SINGLES

It is often thought that only one single was released from *Tormato*. As we shall learn a little later, that's not strictly true. However, for now, let's imagine that 'Don't Kill The Whale' b/w 'Abilene' was the only single and it reached the dizzying heights of number thirty-six on the UK singles chart. It was sandwiched between 'Going For The One' from the album of the same name (1977) and 'Into The Lens' from *Drama* (1980).

Although it has hardly ever been mentioned since 1978, 'Don't Kill The Whale' was a charity single in the UK. Yes historian Geoffrey Mason reminded me of the press coverage on the amazing *Forgotten Yesterdays* site (see page 170).[35]

As pointed out by Henry Potts of bondegezou.co.uk,[36] Greenpeace launched its first anti-whaling campaign in 1975 and Greenpeace UK was formed in 1977. Greenpeace flagship, the Rainbow Warrior, was re-launched in May 1978 and went on to be involved in many anti-whaling campaigns over the next few years, before being bombed and sunk in New Zealand in 1985. Conservation was, therefore, becoming a

---
35 https://tormatobook.com/forgottenyesterdays
36 https://tormatobook.com/henrypotts

Yes: The Tormato Story

YES single written by Jon Anderson and Chris Squire

YES HELP THE WHALE

SHOWING CONCERN about large scale whale slaughter, Yes release a new single 'Don't Kill The Whale', this week.
Written by Jon Anderson and Chris Squire, the track is taken from the forthcoming album 'Tormato' for which no release date has yet been set. The B side is a Steve Howe composition, 'Abilene', which was specially recorded for the single and won't be included on the album.
The single comes in a special black and white bag.

Hook line and single

THE NEW single by Yes called Don't Kill The Whale and written by band members Jon Anderson and Chris Squire is likely to bring considerable financial benefit to Greenpeace, the direct action environment group closely involved with the Save The Whales campaign.

Yes will donate one penny for every copy of the single sold to Greenpeace, and it's reckoned that should be worth several thousand pounds to the cause.

Don't Kill The Whale is included in the new Yes LP Tormato, scheduled for release by Atlantic on September 8, which has shipped gold on advance orders — the first time Yes has achieved this distinction in the UK.

Reports of the Greenpeace 'Don't Kill The Whale' tie-in, left – Record Mirror, right – Music Week, uploaded by Geoffrey Mason to Forgotten Yesterdays

very topical issue in 1978 and Yes wanted to be seen to be supporting this campaign group.

When considering the singles from *Tormato*, an interesting place to start is to examine the promotion of 'Don't Kill The Whale'. It was included on a WEA International singles sampler sent to radio stations in Spain. This allows us to place the Yes single in the context of what else was being promoted by the WEA Spanish arm, Hispavox, at the same time:

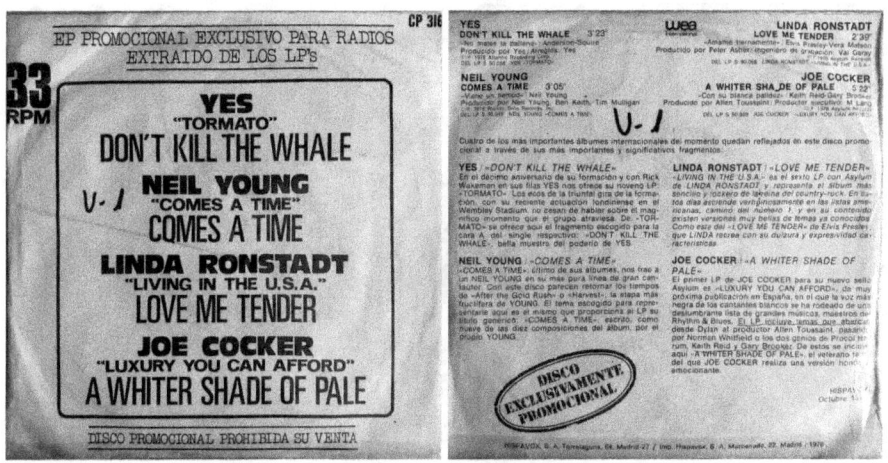

WEA Spanish radio sampler, author's collection

Yes receives top billing on the front cover amongst an eclectic mix of other artists and the back cover has a small blurb about each song. According to Google translate, this is what it says about 'Don't Kill The Whale':

"On the tenth anniversary of its formation and with Rick Wakeman in its ranks, YES offers us its ninth LP: TORMATO. The echoes of the group's triumphant tour, with its recent London performance at Wembley Stadium, do not stop talking about the magnificent moment that the group is going through. TORMATO offers here the fragment chosen for side A of the respective single: DON'T KILL THE WHALE, a beautiful example of the power of YES."

Incidentally, Yes and Neil Young both appeared at the same venue in the Autumn (Fall) of 1978. Presumably both singles got an airing (see over page).

You would be forgiven for imagining that all 'Don't Kill The Whale' singles are fairly similar whatever country they hail from. Maybe there's just a slight variation in terms of language or cover. One would expect to see the black and white drawing of a whale jumping out of the sea on the front and the group photo from the reverse of the album on the back – a bit like this:

'Don't Kill The Whale', author's collection

However, there are myriad, slightly odd variations out there, mostly connected with the B side song, Steve Howe's composition, 'Abilene', that did not appear on the album. Call these mistakes if you like: 'Abilene', 'Abalene', 'Abiline', and 'Abeline' are the variations I've found, and the spellings are even different on some sleeves and the records inside. The correct spelling is 'Abilene', the US city in Texas, and, in another bizarre coincidence, I discovered that the 'Abilene paradox' is a psychological phenomenon involving a breakdown of group communication. Maybe this explains the spelling errors – or perhaps the state of Yes at this time. (Not a serious suggestion.)

Other variations around the world include alternative picture sleeves in Japan (as you might imagine) and Spain where a cropped version of the group photo is used. The back of the Spanish version looks quite old-fashioned and misspells *Tormato* as *Tornato*. The Japanese single comes in a colourful sleeve with an insert featuring an image of the album back cover on one side and the lyrics to 'Don't Kill The Whale' in Japanese and English on the other.

The US version has a significant difference as well. 'Abilene' does not appear as a B side and is replaced by 'Release, Release'. In fact, neither the promotional copy nor the official US single has an A side or

AMUSEMENTS AMUSEMENTS

TONIGHT
8 PM
An Evening with
YES
in The Round
$8.00, $7.00 + Tax

capital centre

Thursday, Sept. 21—8 PM
NEIL YOUNG
&
CRAZY HORSE
$8.00, $7.00 + Tax

Saturday, Sept. 23—8 PM
ELECTRIC LIGHT ORCHESTRA
TRICKSTER
$8.00, $7.00 + Tax

Monday, Oct. 2—8 PM
JETHRO TULL
URIAH HEEP
$8.00, $7.00 + Tax

Tickets available at HECHTS, PENTAGON TICKET SERVICE and CAPITAL CENTRE BOX OFFICE, LANDOVER, MD Add 60¢ service charge to all tickets except at Capital Centre. Capital Center is located on Beltway Exit 32 E. No personal checks accepted. For info., call 792-7490.

A Baltimore Sun advert for Yes and then Neil Young from September 1978, Forgotten Yesterdays, uploaded by Geoffrey Mason

Yes: The Tormato Story

Singles from various countries, author's collection

B side marking at all. The single is referred to as 'Release, Release' / 'Don't Kill The Whale' in several sources.[37] However, Discogs lists it as A side – 'Don't Kill The Whale', B side – 'Release, Release'.[38] The single appears only to have been released in a generic sleeve in the US which doesn't help, but US chart sources are probably more reliable than the fan-sourced Discogs. Paul Cobb's remarkable Yes Catalogue[39] (hosted on Henry Potts' website) backs up the idea that the US single was 'Release, Release' and that it was also released in this format in Canada and the Philippines. The catalogue number (3534) is the same on the US and Canadian releases, with the usual 'AT' added on the Canadian version. The most surprising entry on the catalogue is what seems to be a twelve inch single with 'Release, Release' on the A side and 'Future Times' on the B side. I haven't been able to confirm the existence of this record.

As we can see, there were actually two singles from *Tormato*. It seems that 'Don't Kill The Whale' b/w 'Abilene' was not released in Canada, the US or the Philippines, so I assume fans from those parts of the world will have been unaware of 'Abilene' in 1978, unless they got

---
37 https://tormatobook.com/whalesingle
38 https://tormatobook.com/discogswhale
39 https://tormatobook.com/yescatalogue

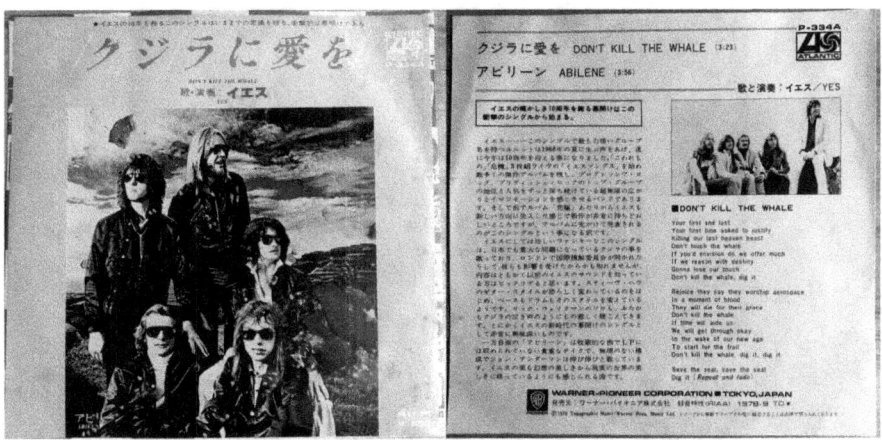

Japanese copy – insert, author's collection

Spanish copy, author's collection

hold of copies from elsewhere. This would have been more difficult in those days than it is today with the internet to help. Personally, I think it would have been a good idea to release two singles from *Tormato* across the world.

When I interviewed Colin Elgie about his design for the inner bag of the album (see chapter 12), I also asked him if he knew who had created the line-drawing of the whale for the cover of the single (in most territories). After looking up his illustration style on his website and elsewhere, I thought the cover looked similar to some other commissions he had completed over the years. Colin confirmed that one of his illustrations was indeed used for 'Don't Kill The Whale'. He had been

Yes: The Tormato Story

US single promotional copy, author's collection

US single, author's collection

Canadian promotional single, author's collection

Canadian single, author's collection

going through his archive the day before I spoke to him and had come across a whale drawing he had done for some kind of, "freebie session", as he put it. Apparently, it was going to be used by a book club who were interested in the Save The Whale cause at the time. Colin didn't realise Yes had used his drawing until I had arranged to speak to him, forty-four years after the single appeared. Before my call with Colin ended, he also disclosed that the first job he ever did for Hipgnosis was in the Summer of 1970 – a poster for a Yes concert. This artwork is now highly-collectable and the few copies which still exist sell to collectors for multiple hundreds of pounds. The image was re-used for a variety of different concert posters and newspaper adverts. It's this one (see over the page).

Poster by Colin Elgie (note the Droste effect posters on the left – see chapter 12), uploaded to Forgotten Yesterdays by Geoffrey Mason

15

VINYL ALBUM VERSIONS

As with other chapters, please read the below in conjunction with the dedicated Japanese copies chapter (chapter 19) which contains much more detail about that country's remarkable output.

Unlike cassettes and 8-Track cartridges (see chapter 17), it appears that the main aim of vinyl record producers around the world was to make their versions of *Tormato* look as close as possible to the UK and US releases. This means that there is little variation. In this chapter I'm going to present just the differences I have found.

As you would expect, the front covers of all vinyl copies are pretty much identical, so the first set of interesting variations occur on the back covers. Only a small number of versions translate the names of the songs into the local language, which is a bit of a shame, especially when the Spanish titles are so enjoyable (see next page).

In the US, vinyl versions were made by Warner Bros., but most countries around the world had their own manufacturing processes for both cover printing and record duplication under licence (see chapter 16), and this is reflected on the back covers. I've tried to make these legible, but the Hipgnosis photography makes it all rather difficult:

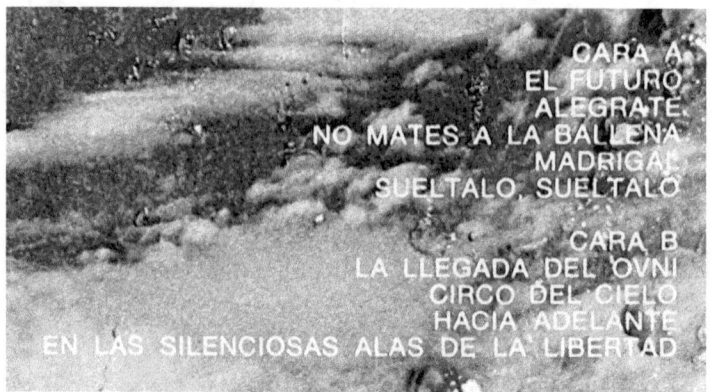

Mexican vinyl version, author's collection

Clockwise from top left, Gothic Press – UK, DISCO ES CULTURA – Venezuela, WEA fillpacci music – France, HISPAVOX – Spain, RADIO TRIUNFO – Portugal, Sonolux – Columbia, author's collection

One of the most recent re-releases of *Tormato* on vinyl was the Friday Music 180g version from 2013:

Friday Music Audiophile release, Author's collection

This fantastic version also features an almost unique (for *Tormato*) gatefold sleeve. All previous Yes studio albums apart from Time And A Word (1970) sported gatefolds at release (at least in the UK). The Friday Music version uses the inner bag for its gatefold image, just like the only other anomalous version I have managed to find from 1978, released in Venezuela:

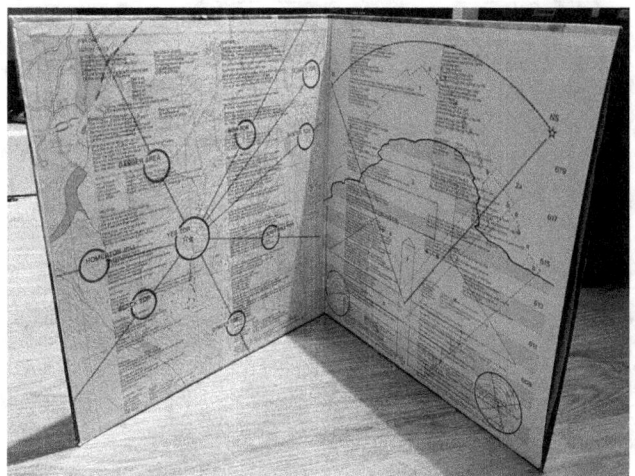

Vinyl with gatefold, Venezuela 1978, author's collection

When the inner bag is not treated as above, there isn't a great deal of variation from the original, thin paper, but some versions do deviate as below:

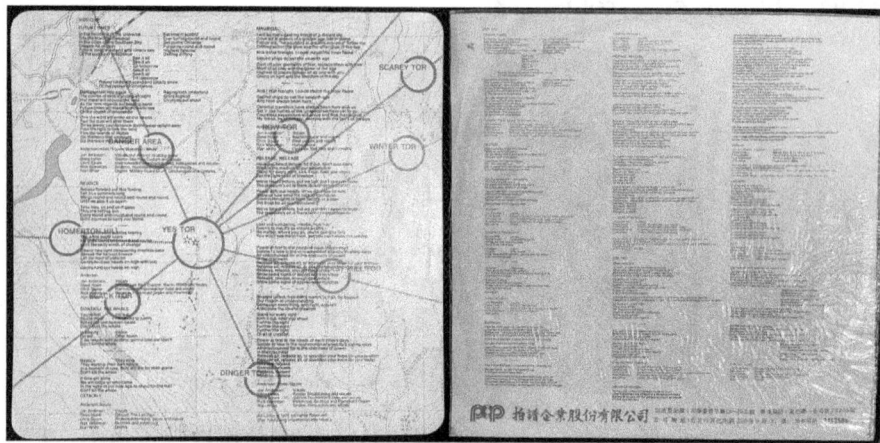

Left – UK Gothic Press inner bag in stiff card with rounded corners, right – Taiwan inner bag without graphic background and with additional text in Mandarin (I assume) at bottom, both author's collection

I'm a big fan of the Colin Elgie design used on the original versions of the record label, but it isn't always there:

Clockwise from top left, Spanish original design, Rhodesian plain white label (promotional copy), Mexican plain red label, Colombian traditional Atlantic coloured label, author's collection

In addition to the above, there are a few other logos, hype labels and other design elements out there:

Left – Taiwanese pop record label logo, centre – Mexican GAMMA record label logo, right – German hype sticker, author's collection

Another vinyl release which deserves some attention is the 40th Anniversary Limited Edition Record Store Day 2018 picture disc. Apparently, 5,400 copies of this version were made by Optimal Media in Germany. As a circular picture disc, the front and back covers had to be re-arranged but I think it worked really well:

2018 Record Store Day 40th Anniversary Limited Edition, author's collection

Finally, as I collect copies of *Tormato* on vinyl from across the world, I occasionally receive items with questionable provenance. A good example of this is my Colombian record. The quality of the vinyl itself is low, it's flimsy and light, but that is common in records from this part of the world. The worrying part is the cover. It looks to me like the front and back have been produced in someone's bedroom on an inkjet printer and then stuck onto a plain, brown, cardboard record cover. The supplier assured me he had lots of records from Colombia which looked just the same – I didn't find this particularly reassuring. Here's the evidence, see what you think:

Colombian cover – caveat emptor (buyer beware!), author's collection

16

DEEP INTO THE DEAD WAX

Before we leave vinyl *Tormato* albums, I was introduced to a fascinating world of information by Mark Anthony K, my co-host on the *Yes Music Podcast*. Not only is he one of the most generous and friendly individuals you could ever hope to meet, but he is also a multi-instrumentalist, great songwriter, and has an encyclopaedic knowledge of vinyl records. This is partly due to producing his own records under the band name Projekt Gemineye, and partly due to collecting a wide variety of records over several decades. Mark was the perfect person to help me understand the record creation process and particularly the strange hieroglyphics often seen on vinyl records, including copies of *Tormato*, from around the world.

First of all, I wanted Mark's help in defining some of the terminology I had heard. For example, are matrix run-out and dead wax the same thing? Mark confirmed this is just alternative terminology for the section of vinyl at the centre of a record, around the label, where lettering is usually found – either stamped or hand-etched.

I have also been confused over the initial steps in making a vinyl record, so I asked Mark about acetates and test pressings. It turns out that an acetate is the first version of a record, made out of a heavy piece of aluminium, covered with a material a bit like nail polish. As so often, the name is misleading as there isn't any acetate involved in the process at all. Acetates are more correctly known as lacquers in the industry. A lathe is used literally to cut grooves into the soft lacquer when connected to a sound source. In the case of *Tormato*, this would have been the master tape of the album. Information is added into the dead wax area to make the acetates and the eventual vinyl records identifiable. Each side of the record needs its own acetate disc and the artist, the manager or the producer takes them away and plays them on a record turntable. If changes are required, perhaps to make the whole record louder, another set of acetates are created from scratch – this is a test record. Once the acetates are approved, another clean set is made. This means that every record has at least two acetates and these are often still in existence with band members or others – maybe even collectors. Acetates are not meant to be played repeatedly but it does seem that if they are looked after they can last a long time and still be playable.

The next stage is to create the stampers which will produce the vinyl records. Firstly, the clean acetate is nickel-plated. Obviously, the stampers need to have the grooves in a kind of negative image so that when it is used to press the vinyl it comes out the right way round. This is achieved by removing the nickel plating from the acetate to produce a 'father', which has the grooves the wrong way. When this nickel stamper is pressed into the vinyl, the grooves are the correct way. More fathers can be produced by plating the father to make a 'mother' with the grooves the other way round. Apparently, a father can be used to make about 10 mothers and a mother can make about ten stampers. It's a rather complicated and confusing process!

Back to test pressings. There will be around ten to twenty test pressings made from the first stampers and, if the reception from the test listeners (band members, producers etc.) isn't good, new acetates will need to be made to correct the errors or sub-standard sound. This means that there are some test pressings (and presumably acetates and stampers) out in the world somewhere with unreleased versions of albums on them. I have two test pressings of *Tormato* in my collection and we will come back later in this chapter to explain how Mark and I tried to work out where and when they were made.

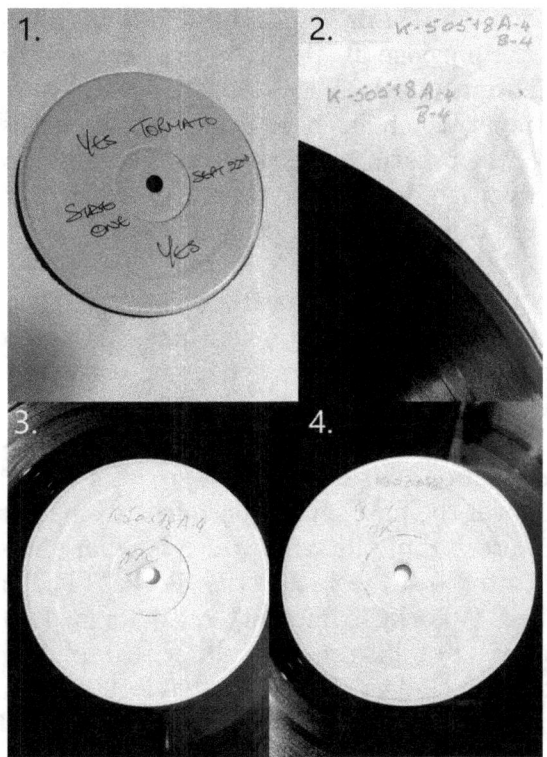

1. Plain white label and sleeve – appears to be fairly modern
2. – 4. Older with catalogue markings

As Mark points out, because records like *Tormato* are released in many different countries across the world, they are often produced in local pressing plants. This means that the record label needs to send physical media to the pressing plant so they can make the vinyl records. Clearly, it would be very risky to send the master tapes to another country so that new acetates can be made, so the record labels often send stampers. As these are metal, they are much less prone to damage. This means that some countries will produce records which look identical to other countries' because they both used the same stampers. At least this is true of the record itself. A boon for collectors is, of course, that the paper record labels and even the sleeves have different information on them so we can differentiate copies of *Tormato* from around the world, even if they are created from the same stampers.

If you have never delved into the dead wax of your records, then you might find some interesting things. I asked Mark to spell out for me exactly what the purpose of writing in the dead wax is. In fact, there are many different purposes, including specifying the date, the generation of stamper which has been used and the initials of the person responsible for the pressing. Unfortunately for us, different companies have different ways of identifying pressings – there are no standards. Internet sources can help a great deal, however.

Perhaps even more interesting than the strings of letters and numbers, some records contain messages or even jokes in their dead wax. Often this is done to appeal to collectors and fans, so take a look at your own Yes vinyl collection and see if you can find, for example, "A Porky Prime Cut". This is the signature of George 'Porky' Peckham whose versions are sought after due to his expertise in creating the master discs for many records over the past several decades. His mastering career began at The Beatles' Apple Records which is where he started adding comments into the dead wax such as, "Pecko", "Pecko Duck" or the aforementioned, "A Porky Prime Cut". Peckham is often credited with being the originator of this tradition. Other examples of amusing dead wax inscriptions include the Elvis Costello 1978 album, *This Year's Model*, where Peckham inscribed, "RING 434 3232 ASK FOR MOIRA FOR YOUR PRIZE". This was a real person and a real phone number for Costello's publicist.

As for Yes, two of my favourites are contained in the run-out groove of the Friday Music 180g re-issue of *Tormato*:

"TOMATO TORMATO, POTATO PORTATO" in the Friday Music dead wax, author's collection

Friday Music are well-known for this practice and Mark mentioned that their version of *The Yes Album*, which consists of two records that play at 45 rpm, contains, "Thank you Yes," in the first side dead wax and, "Your move," on the second disc. He wonders if this was a little message to Yes to encourage them to do more re-releases on Friday Records.

I have many different vinyl copies of *Tormato* (see chapter 15) but, just for reference, I thought I'd take a look in the dead wax of a record which was definitely a first pressing. In 2020, *Yes Music Podcast* listener Steve Perry very kindly sent me his copy of *Tormato*. He bought it at A & A Records in downtown Montreal on release day in 1978. It was produced and distributed by WEA Canada and here is what's in the runout:

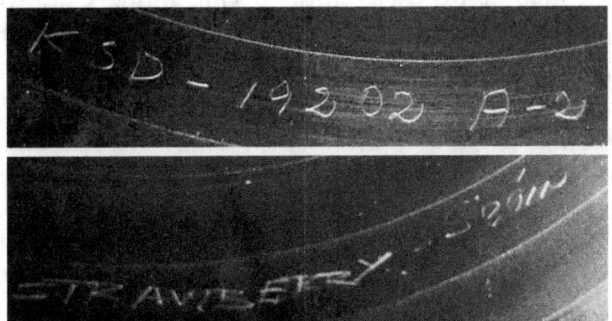

Canadian pressing dead wax "KSD – 19202 A-2, STRAWBERRY – Sean", author's collection

Some information in the dead wax of records is difficult to see but these are clear. "SD – 19202" is the US catalogue number for *Tormato* but, as is the common practice, the Canadian pressing places the "K" in front of it. The capital "A" means side one and the number "2" probably means this record has been pressed from the second stamper.

Before I started looking into the dead wax of *Tormato*, I didn't realise there were different catalogue numbers around the world for the same record. In the UK, for example, *Tormato* has the catalogue number "K 50518," whereas, as mentioned above, in the US it's, "SD – 19202," and in Canada, "KSD – 19202". Perhaps the most well-known Yes record catalogue number is *90125* but, as the cover designer for that 1983 release Gary Mouat points out,[40] the record was originally to be called *80102*. The band were unable to get worldwide consistency with that number, so they went for *90125* which was available everywhere. Does this mean that *90125* is the only Yes album, which has the same catalogue number across the globe? Actually, upon checking the entries in Discogs.com, it's pretty close but there are still variations.[41] You may also be aware that the *Anderson Bruford Wakeman Howe* album of 1989 bears the catalogue number, "90126", as a reference to the Yes album, but there are plenty of versions of that record outside the US that do not feature this number at all.

Back to the Canadian dead wax, the, "STRAWBERRY – Sean," is referred to in the inner sleeve notes of *Tormato* which say, "Disc cutting Sean Davis at Strawberry Studios, London." It seems that this Canadian pressing was made with UK stampers. This appears not to have been unusual, however, with many countries around the world ordering stampers from Strawberry in London and its other locations. I also wonder if the use of Strawberry stampers might be part of the reason for most listeners' dissatisfaction with *Tormato*. Here is the reaction of an internet audiophile forum member to Strawberry pressings from the 1970s, although not *Tormato* specifically:

> "The best way I can describe these pressings is to imagine listening to your hi-fi and someone walks into the room and throws a couple of jackets over your speakers. Behold, no treble, no bass no separation. Flat, lifeless sound and the pressing quality wasn't much better."
>
> James Glennon[42]

What about my own test pressings? Here's what I managed to see (see page 191).

This is the test pressing which looks the older of the two. "K50518," is the UK catalogue number, this is side B and the fourth stamper. The stamper was created at Strawberry Studios by Sean Davis. This doesn't necessarily mean that this record was pressed in the UK of course. The other markings on this test pressing include:

---

40 https://tormatobook.com/80102
41 https://tormatobook.com/discogs90125
42 https://tormatobook.com/strawberry

DEEP INTO THE DEAD WAX

Older test pressing dead wax – "K 50518-B4, STRAWBERRY" – Sean, author's collection

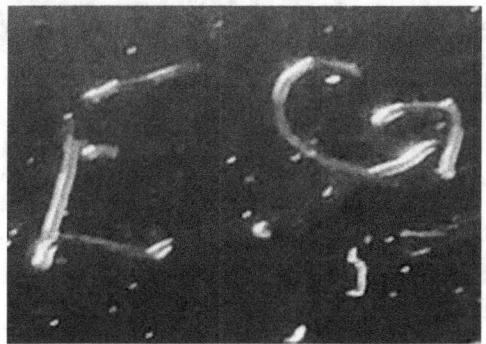

Older test pressing dead wax – "E.G.", author's collection

"EG," refers to Eddy Gorecki who was a galvanizing/metalworks engineer working in the UK at the time this stamper was produced. There are also some indistinct scratches in the dead wax which I can hardly make out at all. It could possibly be the Hebrew text mentioned on Discogs, "מאלח" (this may only be an approximation of the lettering). There is also another mark I have been unable to find in online sources which says "G-T/P". Let me know if you can identify it!

The newer of my test pressings appears to have been produced using the same stampers as the older one because it also features the, "EG", "STRAWBERRY Sean," and, "K50518 – B4," markings but also has this (see next page). This seems to say, "WEA – T/P 1". According to Discogs, this refers to WEA Records Pressing Plant, West Drayton, UK, which was in operation from January 1978 to February 1983. Perhaps my second test pressing is actually just as old as the first.

Newer test pressing dead wax – "WEA-T/P 1", author's collection

If you are interested in finding out more about this vast and often hotly disputed subject, the onrelease.net[43] website has a lot of information as does discogs.com[44] and a fascinating YouTube channel to take a look at is called BarakaPDub.[45] If you'd like to know what these test pressings and other versions of *Tormato* sound like, chapter 20 has my comparisons.

---

43 https://tormatobook.com/onrelease
44 https://www.discogs.com/
45 https://tormatobook.com/deadwax

CASSETTES AND 8-TRACK CARTRIDGES

17

CASSETTES AND 8-TRACK CARTRIDGES

The *Tormato* release format which contains by far the most variation is the compact cassette tape. To a far lesser extent, 8-Track Cartridges of the album also appeared in a few different versions.

24 cassette variations from around the world, author's collection

193

Whichever your preferred naming convention, Compact Cassettes, Musicassettes, Cassettes, Tapes, Audio Cassettes or Cassette Tapes appeared in the 1960s, but began to become the music format of choice during the 70s and 80s. This was largely due to the convenience of their size and the appearance of a myriad small, portable devices to play them on. Vinyl and even 8-Track Cartridges were comparatively difficult to take with you and play on the move (except for the many US cars equipped with 8-Track players), so cassettes came into their own practically everywhere, except the US.

Unfortunately for prog fans, the smaller format meant that cover artwork and sleeve notes also had to be smaller, and the ritual of carefully removing the disc from its protective sleeve, cleaning it and placing it on the turntable was lost. In a way, this might be seen as a parallel to the music being released becoming shorter and maybe the cassette was much more compatible with the general speeding up of life.

Record distribution companies around the world had additional design decisions to make when it came to cassettes. Clearly, the square front and rear covers couldn't be reproduced exactly as they were on the small, rectangular format cassette inlays which had to be used. Consequently, Hipgnosis' artwork appears in a variety of different ways on cassette covers from around the world. There seems to have been very little desire or perhaps incentive from Atlantic to stick to a consistent look.

For example, the 1978 cassettes from the US and UK take very different approaches (see facing page). Cropping the cover for the UK version meant having to make the logo and title transparent while the repetition of the title in a plain typeface on the US cassette looks a little odd. Certainly, both are significant compromises compared to vinyl copies. Some of the approaches from elsewhere around the world in 1978 tried out more daring styles.

Another of the major disadvantages of cassettes was that they were comparatively easy to copy. This has meant that unofficial, pirate tapes have appeared in large numbers over the years. It is interesting to note that many of these illegal tapes abandoned the divining rod cover altogether, instead opting for the band photo from the back of the original record:

CASSETTES AND 8-TRACK CARTRIDGES

US (left) and UK (right), 1978, author's collection

Clockwise from top left – Australia, Canada, Yugoslavia, Portugal, 1978, author's collection

Yes: The Tormato Story

Clockwise from top left – Indonesia, Saudi Arabia, Saudi Arabia, Saudi Arabia, all unofficial, author's collection

Some of the unofficial cassettes look more professionally produced than others, as you can see below. The 'Yess' Indonesian version has a colour photo of the cover literally stuck onto the inlay card, as does the Indonesian 'Perina' one above. (Yess isn't a misspelling by the way, it's the name of the bootleg cassette series which includes other Yes albums as well as many other bands):

While some of the official cassette covers look reasonable, the complete loss of the inner bag artwork, the back cover and almost all the information about what's on the album is disappointing. The original 1978 tapes are typical (see page 198).

Clockwise from top left – Poland, Singapore, Indonesia, all unofficial, author's collection

The convenience of the format must have been the factor which kept music fans (including myself) buying cassettes rather than their much more satisfying vinyl counterparts. According to the RIAA,[46] US music sales for 1978 were as follows:

LP/EP 59.9%
Vinyl Single 6.3%
8-Track 22.9%
Cassettes 10.9%

It's perhaps surprising to see that 8-Track tapes sold more than double the number of cassettes in the year *Tormato* was released, at least in the US. Its predecessor, the Stereo-Pak 4-Track Cartridge[47] was pro-

---

46 https://tormatobook.com/riaa
47 https://tormatobook.com/4-track

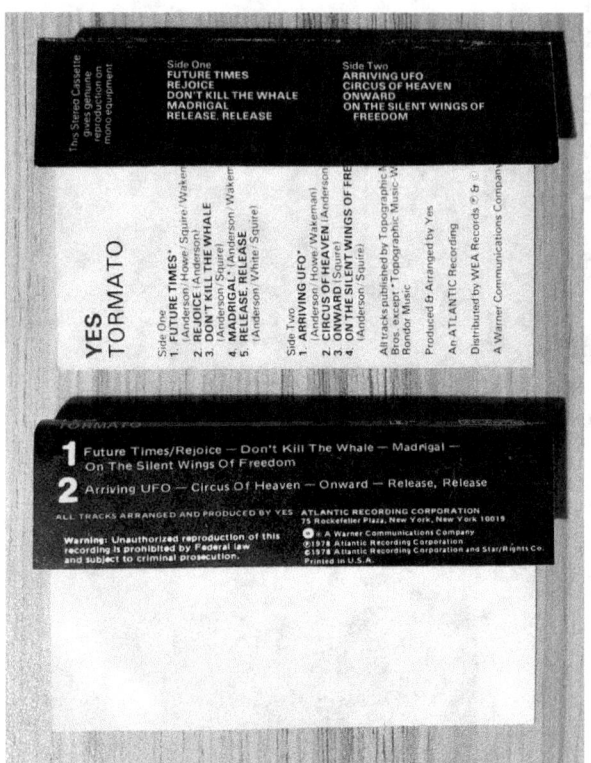

Top – UK, bottom – US, author's collection

duced between 1962 and 1970 and the 8-Track cartridge also pre-dated the compact cassette. It was very popular in car audio setups in the US. RIAA data tells us that 1978 was coincidentally the peak of 8-Track sales in the US, but I don't recall many 8-Track machines in my early childhood in the UK. It's possible I just didn't realise how popular they were, as I was very young. However, after recording an episode of the *Yes Music Podcast* all about Yes 8-Track tapes, my recollections were backed up by listeners:

"Interesting. 8-Tracks clearly passed me by at the time, somehow."

Simon Barrow, YMP episode 558 comments

"I lived through the 8-Track era and although they filled a gap in portable music for the car, I feel as an owner of one you kind of waited for the tape messing up, twisting and jamming. They were probably better suited to the mainstream music and not Prog with the length of the tracks, but it was ok, just not a great product."

                        David Watkinson, YMP episode 558 comments

"As I remember 8 track was not much of a thing in the UK back in the 70's as cassettes were better."

                              Jeremy North, YMP episode 558 comments

On episode 558 of the podcast, we spoke to Tim Durling of *Tim's Vinyl Confessions*[48] about Yes 8-Tracks. Yes albums from the first in 1968 to *90125* in 1983 exist in this format and Tim explained that US mail-order record clubs such as Columbia House (see photograph below) and RCA Music Service continued to make 8-Track versions of albums available until 1988. Retail stores stopped stocking 8-Tracks in around 1982 but major record companies kept issuing tapes of some new albums to these record clubs for another six years. Yes 8-Track tapes of the 'classic' 70s albums are not very difficult to find on the usual internet sources, but titles such as *Classic Yes* and *90125*, which were both issued only by Columbia House on 8-Track, are a lot more difficult to find because of the low numbers produced. *Yessongs* was released as two 8-Track tapes, which makes a set a little trickier to pick up as well, and the first album and *Time And A Word* were also not produced in such large quantities as some of the others.

Depending on your point of view, one fascinating or frustrating facet of the 8-Track format is that the music is split up into four programs. An even more obscure format was the QUAD-8 which only had two programs like a cassette or vinyl record because it was capable of playing back in quadraphonic sound and used the tracks differently. Despite Peter Woolliscroft telling us that Advision's new console was capable of recording in quadraphonic sound, it was never used to do so (see chapter 1) and neither the QUAD-8 nor the entire concept of quadraphonic sound took off.

My 8-Track player has light-up indicators which tell you which program you are currently on, and a mechanical button to press to change between programs (only upwards though, not back). According to Tim, the idea was that if the album was 40 mins long, they would try and split it up into as close as possible to 10 mins for each program.

---

[48] https://tormatobook.com/timsvinyl

This would mean that there were no large gaps at the end or the beginning of each program. This was a reasonable notion, but the technology had some significant flaws including not being able to rewind the tapes (my player doesn't even have a fast forward), and the fact that if you swapped to a different program it wouldn't start at the beginning but rather at exactly the point you stopped the previous program – a bit like turning a compact cassette over. The program functionality led to some strange splitting of songs and *Fragile* even has a note on the 8-Track tape version warning the listener that there is a silent gap of one minute at the end of the fourth program. This is logical but sometimes songs were repeated without warning or unannounced songs would be included, and occasionally programs were even in a different order on different versions of 8-Tracks of the same album. Here's an example of that for *Tormato*:

US Columbia House (left) and UK 1978 (right), author's collection

Tim's 8-Track copy of *Classic Yes* has the two live tracks which were released as an accompanying 7 inch single mixed into the playing order.

As mentioned above, compact cassettes were much less popular at least in the US at the time *Tormato* was released and maybe this is why their production values were so poor when compared with vinyl records. Perhaps we would expect the better-selling 8-Track equivalents to be rather more lavishly presented. Sadly, this doesn't appear to be the case, as can be seen below. In a similar way to cassette tapes, the liner notes and graphic elements are entirely missing from 8-Track packaging as well.

CASSETTES AND 8-TRACK CARTRIDGES

Clockwise from top left – 8-Track cartridges from UK, US, Canada, US Columbia House, all author's collection

There don't appear to be any pirated *Tormato* 8-Track cartridges at all, presumably due to the comparative difficulty of duplication and the high cost of blank cartridges. CDs gradually began to take over from tapes and vinyl after their introduction in 1988 and this meant that albums including *Tormato* had to be converted into the new, digital format which we will take a look at in the following chapter.

18

CD VERSIONS

As with other chapters, this one needs to be read in combination with the Japanese chapter (chapter 19) to make sure you have the full picture.

The Compact Disc format was developed independently by both Phillips and Sony from the concepts of the LaserDisc video system, which had failed to become as popular as had been hoped. Less than a year after *Tormato* was released, the two companies formed a partnership, with the first commercial CDs appearing in Japan in October 1982 and in Europe and the US in March 1983. The success of the format meant that all Yes albums pre-*90125* would eventually be re-released in the digital format. I bought *90125* on CD myself in 1983, so it must have been one of the first wave of new releases to have a CD version at launch.

Tormato's first conversion onto CD seems to have been in Japan where the Forever Young Series version appeared in 1989 (see chapter 19). As is typical with Japanese releases of all kinds, the booklet of this version faithfully recreates the sleeve notes of the original album and there is also a Japanese language sheet folded into the case, containing translations of all the material from the English version. The disc itself is plain, with the track listing but no graphical content, apart from the Atlantic logo. I can't read any Japanese, unfortunately, so I can't tell if there is any mention in the sleeve notes of where or by whom the transfer to digital format was done for this earliest version. However, the digital equivalent of deadwax (see chapter 16) reveals the letters "CSR" around the centre hole of the CD, which is the abbreviation for CBS/Sony Records. This means the Forever Young version of *Tormato* was duplicated at the first CD pressing plant in the world, and features a slightly gold hue, which was replaced by a silver sheen in later discs. I think these earliest *Tormato* CDs should be referred to as 'transfers'. It wasn't until the second phase of releases came around that serious work was put into making the CDs sound as good as possible, a point backed up by Discogs referring to the 1990s versions as remastered, but not the 1980s releases.

The earliest European and US releases of *Tormato* I can find didn't appear until the end of June 1991. Yes aficionado Geoff Bailie found this post on the amazing Steve Hoffman Music Forums site:

> "According to a very detailed Yes discography I found online some time ago, the *Tormato* CD release schedule was (ignoring obvious re-issues, and delayed roll-out in South America, Australia, etc., etc.):
>
> August 1989 – 18P2-2889 (Forever Young Series) – ? mastering – 1st CD issue
>
> June 1991 – 7567-82277-2 (and versions using only 82277 2 depending on territory) – Zal's mastering according to Jamie
>
> February 1992 – AMCY-371 – ? Mastering
>
> August 1994 – 7567-82671-2 (and versions using only 82671 2 depending on territory) – George Marino mastering
>
> March 1996 – AMCY-4037 – ? Mastering
>
> June 2001 – AMCY-6284 – ? mastering (HDCD, limited edition sleeve)

August 2003 – 8122-73794-2 (and versions using R2 73794 depending on territory) – Hersch/Inglot mastering"

Black Elk, May 24, 2008[49]

In the catalogue by Paul Cobb on Yes historian Henry Potts' website,[50] I managed to locate no fewer than one hundred and four mentions of *Tormato*, including all formats of the album as well as magazine articles, videos and many other items. If you would like to delve even more deeply into the release of *Tormato* CDs (and everything else Yes has produced up until 2005), this is a great place to visit.

The 1990s releases contain more information than their 1980s predecessors. Underneath the final statement of the record cover (which is about Yes Tor), an addition has been made in the European booklet I have –

"Digitally remastered from the original master tapes by George Marino at Sterling Sound. Originally released as Atlantic 82277 on September 20, 1978."

The late George Marino was a legendary mastering engineer who worked at Capitol Records in the 1960s. Later in his career, he was senior mastering engineer at the (originally) New York-based Sterling Sound, where many tens of thousands of recordings have been created. Interestingly, the printing on the UK CD itself is rather different to a German/French copy I have, which I believe dates from the same year. The UK one replicates the traditional Atlantic vinyl label, while the German/French version is very plain. The rear insert also uses a different approach as well, with the UK version using part of the original artwork and the German/French one being a more straight forward, informative affair (see page 205).

As mentioned above, many of the first digital transfers of vinyl records were reportedly done as quickly as possible, to ensure availability in the new medium and I've even heard stories of some unusual processes and techniques used which couldn't and didn't produce the best results possible. (See chapter 20 for my rating of different recordings of the album.) Also, digitising techniques have improved over the years

---

49 https://tormatobook.com/hoffmancd
50 https://tormatobook.com/yescatalogue

CD VERSIONS

Top –
UK first
CD edition,
bottom –
French/
German first
CD edition,
author's
collection

and new formats within the overall CD umbrella have appeared, so there are many different versions of the album available in what one might refer to as 'CD' copies.

A myriad different 'CD' releases emanated from a number of countries, particularly Japan, over the next few years (see chapter 19) but the most important development occurred in 2004. This was when Rhino Records (by then part of the Warner Music Group) reached *Tormato* in its series of *Yes Expanded & Remastered* releases. I have a CD-R promotional copy of the new version and we spoke to Brian Kehew on the *Yes Music Podcast* about his part in finding and preparing the additional, bonus material for this release (see chapter 9). The remastering, but critically *not* remixing, of the original album was done by Dan Hersch and Bill Inglot at DigiPrep. The DigiPrep duo earned a reputation for being specialists in remastering classic albums for CD and correcting some of the deficiencies of the earliest transfers.

The series of expanded and remastered Yes albums also had the aim of finding and including music which had never been released (or at least never been made widely available officially) before. As pointed out by Brian Kehew, this sometimes resulted in Yes music from around the same time as the album appearing on the expanded versions, rather than always including music from the same album sessions.

Of the additional songs included on the expanded CD, 'Abilene' (spelled correctly!) is an obvious but important inclusion, particularly for those in the US, Canada and the Philippines who probably didn't hear it in 1978, due to its replacement with 'Release, Release' on singles in those countries. 'Money' is a quirky, fun song, even if you ignore the Rick Wakeman extemporised comedy performance that is indistinct for the majority of the piece. It has a great groove, some excellent Squire bass work and rip-roaring Howe soloing. It's great fun and shows the band in a relaxed mood. While it's not great progressive rock (and doesn't try to be), its joyfulness is a pleasure to hear. I have no idea why the orchestral version of 'Onward' is missing from the sleeve notes but I'm very glad it does appear on the expanded version of the CD. It gives the listener the opportunity to appreciate the beauty of Andrew Pryce Jackman's string orchestration with the addition of the sublime French horn solo. It complements Squire's bass line perfectly. The string writing is exquisite with properly interweaving parts containing counter-melodic themes and figures as well as the use of pizzicato and tremolo.

If this CD series had appeared in more recent years, I think the packaging would have been a little more elaborate, perhaps along the lines of the *Keys To Ascension* or Steven Wilson remixes sets with, for example, additional cardboard slipcases. However, this release does look good despite being in a simple, fully transparent jewel case. The album artwork is well reproduced, and the booklet contains an essay by Tim Jones along with live shots from the *Tourmato* tour and a large, cheerful, outtake photo by Jim Halley from the Blow-up Bridge shoot (see chapter 12). This group shot was also used on the front cover of the 'Don't Kill The Whale' sheet music (see chapter 21), as well as elsewhere. The original Colin Elgie inner bag artwork (see chapter 12) is also reproduced in the booklet, on the CD itself and on the inside of the CD tray. This is highly effective, and it is good to see Colin's 'Don't Kill The Whale' single artwork included as well (see facing page).

The *Expanded & Remastered Tormato* also appears in other configurations, for example the 2004 Spanish Essential Albums series and the 2013 epic box set, *Yes – The Studio Albums 1969–1989*. This collection boasts a beautiful Roger Dean box with brand new artwork, also reproduced as a fold-out poster, as well as great cardboard reproduc-

European Expanded & Remastered CD, author's collection

tions of all the album sleeves. Sadly, however, there are no sleeve notes whatsoever. *Tormato* is included in the 2013 *Yes Original Album Series* box alongside *Going For The One*, *Drama*, *90125* and *Big Generator*, with similar but more flimsy reproduction sleeves. There is also another version I have yet to add to my collection because of the prohibitive cost of the set – the 2013 Japanese *Yes High Vibration SACD Hybrid Limited Edition Collector's Box* (perhaps the longest collection name of all time). This amazing box includes all studio albums up to *Big Generator* plus *Yessongs* and a bonus disc, all in the high-quality SACD format (with standard CD play-ability as well). I do have an SACD version of *Tormato* already, so the asking price of between £500 and £1000 for this box set seems a lot to pay for a set of discs that I can only play as standard CDs anyway because I don't have an SACD player.

Yes The Studio Albums 1969 – 1989, CD box set, author's collection

Finally, the latest version of *Tormato* on CD is part of the new range of Yes MQA-CDs which are being produced in Japan, as one might expect.

See chapter 19 for all the details. It's even possible to find a box set (although I don't think it's an official collection) of all Yes albums up to *Big Generator* in this format which is claimed to produce even better audio reproduction than the SACD versions.

Pirated copies of *Tormato* exist on CD but these are surprisingly difficult to get hold of, perhaps because they mainly seem to originate in Russia. One I would particularly like to find is the double set containing both *Tormato* and *Relayer*.

I have only considered CDs in my exploration of digital versions of *Tormato* because I am rather old fashioned in my desire to own physical copies of music. *Tormato* is available on streaming platforms such as YouTube, Spotify, Apple Music and Amazon Music as well as a wide variety of different downloadable formats including those described as high quality.[51] Perhaps, in the future, I might investigate these.

---

[51] https://tormatobook.com/hdtracks

19

JAPANESE VERSIONS

Japanese versions of *Tormato* deserve a separate chapter because of their high production values and comparatively lavish packaging. Whether on vinyl or CD, there seems to be a desire to produce the highest quality possible. My *Yes Music Podcast* co-host Mark Anthony K tells me that this is because local, Japanese versions need to be special to compete with imports. You will find all sorts of additional tracks, expanded booklets and other goodies in a vast range of Japanese editions of all kinds, not just *Tormato*. I also believe there is a cultural aspect to this attention to detail. In another life, I collected copies of *Alice's Adventures in Wonderland* from across the world. My late father went to Japan as part of an Arts Council delegation back in the 1990s and he brought me back a copy of Lewis Carroll's masterpiece in Japanese. I already had a number of beautifully produced copies from all sorts of different countries, but the Japanese one was on a different level. It came expertly wrapped in strong, delightfully designed Japanese art paper and the hard-backed book was presented in a protective cardboard slip case, printed with Tenniel's original illustrations. The book itself was carefully designed and the paper was of the highest quality, bright white and sensuous to the touch. All this for a western children's storybook. It's one of my most treasured possessions.

Similar attention to detail has been afforded to the Japanese versions of *Tormato* I have collected.

1978 Japanese pressing, author's collection

The most obvious sign of a Japanese copy is the obi strip on the left-hand side. The word comes from traditional Japanese clothing where it is a kind of belt, hence the thin strip of paper on records. The practice of adding the strip that contains information for Japanese buyers originated from the need to provide accessible details of imported albums, but the practice quickly spread to the packaging of locally produced records as well. Other kinds of Japanese products also feature obi strips and, now that I think about it, my *Alice* book has one on the slipcover but it's stuck down and in a horizontal configuration. Record and CD obi strips are usually removable bands of vertical paper (see facing page).

The back of the obi strip is used creatively in the case on the facing page to advertise other Yes albums. In addition to the usual English-language inner bag, this release features a unique, Japanese version which recalls the sheets included with the original versions of Yes and *Time And A Word*. It's interesting to note the production company is listed as WARNER-PIONEER CORPORATION at the bottom of this sheet. This was a collaborative arrangement which was founded in 1971 between the US Warner company and Japanese electronics firm

JAPANESE VERSIONS

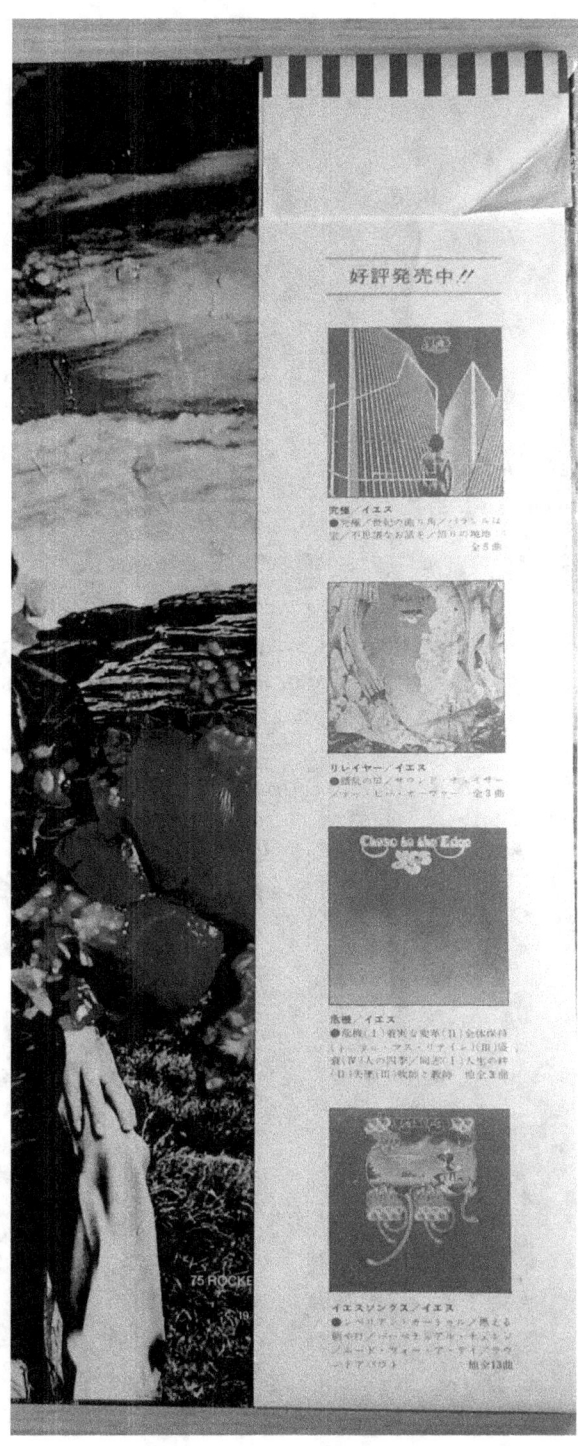

Back of obi strip, author's collection

Yes: The Tormato Story

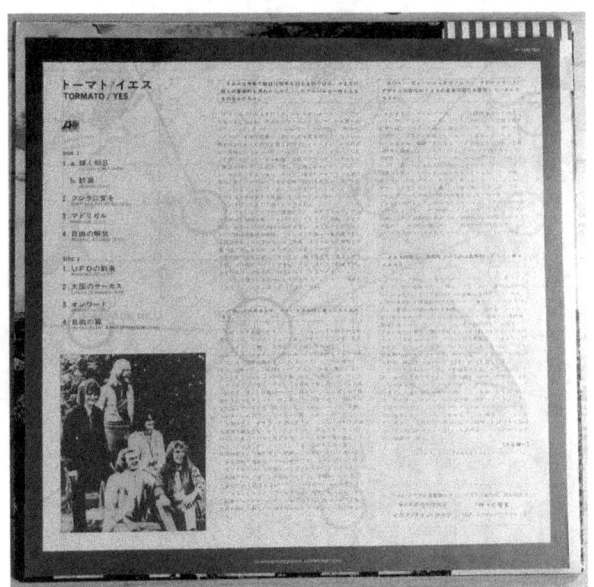

Inner liner notes, author's collection

Pioneer Corporation, which had an entertainment division at the time. Warner bought Pioneer out in 1991 and it is now known as Warner Music Japan.

Once CDs began to appear, obi strips were maintained, and small-

Clockwise from top left – East West Japan CD, Forever Young Series CD, East West Japan HDCD, MMG CD, all author's collection

er versions of the Japanese inner liner notes were often included. However, once we reach re-formatted, new CDs such as the East West Japan HDCD, great strides began to be made. This package includes an exact, miniaturised copy of the artwork of the original vinyl inner bag as a paper insert, as well as a booklet containing Japanese notes and the full English CD notes. It's a great item but there is another version which shines even more brightly – the Atlantic Records 70th Birthday SACD:

Atlantic Records 70th Birthday Edition SACD, author's collection

The proliferation of different digital formats can be confusing. SACD (Super Audio CD) was introduced in 1999. Much like the Betamax videocassette system, which was a superior format to VHS, SACD failed to make the impact that was hoped for, even though some of the discs (called Hybrid) are playable on standard CD equipment as well. The arguably much better sound quality of SACDs means that it is still popular amongst die-hard audiophiles, but it is a very small niche, as dedicated SACD players are now expensive and difficult to find.

More interesting than the format is the remarkable packaging of this item. It's presented in a Mini-LP format which is about the same size as a 7-inch single package. The aim of this approach is to create an experience as close as possible to the original album. The CD itself is housed in a black circle of card to make it appear like a vinyl record with an over-large label:

SACD package, author's collection

Behind the CD is a replica of the inner bag (which can be used as a slip case for the CD), and the booklet has a black and white copy of the cover photo with English and Japanese language contents. It's a lovely item and the one I managed to find is a hybrid version so I can play it on my standard CD player, although that means I can't appreciate the enhanced sonic quality. Needless to say, I don't have an SACD player.

As mentioned in chapter 18, a new CD format is now available from Japan which claims to have far better sound than even the SACD above. Here is what record label Ottava's CEO, Mick Sawaguchi, says about the new MQA-CD format:

"MQA coding enables us to preserve the original master sound quality with thorough timing de-blurring and very small data size. Advantages of MQA-CD are:

• No additional cost for users

• Can be played back by conventional CD-players with higher quality sound.

• With an MQA decoder, listeners can get a master quality hirez from CD.

No special knowledge of PC, network, or software operation skill is necessary. MQA is a remarkable innovation of CD media."
Mick Sawaguchi on stereophile.com[52]

The latest version of Tormato – MQA-CD, author's collection

This looks like a great advance and if you would like to know what I think of the sound of this format compared with others, see chapter 20. The packaging follows the Japanese tradition of high quality. It is another miniaturised version of the original 1978 Japanese vinyl version, right down to the cardboard sleeve. This time, it includes an additional obi strip on top of the removable, red, paper one that gives details of the new format. Fold out inner bags in the original English and in Japanese are included, as is an additional Japanese booklet. The CD itself is in a separate, plastic sleeve and the combination of all these elements makes it feel heavy and high-quality. This is what all Yes recordings should feel like, in my opinion, as opposed to the cassettes, 8-Track cartridges and first CDs, which seem cheap and flimsy in comparison.

---

52 https://tormatobook.com/stereophile

Yes: The Tormato Story

The only other Japanese version I've managed to see online is a cassette from 1978. It has a pleasing, mainly black cover and regularly sells in Japan for a very reasonable price. However, I haven't managed to snag one yet. If you know anyone who is selling a copy, please let me know.

20

WHICH VERSION SOUNDS BEST?

There are many different versions of *Tormato* in my collection and I am often asked which one sounds best. This is a difficult question to answer, but one I feel I should at least try to tackle in this book. In order to achieve an answer in a sensible amount of time, I have restricted my listening to 'just' nine different copies of the album:

1. Vinyl test pressing
2. 1978 US vinyl
3. 1978 US cassette
4. 1978 Canadian 8-track
5. 1991 Germany/France CD
6. 2004 UK Expanded & Remastered CD
7. 2013 Friday Music 180g vinyl
8. 2001 Japanese HDCD
9. 2022 Japanese MQA-CD/UHQCD

The nine versions, ready for analysis

I came up with a set of criteria in my attempt to make the comparisons useful, although I realise my results are highly subjective and prone to influences such as the different equipment I used and the condition of the different copies. However, I hope what I found out is of some interest and perhaps even of use to you. The equipment I managed to keep the same included the headphones and amplifier, and I maintained identical EQ settings, so I had a better chance of hearing some of the differences between the formats.

All scores out of 10:

Version 1 – Vinyl Test Pressing
Overall sound – 5
Clarity – 5
Enjoyment – 5

Comments – The sound is quite thin and doesn't seem to fill out the full spectrum I would expect. All instruments are audible, but the music doesn't pack the same kind of punch that Peter Woolliscroft described on playback at Advision. The bass in 'Don't Kill The Whale', for example, sounds light and underrepresented. Also, where there is a lot going on in the music, the sound seems to become noisier with static. 'Madrigal' comes over better but is still light on the bass. 'Release, Release' sounds 'tinny' as well. Vocal harmonies at the beginning of

'Arriving UFO' come over quite well but the 'bigger' sections sound noisy again. 'Circus Of Heaven' sounds similarly held back. Anderson's vocals on 'Onward' sound a lot more effective, in terms of their recording, than the previous songs. The strings in the background also sound fuller than the band instruments have up until this point. French horn also sounds good. 'On The Silent Wings of Freedom' takes us back to some of the limitations of the full band songs from earlier. Squire's bass is clear but maybe fades into the background during guitar solos too much for me. Anderson's voice cuts through nicely but, as the volume grows, the static is back with a vengeance and the fast play-out section suffers from thin sound again. Alan White's drums are particularly obvious here. They do sound like very cheap instruments with no depth at all so the effect of the end of the album which should be a real barn-storming crowd pleaser is lost. If I had heard this test recording in 1978, I would have sent it back with some stern words, I think.

Version 2 – 1978 US Vinyl
Overall sound – 7
Clarity – 7
Enjoyment – 8

Comments – The sound on this version is much smoother and a little fuller. The bass is a little more prominent and 'Future Times' rolls along more pleasingly. Howe's guitar solo on 'Don't Kill The Whale' is much more enjoyable and Squire's bass is more audible. I was wondering if I would hear any difference at all between this and the test pressing, but this is like listening to a different album. It's not brilliant but it's better. 'Madrigal' doesn't stick out as much as it did on the test pressing. It sounds as good as the previous songs, not significantly better. There is a little bit of a 'wobble' in the sound which I think is probably down to the record having been played a lot over the years but, even so, it still sounds better than version 1. 'Release, Release' is much improved. The feel is much more exciting and the sound doesn't seem to suffer as much in the louder passages. I'm surprised how much difference the modest improvement in sound makes to the enjoyment level. Even the bass drum in 'Arriving UFO' sounds like a bass drum and complements the bass guitar well. The explosion towards the end of the song also sounds dramatic and doesn't fill my headphones with static. In 'Circus Of Heaven' the backing vocal lyrics are much clearer and I can even hear the comedy I assume is intended. Like 'Madrigal',

'Onward' sounds good but not noticeably better than the other songs. The recorder consort is obvious in this version, and the strings are appropriately lush. I'm pleased to say that Alan's drums sound better in 'On The Silent Wings Of Freedom'. It sounds a lot less like he's bashing cardboard boxes. Squire's bass is also more prominent and balanced with Steve's guitar. Moments of Wakeman sparkly keys also cut through and the level of static is greatly reduced. It's a much more enjoyable experience.

Version 3 – 1978 US Cassette
Overall sound – 5
Clarity – 5
Enjoyment – 5

Comments – There is an annoying scratchy sound on this cassette version but I'll ignore that. The sound is muffled in comparison with the vinyl versions. However, the mix on 'Future Times/Rejoice' is as well balanced as the US 1978 vinyl, with plenty of bass and drums, which sound like drums. Guitar and keyboards fight it out, but at least they are both clear when it's their definite turn. 'Don't Kill The Whale' is similarly muffled as is 'Madrigal' which is a shame and obscures the orchestration. 'Release, Release' sounds full of energy which is a surprise. The bass is again clear and the backing singing comes across well. Alan's drum solo sounds okay and, for whatever reason, the songs sound better than the rest so far. Side two is still muffled but I may be used to that now, as it's less noticeable. 'Circus Of Heaven' sounds terrible at the beginning. The triangle sounds very odd and the gaps in the music sound strange, as if it's not supposed to be so sparse. It's the first time I have experienced that. The backing singing is audible which is a good thing, but the odd feel continues throughout the song. It comes over as forced. I'm surprised that the media can have such an effect on a specific song. Even the synth bass at the beginning of 'Onward' sounds odd and the recorders sound mushy. I'm finding this version tiring to listen to. 'On The Silent Wings Of Freedom' revives me a little. Drums and bass are energetic and sound fairly well mixed. Howe's interjections blast through and Wakeman's keyboard washes come across well. I have a feeling the tape is changing speed a little so maybe that's the reason I have found side two tiring. When the vocals finally arrive, the mood feels appropriately upbeat. The audio mayhem is less diminished than earlier in the album and Anderson's voice cuts through the quieter passages effectively. Overall, not a great experience and rather patchy.

Version 4 – 1978 Canadian 8-Track
Overall sound – 7
Clarity – 7
Enjoyment – 7

Comments – Moving from the cassette version to the 8-Track is a bit of a revelation. Although the sound isn't sparkling, it is a lot fuller and, in particular, the bass is much more audible – and enjoyable – in 'Future Times – Rejoice'. The song rocks along with proper layers of accompaniment to Wakeman's soloing. The moments when Anderson's voice takes centre stage are lovely, complete with great sounding backing vocals. Howe's opening solos in 'Don't Kill The Whale' are also presented clearly. There are a few moments when the tape is slightly warped, but after more than forty-five years that's no surprise. It's a bit odd to move straight to 'Arriving UFO' at the start of program two but the vocal harmonies and backwards reverb come across well, as does Squire's bass again. There is still a bit of a flat sound and I wonder if that's to do with the mix or the inability of 8-Track tape to reproduce the full range of frequencies. It's undeniably a better listening experience than the cassette, however, and it's a pleasure to remember why this is my favourite album. 'Onward' is next in this version and I find I quite like the order. I also like being able to hear the character of Squire's bass and the recorder consort. The synthesised bass also sounds great and the calm mood is enhanced greatly by the strings. This version gives the song the quality it deserves. I've even just noticed the vibraphone White is playing, according to the sleeve notes, near the end of the song – for the first time ever! Moving from this to 'Release, Release' works fine and the song springs out of the headphones with energy. The backing singing duo of Howe and Squire are enjoyable, and it all hurtles along in great style. White's drum solo transports me to a 'live' gig and I can't help nodding my head to the final play out with Wakeman whizzing away on his keys and Squire's final bash. 'Circus of Heaven' sounds good as well. The triangle (or is it actually an individual crotale?) which sounded dreadful on the cassette is now a pleasing effect, and this version reveals a lot of background detail entirely missing from the previous one. Program 4 begins with 'Madrigal'. It is rather surprising to hear that this song is muffled more like the cassette than the rest of the 8-Track. Such a shame – it sounds like someone has thrown a towel over the speaker. The vocals really suffer and the detail of the accompaniment is difficult to make out. I wonder if 'On The Silent Wings Of Freedom' is also like this. Sadly it is. This could be due to manufacturing issues as it covers all of the fourth program, but I do remember this problem when listening to other 8-Tracks. The sound is almost but not quite as bad as the US cassette and ruins the end of the album.

Version 5 – 1991 Germany/France CD
Overall sound – 8
Clarity – 8
Enjoyment – 9

Comments – There might be a bit too much treble on this CD transfer, at least when it begins, but it sounds good in terms of separation of instruments. Bass is nicely defined, and Anderson's voice certainly cuts through. Drums sound better mixed than in previous versions I have listened to in this process, and effects like Wakeman's swooping Hammond organ stick out the right amount. 'Don't Kill The Whale' has a good balance between bass and lead guitar initially, but the bass does disappear quickly, which is a shame. There is still a very pleasing amount of detail, and each element is given a good chance to be heard. 'Madrigal' doesn't suffer from the same muffled character as the tape versions. There is also more depth to the harpsichord sound and the strings are audible, making a great overall sound. It's a treat to hear this properly again. There's quite a lot of punch in the opening to 'Release, Release'. Bass drum and bass guitar work particularly well together. The motion is infectious. The sound is probably still too bright but the way the drum solo comes over is the best yet. 'Arriving UFO' is clean and clear, so I can hear all the parts including the synthesized drums and it rips along. The crazy guitar and keyboard sounds battle it out once again and the explosion ... explodes. 'Circus Of Heaven' sounds great as well. For once, the bass line is given proper prominence as the music grows. I can't imagine how other versions are going to sound better than this one, but we shall see. I'm delighted that 'Onward' is presented in full quality, with all components sounding as they should and clearly audible, culminating in the key change and lovely French horn solo. All set for the final blast – 'On The Silent Wings Of Freedom'. The drums are light at the beginning, but I believe that is deliberate.

Squire's bass is centre stage and it's a wonderful, insistent and lively-sounding performance. The vocals ratchet up the mood further when they arrive and feel well-mixed in. The backing singing is a bit too far down in the texture but that's a minor problem. The instrumental accompaniment is balanced and the song rips along to the quieter section. This part also feels right and the gradual build-up introduces the spritely Wakeman soloing and the rush to the end. This version is hugely enjoyable.

Version 6 – 2004 UK Expanded & Remastered CD
Overall sound – 9
Clarity – 9
Enjoyment – 9

Comments – I should be able to hear a definite difference in this CD because, otherwise, what is the point in remastering the music? The beginning of 'Future Times – Rejoice' does indeed sound better. There is more separation between the instruments and the bass seems to be louder. The difference is not dramatic but certain instruments like Steve Howe's guitar do tend to stick out suddenly at times. I'm not sure I like that effect. Everything is clean and audible though, which is great and it all sounds like it's had a bit of a boost – presence rather than volume. 'Don't Kill The Whale' reveals some hidden aspects of individual instruments, particularly Steve Howe's electric guitar technique which were possible to miss in other versions. The vocals on 'Madrigal' sound lovely, as do the acoustic instruments. There isn't really any sign of the bass pedals which remain almost inaudible, but that's not a surprise as this version is remastered, not remixed. 'Release, Release' welcomes Squire back after being lost in action in the previous song. The backing vocals seem even more boosted than on the previous CD, and the drum solo feels more like it's really going on live. The increased clarity is particularly obvious in the vocals – it is possible to hear the individual character of Anderson, Howe and Squire. 'Arriving UFO' is similarly clear with some lovely bass tones coming through, perhaps for the first time, in full quality. It's somewhat of a revelation. In 'Circus Of Heaven' there are some background effects I don't think I've heard before. Some short textures, maybe on a keyboard appear and I'd love to know who is adding the bass vocals – Squire? It's not a common Yes component. This version makes 'Onward' even better to drift away to and then the sudden change to the dramatic, Squire-driven 'On The

Silent Wings Of Freedom' takes the listener by surprise – in a good way. The drum sound here is so much improved from the flat, lifeless character of earlier versions and the bass disappears less. This is a much more satisfying conclusion to the album which leaves the listener in a state of excited exhaustion, which is the idea, I'm sure. So far, I would definitely recommend this remastered version to anyone wanting to hear as close as possible to the original vision for the album.

Version 7 – 2013 Friday Music 180g vinyl
Overall sound – 8
Clarity – 7
Enjoyment – 8

Comments – What can vinyl do to rival the remastered CD? Friday Music's series is marketed to audiophiles so it should be good. I don't possess audiophile vinyl equipment, so this comparison is probably the least reliable of the whole process. 'Future Times' does sound great but very different to the remastered CD. It's much warmer in character with all parts integrated well. I'm not sure I like it as much though. There's nothing wrong with it but the separation and brightness of the CD appeals more to me. Anderson's vocals, for example, sound more natural and rounded and Squire's bass also sounds fuller. This is definitely a great-sounding record and clearly better than the others, but I'm not enjoying it as much as the remastered CD. The same comments apply to 'Don't Kill The Whale' – the sound is more homogeneous and the clarity of instruments is less effective. As I guessed, 'Madrigal' lends itself more to this warm sound. It's pleasant and if I tweak the EQ settings it comes to life. However, I said I wouldn't do that to try and have sensible comparisons. The drums cut through well on 'Release, Release' and the overall feeling is exciting while 'Arriving UFO' actually seems to sound better than side one. More clarity and slightly more edge to the sound benefits the song, and I also like the sound of 'Circus Of Heaven'. I suppose this kind of variation is possible with analogue technology. 'Onward' benefits like 'Madrigal' from the warmth of this vinyl version with the strings, French horn and backing singing coming across well. 'On The Silent Wings Of Freedom' takes us back to full rock band territory and is less appealing in terms of sound. This record is definitely a better listening experience than the other vinyl versions above and, if you prefer the character of this media, then the Friday Music version is probably the one for you, but I prefer the experience

WHICH VERSION SOUNDS BEST?

of the remastered CD, so far.

Before listening to the Japanese HDCD, which I now realise is out of chronological order, I received an email from the very helpful John Ford, concerning how to play this format. Here is an edited version of his main points:

> "There is an HDCD protocol that is necessary for listeners wanting to hear the full, 20-bit decoded stream of the album. The format is a superb way of extending the humble CD's usability, but not everything is rosy in the garden. To be able to add the additional HDCD information to the CD, there had to be a reduction, by 2-bits, of the available space used for the normal CD information. The protests that the reduction from 16-bit to 14-bit results in a reduction of sound quality proved, basically, to be null & void. Personally, I had one of the early Phillips CD players, which had 14-bit DACs (digital to analogue converters), which, in listening tests etc., beat the Japanese machines with 16-bit DACs hands down! You need to have either have a CD player or an amplifier with an HDCD decoder, otherwise all you'll hear is the standard 'un-enhanced' audio. Even those who did have HDCD built into their equipment were possibly not hearing the decoded output because of the following problems:
>
> A) If the listener has a CD player with built-in HDCD decoder connected to a standard stereo amplifier, where the two are connected using the analogue stereo out/in ports, then the listener will hear the full 20-bit decoded version of the album.
>
> B) As above, but the CD player is connected to the amplifier 'digitally' using the separate 'out' and 'in' sockets – the listener will only hear the standard audio from the CD. This down to the limitations of the digital communication protocols.
>
> C) If the listener has a standard CD player and an amplifier with built-in HDCD decoder and the connection between the two is 'digital', then the listener will be listening to the full 20-bit decoded HDCD audio.
>
> D) As above (C) but the two units are connected using the ana-

logue cable, the listener would 'normally' hear just the 'standard' audio unless the manufacturer has used the HDCD as the only DAC in the amplifier.

For those of us without any of the limited number of pieces equipment equipped to decode HDCDs, there is now a way of doing so using software."

I do not have any of this advanced equipment so I'm expecting the HDCD to sound much like the remastered one I listened to earlier, given that it is presumably playing back in standard definition, as outlined by John above.

Version 8 – 2001 Japanese HDCD
Overall sound – 9
Clarity – 9
Enjoyment – 9

Comments – I can't tell any significant difference between this CD (played back in standard definition) and the remastered one. It's perhaps slightly less broad in its frequency response due to its digital remaster by Isao Kikuchi but it's so close that, for normal purposes, I'd say there's nothing to separate the versions. Both of them sound great.

Version 9 – 2022 Japanese MQA-CD
Overall sound – 10
Clarity – 10
Enjoyment – 10

Comments – According to the words of Mick Sawaguchi (see chapter 19), my standard CD setup should be perfectly capable of playing the MQA-CD format at higher sound quality than the CDs I've listened to so far. The first difference is an odd couple of clicks before the music starts. Ignoring that, the sound is smoother than the other CDs and perhaps better balanced, with less harsh treble. 'Future Times' sounds like the best vinyl copy but with more clarity. The enhancement isn't startling but if I had the choice (and I do!) between this version and the other CDs, I'd certainly choose this one, at least from the evidence of the opening song. 'Don't Kill The Whale' carries on in the same vein with an attractive feel to the sound. Maybe this is the closest we are going to get, without a proper remix, to the original intentions of the musicians and the studio staff. 'Madrigal' sounds beautiful, particularly Howe's Spanish guitar, which is presented in a glorious, full timbre. The bass pedals are also slightly more noticeable but, then again, I am consciously listening out for them! 'Release, Release' zips along and 'Arriving UFO' features some resounding bass (guitar and drum) and remarkably clear synth parts. 'Circus of Heaven' comes over well and this is the version of 'Onward' I'd like to be played at my funeral, as long as the Church has a decent PA system. If you need to explain to anyone what a towering bass guitar and drum passage the beginning of 'On The Silent Wings Of Freedom' is, then this MQA-CD will give you all the help you need. The drums are unrecognisable compared to some of the earlier versions, and the music is consequently very exciting. I don't know if some of the other versions use different takes of this song, but the highest notes Anderson sings in his opening vocals often sound strained whereas they don't on this CD. It makes me wonder if the reproduction technology was detracting from his performance. Surely not? Whatever the answer, this version has Jon – and Wakeman's spiky soloing – in appropriately great quality, and the dynamic range between softer and louder sections is controlled brilliantly. It makes for a festive end to the album. A wonderful version.

Overall, it's perhaps unsurprising that my scores generally increased as the versions became newer. I have tried to feed back what my ears told me and my conclusion is this: if you want to hear *Tormato* in the best quality possible today (and you can afford it), the MQA-CD is the one to get. If you are on a tighter budget, the remastered CD is also great and I'd go for a well-preserved original 1978 vinyl copy. If you are happy with the version of the album you currently listen to but are interested in collecting some brilliant packaging, the Friday Music record is excellent and any of the more recent Japanese CD copies are worthwhile.

21

SHEET MUSIC

Even today, it is possible to visit the small music shop in my small town and pick up sheet music transcriptions of popular music. Once upon a time in the UK, there was a sheet music chart. It predated the NME's record chart which began in November 1952. Before the 50s, it seems there were more pianos in homes in the UK than record players (although I imagine this idea is referring to middle class homes and working-class homes generally had neither) so most popular music was consumed in the form of playing it yourself on your piano. It might seem bizarre from the standpoint of the twenty-first century, but the first top 20 shows broadcast by UK radio stations in the 1950s played music taken from the sheet music charts of the day. When my mother (now in her 80s) tuned into Radio Luxembourg from her teenage Belfast bedroom, the music she heard had been bought by people like her in paper format, not on vinyl (or shellac). In the US, the Billboard charts were first collated in 1913 and they were also initially created from sales of sheet music. As usual, the US led the way and the first Billboard record sales chart appeared in January 1936.

I've been able to find a *Tormato* album songbook which was published by Warner Bros. in the US in 1979, as well as sheet music for 'Don't Kill The Whale', which was published in the UK in 1978, also by Warner Bros.

SHEET MUSIC

UK sheet music, author's collection

The 'Don't Kill The Whale' sheet music has a cheerful, red cover with one of the alternative photos from the album back cover album shoot. It was taken while the photographer was setting up and the band are shown before donning the tour jackets. All are laughing so perhaps Rick had just cracked one of his archetypal jokes.

As with most sheet music arrangements, the Anderson/Squire song is set out as a piano score with guitar chords above. Also, as usual, the song is somewhat simplified in its parts and its structure, but it gives a pretty good approximation of the single. I'm reminded that one of the first jobs that legendary composer, conductor and performer Leonard Bernstein had was creating piano reductions of symphonic works, and he was reportedly amazingly quick and proficient at it. I imagine that he usually had some kind of score to work from, but most rock music is never written down, and where it is written down the resulting score is almost never created in standard notation. This means that transcribing rock music is a significant skill, even if the song is a relatively simple one like 'Don't Kill The Whale'. The process involves listening to a song, transcribing the parts and 'reducing' it all to a score, playable by a single pianist. I had to do some transcription of a recording of a Northern Indian Raag as part of a course in ethnomusicology when I was a student, which I found very challenging indeed, so I have a sincere sense of appreciation for all rock sheet music.

However, there is a difference between reduction/simplification and getting things wrong. The coda section in the UK sheet music for 'Don't Kill The Whale' features the words, "Hey____to see ya_____" which is repeated. In fact, the lyrics at this point, as transcribed on the inner bag of the album, are, "CETACEI" which I believe is the plural of the word 'cetaceo', meaning whale, in Italian. I imagine the idea was to include a call of 'whales' but using a word which sounds a little 'scientific' as part of the message of the song. Perhaps the misheard version is preferable, or at least less opaque. This use of language is similar to the Chris Squire solo song, 'The Fish (Schindleria Praematurus)' from *Fragile*.

The transcriber clearly misheard the lyrics, which is not an unusual occurrence, in my experience. I remember a member of staff at the UK magazine *Smash Hits* admitting that, in order to publish the lyrics of the latest singles, they used to play the 45rpm records at 33rpm and transcribe the words, rather than relying on record companies to send lyrics in. I recall frequent mistakes when attempting to sing along to Frankie Goes To Hollywood or Queen in the mid-80s.

The *Tormato* songbook I have wasn't published until 1979 and doesn't seem to have used the earlier arrangement of 'Don't Kill The Whale' as source material. The version of the song here is different in several respects, including the reintroduction of the word, "Cetecei," towards the end. Quite a lot of the piano reduction is more complex as well. The other transcriptions also seem reasonable, despite being listed in the contents of the book slightly bafflingly (but in common with most music books) in alphabetical order, and 'Rejoice' being split up from 'Future Times'. The production values of the songbook are fairly high, with versions of the cover artwork and inner bag artwork included, and acknowledgements to Hipgnosis, Rob Brimson and Colin Elgie (see chapter 12) printed appropriately. There are also seven pages of colour and black and white photographs at the beginning.

US Tormato sheet music book, author's collection

Firstly, there is a double-spread photograph from a live show on the Tourmato tour in 1978. Owing to the circular stage, at least one member of the band is always going to have his back to the camera and, in this shot, it's Chris Squire. The image is also grainy, but is otherwise a good representation of the concert in question, containing a great view of Steve Howe's five guitars as well as Jon Anderson's cuatro (see chapter 5) lined up next to Rick Wakeman's keyboards. Also visible are Alan White's red, scooped North toms and his set of crotales.

Then we have a single page of photographs for every band member. Each page features a small colour shot from a concert and a large, black and white publicity photo. Steve Howe is shown leaning against a wall, outside RAK Studios, while Rick Wakeman is seated at a pipe organ somewhere. It is definitely not St. Giles' Cripplegate (featured on *Close To The Edge*) as the console is much more modern-looking. The black and white photo of Jon Anderson is the strangely bleached one

Yes: The Tormato Story

Tourmato tour photo inside the sheet music, author's collection

from the Yes press pack of the time, and the shot of Alan White is a real beauty. He is perched on the wall outside RAK Studios with his trusty Great Dane sitting on the ground in front of him. Both dog and owner look relaxed and happy.

Perhaps the most interesting inclusion, however, is the black and white photograph of Chris Squire. "INSIDE PHOTOGRAPHY" is credited to Fin Costello, the famous rock photographer, known for his iconic images of many of the most recognisable artists of the day. However, the photograph printed in the songbook of Chris Squire isn't by him. While flipping through the music book recently I was astonished to recognise the shot as one of the set taken by Yes fan Chris Hoskins (see chapter 1) when he visited Advision Studios during the *Tormato* sessions. I contacted Chris about this, and he had no idea it had ever been used. He said he had given copies to the band at the time and so they must have used this photo without telling him. It is a fantastic, moody shot of the great bassist and also turns up (cropped) in the 1978 *Tourmato* tour programme (see page 234).

Left – Alan White and his dog outside RAK Studios in 1978, right – author attempting to recreate the shot in 2023, photo by William Mulryne

Author recreating the Steve Howe RAK photo 45 years after the original was taken, photo by William Mulryne

Chris Squire at Advision, photo courtesy of Chris Hoskins

SHEET MUSIC

"I suppose," Chris Squire once said in a moment of characteristic understatement, " that a lot of my music *is* on what you might call an epic scale."

There's a terrible temptation to start unpacking all that wide-screen phraseology again. Maybe slip in a few flash references to 'heathen magnificence' or 'pagan grandeur', or put Chris' musicianship on a par with the eruption of Vesuvius, the sinking of North America, or the Utter Annihilation Of The Universe As We Know It.

It's probably less pretentious to say that Chris is one of the most powerful and influential rock bassists in the business. In many ways, he's more responsible for putting the instrument on the musical map than just about anyone else around – though that sizeable achievement is the result of a long, slow buildup of musical experiences over the years.

Chris Hoskins' photo of Chris Squire at Advision as it appears in the Tourmato programme, author's collection

PART 5 – PROMOTION AND RECEPTION

22

ADVERTISEMENTS AND PROMOTIONAL ITEMS

Whether you think it was a good idea to change the name of the album from *Yes Tor* to *Tormato* (or even *The 11th Illusion* to *Yes Tor*), it certainly gave promoters and advertising companies the chance to tie in their efforts to the theme of tomatoes. As I have said elsewhere, I'm not sure that a squashed fruit is a great way to promote music of any kind and certainly not an album which was meant to be serious, not a novelty record.

Nevertheless, a lot of the point of sale, newspaper and other items used tomatoes – some more creatively than others. A British fan originally from Derby contacted me to say that he once had a *Tormato* point of sale advert which, as far as he can recall, had a cardboard half-pipe with a background based on the photograph of Yes Tor from the album cover. Stretched across it was a clear plastic sheet and inside the space created between the plastic and the background was a cardboard stand-up figure of the diviner which could be positioned freely. The item was about eighteen to twenty-four inches tall, and approximately six to eight inches wide, from his memory. It sounds a bit like a bizarre *Tormato* play set and its owner even has a hazy memory of the squashed tomato maybe being printed on the plastic portion. Sadly, due to parental attic clean outs, the item no longer exists.

I did manage to find an unused US point-of-sale stand-up which is not as elaborate as the UK one, but is almost as inventive:

Standup with 3D effect bottle top and author, author's collection

Music shops were encouraged to order *Tormato* displays by articles such as this in a trade magazine of the time (such as the one on the next page).

More standard-looking adverts and posters were also produced including Yes discography tie-ins and the use of the back cover of the album to show the band.

Yes: The Tormato Story

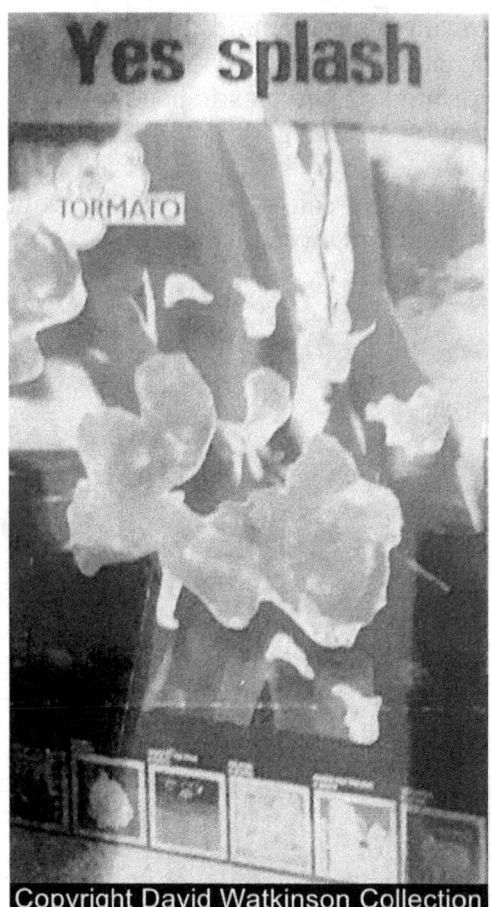

Encouragement for dealers to display an advert for Tormato in their shop windows, photo courtesy of David Watkinson

A GIANT 3D window centrepiece, designed around the artwork for the new Yes album Tormato is to be available for 600 dealers. The display has a clear PVC front, which has a tomato thrown against it. Dealers with windows which get a lot of sun (if there is any sun) and who are beginning to worry about the state the tomato will be in before long should be glad to know that the offending fruit is painted on.

The first point-of-sale item I received was kindly given to me by long-time *Yes Music Podcast* producer, Joseph Cottrell. As he said in the note which accompanied the gift, the original 1978 48inch × 48inch poster had been in his possession for around thirty-nine years. It had been tacked up on several walls and at least one ceiling during that time but, due to space issues, he was unable to display it anymore. He bought it from a Las Vegas store, Odyssey Records, which had a merchandise store connected to it, selling all sorts of items including Roger Dean posters. Once promotional periods had ended, materials would be removed from the main store, rolled up and offered for sale in the merchandise area. Joseph just happened to be there on the right day to pick up this wonderful item.

ADVERTISEMENTS AND PROMOTIONAL ITEMS

Left – UK shop advert, a gift from Brian Neeson, right – US poster signed by Rick Wakeman and Steve Howe, author's collection

Since receiving this gift, I have also collected two other point-of-sale posters of the front cover of the album, one of which is pictured with Joseph's below:

1978 point-of-sale posters, rear – a gift from Joseph Cottrell, middle – smaller with white border, front – promotional LP for scale, author's collection

The print media was a critical place to advertise a new record in 1978 and Yes' publicists throughout the world tried out a number of approaches, some traditional and other less so.

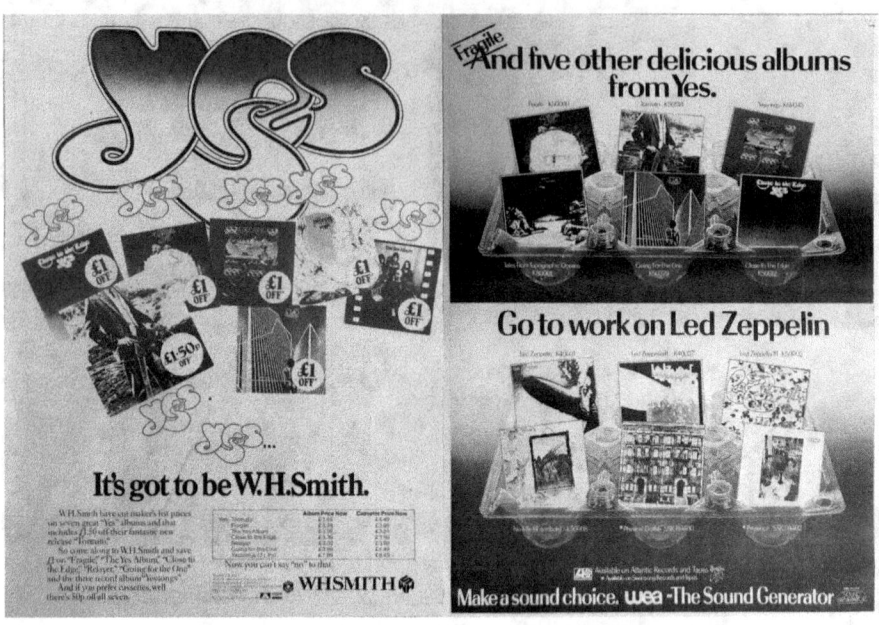

UK newspaper adverts, author's collection

In the UK newspaper advertisement above right from WEA (who had taken to calling themselves 'The Sound Generator', in a foreshadowing of a Yes 1980s album, perhaps), a variety of Yes and Led Zeppelin albums are featured, portrayed as eggs. A well-known advertising slogan of the day was, "Go To Work On An Egg". Squashed tomatoes? Eggs? I don't quite understand the food/music analogy. It's interesting to see both that *Fragile* was chosen as the headlining album for Yes and that stablemates Yes and Led Zeppelin were marketed together in 1978. Above left is the bookshop and newspaper retailer W.H. Smith's advert for *Tormato*, alongside a lot of other Yes albums, for a budget price.

The food and/or beverage theme continued into the *Tourmato* tour and *Ten True Summers Tour* programmes as well. This time, a very 70s looking barman will serve you a choice of Yes albums:

ADVERTISEMENTS AND PROMOTIONAL ITEMS

Inside back cover of the Tourmato tour programme, author's collection

The UK advert on the right (see bottom of page 244) was a complete surprise to me. I bought a 1978 UK Wembley concert programme from eBay which included a ticket from the concert. I was flipping through the pages and discovered this advert which acts as a money-off voucher. Imagine receiving £1.50 off the album price and a free copy of 'Don't Kill The Whale'!

Advertising for the album and its associated tour was often combined, as can be seen in the UK newspaper adverts below (see page 245) which both contain dates for the UK concerts at Wembley. The left-hand one contains the information that the original dates were sold out and an additional, matinee performance had been added on Saturday 28th October at 3pm, "BY PUBLIC DEMAND". How many times have Yes performed twice in a day? There can't be many instances like this one since their earliest days gigging at small venues around London.

Yes: The Tormato Story

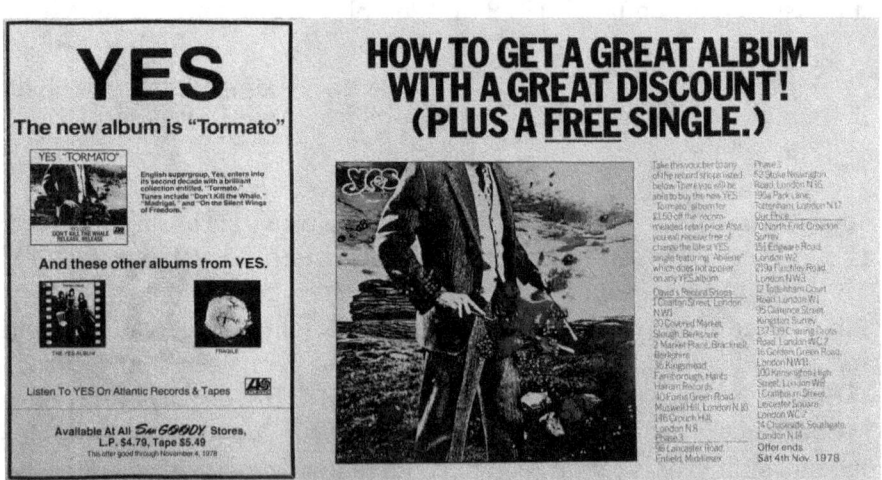

Three magazine adverts, clockwise from top, US, France and Germany, author's collection

Tormato adverts from other record stores, left US, right UK, author's collection

ADVERTISEMENTS AND PROMOTIONAL ITEMS

Left, UK Melody Maker advert, right, UK New Musical Express advert, author's collection

A press pack was produced to promote the album and it was included in trade magazines which gave some marketing suggestions to the record sellers of the day:

Music trade magazine entry for Tormato, author's collection

Unfortunately, I have lost track of the person who posted the following images of the *Tormato* Press Kit online (see page 246). I'm also not absolutely sure the dark picture was the cover but it may have been. Perhaps the Hipgnosis cover wasn't ready for this publication. The band photos are mostly from the Blow-up Bridge photo shoot (see chapter 12), or outside RAK Studios. The two notable exceptions to this are the live shot of Chris Squire and the odd, faded photo of Jon Anderson. There is a discography of the band's music up until 1978 and four pages of biography, along with a large Roger Dean logo. Only the last few paragraphs of the biography concern *Tormato* but they give an interesting insight into how Atlantic wanted to position the album.

Yes: The Tormato Story

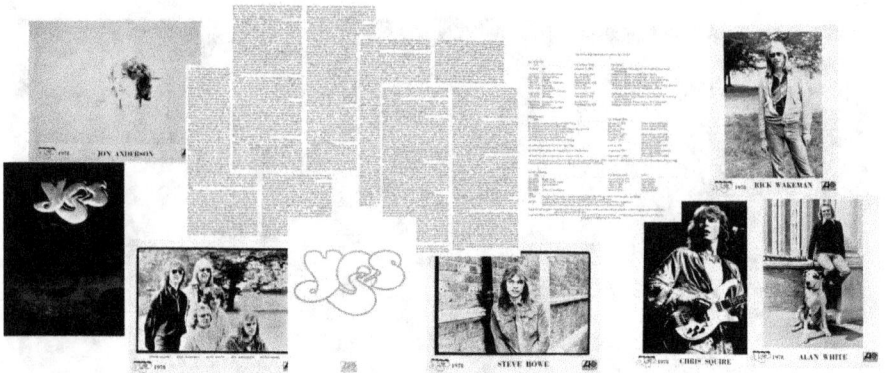

Tormato Press Kit, origin unknown

It points out the number of songs on the album and refers to the band continuing the shorter song trend partially begun on *Going For The One* with no song more than eight minutes long for the first time since 1970. Concerning the title, it says that Yes Tor is a real place and the Hipgnosis cover is there to, "provide whatever clarification it may." *Tormato* is described as one of the most innovative Yes LPs, departing from what it calls, "the previous effort." There follows quite florid description of each song:

'Future Times' – "a dense pulsing rocker"

'Rejoice' – "a positive celebration of those 'ten true summers long'"

'Don't Kill The Whale' – "one of Yes' most striking message songs ever"

'Madrigal' – "a beautiful ballad"

'Release, Release' – "Yes power"

'Arriving UFO' – "diversity of the dramatic" – "its unusual electronic effects (note Alan White's drum synthesizer)"

'Circus Of Heaven' – "one of Yes' most intriguing pieces ever"

246

'Onward' – "a slow majestic love song, highlighted by a most effective strings and horn arrangement by Andrew Jackman"

'On The Silent Wings of Freedom' – "decidedly jazzy underpinnings" – "yet further proof that the Yes soundscape is ever-changing, ever unpredictable, and ever-impressive in its power to move and challenge players and listeners alike"

I agree with a lot of the description here and it would certainly have convinced me as a Yes fan to rush out and buy the record. I'm not sure it's pitched very effectively to appeal to the new generation of listeners in 1978, which doesn't appear to be the intention. It reads more like an attempt to prove that *Tormato* is a development of all the traits existing fans love about the band and is striving to break new ground, while being deeply connected to previous work.

Other items produced included badges (pins in the US) in various shapes and colours:

Two Tormato badges, author's collection

A number of items were only produced for band, management and crew, as Dave Watkinson shared with me:

"A collection of four pieces of Yes memorabilia from 1978 came up for sale around the time of Yes' 50th Anniversary in England. It included two limited edition (likely edition of 25) badges one designed by Mick Milligan to depict the logo of Yes' manage-

Yes: The Tormato Story

ment company 'Sun Arts', and the other the Roger Dean Yes logo (measures approx. 3cm across). Mick worked for Yes at this time in the late 1970s and the badges were given to band and staff only. Also sold, a crew pass for Wembley 1978 and a 1978 record company document folder featuring the Roger Dean Yes logo."

David Watkinson

Yes logo and Sun Arts badges, photos courtesy of David Watkinson

Record company document folder with a variety of 1978 materials, photos courtesy of David Watkinson

23

ALBUM RECEPTION

A gold record in the UK before its release, *Tormato* certainly sold well, but what did the critics think when they actually heard it? In the UK, two of the main weekly music papers featured album reviews by some of the most high-profile critics of the day. The Royal Academy of Music educated Paul Morley is well known both for his florid and erudite writing style and his collaboration with ex-Yes front-man, Trevor Horn, on their record label, ZTT. Therefore, it's no surprise to see the style of his *Tormato* review for the NME in October 1978:

> **YES, YES, YES — BUT SO WHAT?**
>
> A good trick is always worth replaying twice.
> But make no mistake, I chant mindlessly, the Yes people have a lot to be excited over. Gorgeous melodies, intelligent, carefully crafted, surprising arrangements, concise and energetic performances, cryptic but evocative lyrics — when all these are present Yes are quite boggling and their potential seemingly unlimited.
> But who's looking? The inevitable concluding epic "On The Silent Wings Of Freedom" has all of Yes idiotically indulging their own particular virtuosity without any cares in the world, and is a jolly way to finish a jolly album.
> Will we ever forget it?

Paul Morley writing in the NME, author's collection

As I've always found with Mr Morley's writing, I'm not exactly sure if he likes *Tormato* or not from his review. Certainly, the headline appears to be dismissive. A, "jolly album," which has the band members, "idiotically indulging their own particular virtuosity without any cares in the world." That sounds like a good thing, doesn't it? His list of features of Yes music in the first extract above is a glowing endorsement of the capabilities of the band, but I'm not convinced Morley is saying these are all present in *Tormato*. Perhaps I'm reading too much into the text and it is supposed to be a bit light-hearted. He definitely doesn't mention thin sound or inadequate production, so overall I think it's a positive reaction to the new album.

> With Rick Wakeman now firmly committed to the band, Steve, Alan and Chris all charged with new energy, and with Jon Anderson an imaginative and distinctive writer and vocalist unswerving in his beliefs and musical standards, the result is a band for the Eighties.
>
> I like the new Yes album more than "Relayer" or "Going For The One" because of its variety, live, spontaneous feel and because of the raw, aggressive energy that in the past had sometimes been replaced by a neurotic, mechanical effect, caused by over indulgence in the studio.
> With this album they have achieved a perfect balance between the band's energy as creative players, the material, which is carefully edited and shaped, and the technology of the studio. A thunderous ex-

Chris Welch writing in Melody Maker, author's collection

There's no doubting author of *Close To The Edge The Story Of Yes*, Chris Welch's, strength of reaction to Tormato, however. Chris knew Yes on a personal level from their earliest days and had been on tour with them. It's a little surprising that he rates *Tormato* above *Relayer* and

Going For The One, but his other musical interests are wide and, when we interviewed him on the *Yes Music Podcast*, he mentioned that he liked Punk music when it came along. His view above is that previous Yes albums were hampered by overindulgence in the studio, but *Tormato* gets the balance right. This is very different to the reactions of a lot of Yes fans over the decades. He is absolutely correct that Yes fashioned themselves into a band for the 80s but that transformation necessitated a very different lineup and approach, five years later than this, and it arguably had very little to do with *Tormato*. However, it's very easy for me to sit here in 2023 and make pronouncements with the benefit of more than fifty years of Yes history.

Welch visited the band in Advision Studios along with photographer, Barry Plummer, and his obvious excitement about hearing the musicians at work seems to have been borne out, for him, in his eventual review.

Above and below, Melody Maker, 6th May 1978, author's collection

I heard brand new Yes music pouring out of the studio on playback, and it's astonishing stuff. Unless something disastrous happens to the tapes between now and the eventual release of the black plastic, it will be the most vibrant, exciting record they have yet conceived.

In an attempt to gauge the overall critical reaction to the album, I looked at the numerous reviews available on *Forgotten Yesterdays*[53] and chose 10 examples at random. The responses covered a range of reactions from positive to rather less than positive:

> "...a superlatively executed work of art..."*Tormato*", the eleven[th] Yes album, is a masterpiece of interwoven delicate and intricate instrumentals and vocals."
>
> UMBC Retriever

> "The group appears to be consciously attempting to capture, revise and integrate the best sounds from the ten years it has been together – and it works."
>
> Cal State University Fullerton *Daily Titan*

> "All in all, another successful outing for the band and those Yes fans who may have been hesitating can go out and buy it with confidence."
>
> *Scunthorpe Evening Telegraph*

> "Keyboard wizard Rick Wakeman and guitarist Steve Howe are in sparkling form as the group present an inspirational and contrasting set of new compositions."
>
> *Derby Evening Telegraph*

> "But the record gets better and better. It could easily be Yes' best."
>
> *Tulsa World*

> "No doubt hardened Yes fans who have followed the band over the decade of its existence will love this album, but if you're not one of them, you're not missing too much."
>
> *Southall Gazette*

> "On "*Tormato*," the lyrics are indulgent and pointless, and give the music as a whole a passe effect which the brilliance of Alan White (drums) and Steve Howe (guitar) do not deserve."
>
> *Sandwell Evening Mail*

---

[53] https://tormatobook.com/reception

"It took a while to get into this. The album certainly lacks the immediate appeal of the classic *"Going For The One."*"

Crewe Evening Sentinel

"But as a whole the album lacks energy. So where do they go from here? Oblivion? I hope not. But retreating into the past will only distance Yes from the progressing tastes of music lovers. And how long can any group survive on past success? I guess Yes are slow learners, as well!"

Windsor Lance

What surprises me most is that I can't find any mention of the issues most Yes fans have pointed to over the years – the bad production and terrible sound of the record. I suppose this might have to do with the speed at which reviewers have to scribe their reactions but it's strange that not one of the critics mentions those deficiencies. Perhaps others do point out these problems and I just haven't found their opinions in my searching, but I would have thought the immediate reaction to placing the needle on this record, for at least some of these professional listeners, would have been, "Urgh, this sounds thin, flat and terrible!" As pointed out by Yes author, Simon Barrow, however, music fans (and even critics, perhaps) were used to listening to music on poor quality cassette machines or record players, so aural quality was not the issue it is now.

24

PROMOTIONAL VIDEOS

You will have noticed Geoffrey Mason's name multiple times already in this book. He has been one of the most loyal and prolific contributors to the *Yes Music Podcast* online spaces over the years. Geoffrey has researched and collected hundreds of articles, interviews and other material about the world's greatest progressive rock band, and a lot of them are now posted to *Forgotten Yesterdays*.[54]

As I've mentioned, this site is the most important source of information about Yes' live concerts, posters and other memorabilia, and was established by Pete Whipple (later to be joined and then succeeded by Steven Sullivan) in 1996. When Geoffrey posted an interview published in the UK's *Scunthorpe Evening Telegraph* from 1978, my *Tormato* senses were activated. It turns out to be a fascinating piece in which journalist Nick Cole interviews someone I had never heard of before – Clive Richardson. Apparently, he had decided it was time for him to move on and he was saying no to yes.

Clive was planning to end his, "lucrative association," with Yes at the end of 1978, having reached the age of 34, stating that he was too old

---

54 https://tormatobook.com/forgottenyesterdays

SAYING NO TO YES . . .

Scunthorpe Evening Telegraph, *date unknown but certainly before June 1978*

for rock and roll. He had been working with Yes since 1973 as 'art designer', having been introduced to the band by Roger Dean, one of his contemporaries at the Royal College of Art in London. After a small amount of research, it's clear that I should have heard of Clive before now. He worked with Roger and Martyn Dean to produce the extravagant and amazing stage sets the band had become famous for in the mid-70s. His name appears in several tour books:

- The 1974 *Relayer* Tour programme for Stage Design Modification and Stage Set Management with Adam Wildi
- The 1975 US Tour programme for Stage Design alongside the Dean brothers
- The 1976 *Solo Albums Tour* programme where he is mentioned for assisting with Martyn Dean's scenery design and construction
- The 1977 *Yesshows World Tour* programme alongside Mike Tait and Adam Wildi for Set Design

There are photographs of the fibreglass scenery being constructed in the 1975 programme (presumably in the Yes equipment warehouse, see chapter 7), so I assume one of the people pictured doing the work is Clive.

At the time of the 1978 interview, Clive was working on a spectacular set for Yes' upcoming live shows, which included a two-hundred-foot screen. We know that no such thing was present on the *Tourmato* tour, which famously featured the world's first revolving, circular stage, so I assume Clive's plans were shelved. Perhaps he was working on the concept of 'The 11th Illusion' which the band was developing and used as a working title for *Tormato*. The original idea of a double album was supposed to tie in with a proposed stage setting idea using the theme of illusions, so this seems to fit. However, the interview seems a little confused because it then proceeds to say that the screen will 'go on display' when the band reach the US to celebrate their tenth anniversary. Was it part of a stage set or a separate item? It's not clear.

Another tantalising item in the interview is a planned trip to Los Angeles to negotiate the hiring of a, "laser-video scanner" for use in the *Tourmato* tour. I'm not quite sure what this equipment might be, but it sounds great! Once again, was this used in 1978 or not?

By this point in the chapter, you may be wondering what all this has to do with the promotional films for *Tormato*. Well, later in the same interview with Clive, we find the following statement:

> "Clive is now filming Yes recording their latest album in Jon Anderson's studio and the finished work will be incorporated into the American set."

We appear to have a plan to incorporate footage of Yes, projected onto a 200-foot screen as part of the *Tourmato* set, plus a laser-video scanner. That's quite a set-up and very different to what ended up appearing. The other aspect to ponder is what became of the footage. The interview goes on to say that Clive also spent two months filming the band in Montreux in 1977 (and also worked with legendary Italian director, Fellini). That is highly likely to be the material widely available on YouTube[55] and elsewhere that shows the band rehearsing, recording and also in their downtime between sessions for *Going For The One*. As for the 1978 filming, perhaps interviewer Nick Cole misheard 'Advision Studios' as 'Anderson's studio'. Maybe the behind-the-scenes film of the band developing 'On The Silent Wings Of Freedom' and the footage of the *Tormato* photo-shoot was taken by Clive Richardson as well. This seems entirely feasible to me. I haven't previously managed to find any credits for the Advision film.

When I asked Rick Wakeman if Clive Richardson created the promotional films for *Tormato*, he said, "I think so ... but not 100% sure."

---

[55] https://tormatobook.com/gfto

Is the cameraman in the stripey shirt Clive Richardson? Note the Yesshows logo on the back of Rick Wakeman's jacket, far right, photo by Jim Halley at 'Blow-Up Bridge'

Searching on the internet for Clive Richardson reveals that someone with the same name ended up being highly successful in the area of pop videos. In fact, I contacted Roger Dean, who confirmed that this is indeed the same Clive Richardson. His extensive 80s portfolio includes promotional films for:

- **Depeche Mode** – 'Just Can't Get Enough' and many more
- **Marillion** – 'Lavender' and 'Kayleigh' from *Misplaced Childhood*
- **Siouxsie and the Banshees** – 'Christine' and many others
- **Tears For Fears** – 'Mad World'
- **Steve Winwood** – 'Valerie'
- **Adam and the Ants** – 'Kings Of The Wild Frontier'

That's an amazing track record and prompted me to wonder if Clive was indeed also responsible for the other *Tormato* promo films, 'Don't Kill The Whale' and 'Madrigal'. I think this is less likely because Clive had yet to concentrate fully on video production. These two promotional films are very different to the behind-the-scenes footage from Montreux and Advision which, although well edited, don't contain the type of video effects used in 'Don't Kill The Whale' and 'Madrigal'.

However, Derek Dearden (see chapter 7) told me that Clive filmed the Alan White 'Spring-Song Of Innocence' film[56] for *The Old Grey Whistle Test* BBC show. It featured Steve Howe and Jon Anderson, so perhaps I'm wrong and he was, indeed, responsible for both of the *Tormato* videos. Unfortunately, there don't seem to be any credits at all on the Yes YouTube channel or the *Greatest Video Hits* collection and I haven't managed to find any contact details for Clive, despite asking several people who knew him well. Sadly, the last time Clive was with his former colleagues was at Nigel Luby's funeral (Yes live sound and *Tormato* studio engineer).

What remains of all that potentially exciting work is the behind-the-scenes video of 'On The Silent Wings Of Freedom' which gives us a fascinating and unique glimpse of the band at work. As far as I can tell, it was never officially released and appeared on YouTube for the first time in 2006 on the yesfan21 channel. Subsequently, a cleaner version was uploaded to the same channel in 2008.[57] The earlier video has a significant additional feature close to the beginning – the following details of the song are superimposed:

Yes
"On The Silent Wings Of Freedom"
Tormato
Atlantic Records

It looks like the kind of caption one would see on television programmes, so does that mean this video was once broadcast? In any case, we are fortunate that this video was at some point uploaded to YouTube as it contains a treasure trove of *Tormato* detail unavailable elsewhere.

Even the opening shot is remarkable, with the throwing of the tomato at the album cover presumably re-created and timed to match the music. Seeing and hearing the development of a Yes song is a rare thing and here we have nine minutes of just that. Behind-the-scenes footage of the photo shoot at 'Blow-up Bridge' is also fascinating, with Po from Hipgnosis directing the band. They even have the opportunity to play

---

56 https://tormatobook.com/springsong
57 https://tormatobook.com/silentwings

around a bit, recalling their youthful antics on the 'Everydays' film,[58] a video made very shortly after Steve Howe joined the band, in 1970. Alan White's Great Dane dog plays football and there are some wonderful shots of both Advision and RAK studios. The glass door the band walk through is at RAK but they emerge, as if by magic, back in time at Advision. It is a delight to see the mixing desk adorned with tape, notating what each track is for, and all the instruments are seen being set up. This includes Steve polishing his Gibson and re-stringing it, as only he was allowed to do. Rick Wakeman is seen playing a few notes on the Birotron (see chapter 3) and the discussion of the arrangement of the song is fascinating.

Aspects of Studio 1 on show include the huge cinema screen behind Steve and there are several shots of the control room behind Jon Anderson. The same sound baffles which are still there today (see chapter 2) are visible and Alan's multi-coloured North hybrid kit sits inside its isolation area. There is even a wonderful segment of discussion in the control room where they agree to go and do (yet) another take of the song, in the hope of regaining some of the 'magic' of earlier versions. The resulting playing does indeed seem more energised, and the Roger Dean Yes logo ring (see below and chapter 22) makes an appearance at the end of the film on Rick Wakeman's finger, as he removes his hand from the Birotron keyboard.

As for the 'official' videos from *Tormato*, there are two – 'Don't Kill The Whale'[59] and 'Madrigal'.[60] Quite why there is a promotional video for 'Madrigal' at all is a puzzle. It wasn't a single from the album, and not even a B side. When I asked Rick Wakeman why the video for 'Madrigal' had been made, he said, "I've no idea why we did a film ... and dressed up!" As we shall see, quite a bit of work was put into this video and it's very definitely meant to be a promotional film, but before appearing on the compilation, *Yes Greatest Video Hits* in 1992, had it ever been seen before? It's not clear that it had.

The short 'Madrigal' is shown in a fanciful context and features some remarkable visuals. Rick told me it was filmed in a Georgian house by the River Thames, near Richmond. Never one to shy away from a bit of

---

58 https://tormatobook.com/everydays
59 https://tormatobook.com/whalevideo
60 https://tormatobook.com/madrigalvideo

pantomime, he is dressed as an 18th Century musician, all lace collars and tailcoat, as he walks to a harpsichord (see chapter 4), in the appropriately dramatic drawing room. The small audience are heard talking quietly, and Rick is taking it all very seriously indeed – he's clearly from the school of deadpan acting popularised later by stars such as David Duchovny. This was 1978 and so perhaps we shouldn't be too surprised to see Jon Anderson's face superimposed into the keyboards of Wakeman's harpsichord and then Anderson and Howe floating out of the window behind Rick.

There is a zoom into the sound hole of the harpsichord which reveals Steve Howe playing his Spanish guitar. Anderson, Squire and Howe then sit in a row on high stools, recalling for me the cosy noodling of the great 70s entertainer and doyen of the cardigan, Val Doonigan. Alan White does get to appear in the video, despite adding very little to the song itself. I'm not 100% sure he's on 'Madrigal' at all, but he is shown adding some cymbals. Wakeman's hands are seen next, appearing like Gulliver's Lilliput experience with the other musicians tiny, and seemingly contained inside his harpsichord.

At the end of the song, Rick receives a little fairly half-hearted applause and the hand of one of the audience is revealed, as fake crowd noise is added. Finally, we are left with a shot of a Roger Dean Yes logo ring (see page 261) which appears to be studded with diamonds. Dave Watkinson tells me this special logo ring was arranged by John Martin, Jon Anderson's instrument tech at the time, who went on to be his personal assistant. It appears some were made in 14K yellow gold and others made in sterling silver, all given out to band members, management, record company personnel and road crew. The precise number made is not clear, but is likely to be under twenty-five. None have come on the market for sale, as far as Dave can tell – clearly if one did it would be very desirable indeed.

'Madrigal' is a very odd but definitely enjoyable promotional video. It is clearly meant to be humorous, and the editing and compositing are fairly good for the time. A great little Yes curio.

Finally, there is 'Don't Kill The Whale'. This is definitely recorded with the same equipment as 'Madrigal', and uses some of the same vision mixing techniques. We start with a view of the sea with two dark shapes moving about, off in the distance. Are they whales? It is really not clear. One pleasing aspect is that we get to see the musicians wielding the instruments which feature in previous chapters in this book. Alan is using a somewhat reduced version of the North hybrid kit, Steve is playing (miming on) The Les Paul, Rick has his Polymoog (I think) and his Birotron and Chris' almost omnipresent Rickenbacker bass contrasts well with his black coat.

As Steve Howe's fabulous solo reaches its high point with the weird rasping and warping bass beneath, the band are revealed as if getting their feet wet in the sea. Jon Anderson is sporting some large shades and footage of whales' tails plays semi-transparently through the figures of the musicians. Essentially, it's a watery performance video. Waves crash and the effect of hiding the feet and even sometimes the complete lower halves of the musicians in the water is slightly peculiar, but it is an effective video – a bit of fun.

Roger Dean Yes logo ring, as seen in the video for 'Madrigal'

25

SALES FIGURES

> Don't Kill The Whale is included in the new Yes LP Tormato, scheduled for release by Atlantic on September 8, which has shipped gold on advance orders — the first time Yes has achieved this distinction in the UK.

Pre-release success for Tormato *in the UK as reported by* Music Week, *uploaded by Geoffrey Mason to* Forgotten Yesterdays

The number of sales required to qualify for Platinum, Gold and Silver discs was changed to the current thresholds of Platinum (300,000 units), Gold (100,000 units) and Silver (60,000 units) in 1979 for albums above a minimum RRP. Below the minimum RRP, the thresholds are doubled. Prior to this, the thresholds were based on monetary revenue: Platinum (£1,000,000), Gold (£150,000 from April 1973 to September 1974, £250,000 from September 1974 to January 1977, and £300,000 from 1977 until 1979) and Silver (£75,000 from April 1973 to January 1975, £100,000 from January 1975 to January 1977, and £150,000 from 1977 until 1979).

Wikipedia article[61]

The easiest way to define record sales, it seems, is via the award classifications achieved by albums. Beyond this, it appears to be rather difficult to keep track of how many copies are bought. As above, *Tormato* achieved Gold status in the UK based solely on advanced orders, before it was released on 8th September 1978. This means that Yes fans were very keen to get their hands on the new Yes album after the success of *Going For The One* and its tour.

In the UK, Gold discs were awarded after 1979 for in excess of 100,000 units sold but when *Tormato* was released in 1978 the threshold was different. It was actually based on revenue, not unit sales. *Tormato* achieved at least £300,000 in sales revenue. According to the WH Smith advertisement (see chapter 22), *Tormato* cost £3.49 on vinyl and £4.49 on cassette. This included £1.50 off the manufacturer's recommended price of records and 50p off cassettes. Using the full record price of £4.99 for convenience, and assuming the Gold certification meant exactly £300,000, this equates to approximately 60,120 copies. Using this very unscientific method, Platinum sales would be around 200,400 copies. As far as I can see, *Tormato* did not achieve this in the UK, but I'm not sure what difference the change to unit numbers for classification made to the statistics in the year after *Tormato* was released. By my own calculations, *Tormato* would have been awarded Silver disc status if it had been released in 1979, after the changes in criteria.

In the other main (and much larger) market for Yes, the US, *Tormato* achieved a Gold certification (500,000 units) on 10th October 1978, shortly after release on 26th September. It then went on to sell a lot more, unlike in the UK, and achieved Platinum status (1,000,000 units) on 8th November 1978.

It is useful to compare these numbers to previous and future Yes albums.

---

61 https://tormatobook.com/recordsalesuk

	UK	US
Tales From Top. Oceans	Gold	Gold
Relayer	N/A	Gold
Going For The One	Gold	Gold
Tormato	Gold	Platinum
Drama	Silver	N/A
90125	Gold	Platinum

Sales classifications within 24 months of release – changes of criteria affect the ratings, see above

From the viewpoint of 2023, *Relayer* in the UK and *Drama* in the US both performing less well than *Tormato* in terms of sales is interesting, and I wonder what the total figures are like for these albums today. Would *Tormato* now be lagging behind both? Unfortunately, it seems very difficult to find out.

PART 6 – TORMATO LIVE

26

THE TOURMATO TOUR, THE TEN TRUE SUMMERS TOUR AND BEYOND

"It's not often we play anything from [*Tormato*]. We only play 'Onward', which is the other thing [apart from 'On The Silent Wings Of Freedom'] I love from *Tormato* ... We play [it] in a new way, without three hundred zillion notes on the keyboard and the guitar. We play another version of 'Madrigal', which doesn't have a lot of notes, which is a relief because that version [on the record] has too many notes!"

Steve Howe, *Yes Music Podcast*, October 2022

Whatever your personal opinions of *Tormato* were at the time it was released, or are now, it sold a lot of copies (see chapter 25) and the tours which supported it were also undeniably sensationally successful. Facts, figures, reviews and memorabilia from the tours in 1978 and 1979 could easily fill more than one complete book on their own, so all I can do here is to provide what I hope is a useful flavour of the live Yes activity following on from the creation of *Tormato*.

THE TOURMATO TOUR, THE TEN TRUE SUMMERS TOUR AND BEYOND

Here are some statistics from the *Tourmato* tour, the *Ten True Summers Tour* and the following years to date (March 2023), according to the wonderful Yes live source, Forgotten Yesterdays.[62] If you consult setlist.fm, you will find some differences in statistics for these tours and songs. I prefer to use Forgotten Yesterdays because it is created and curated by Yes fans themselves, and is therefore likely to be more accurate.

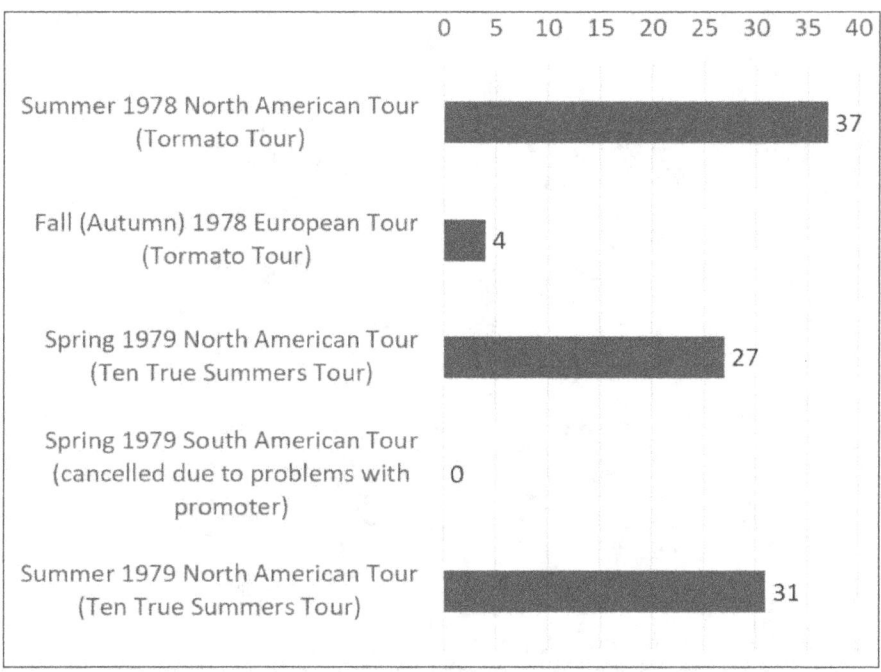

Chart showing the 99 concerts in 1978 and 1979, data from Forgotten Yesterdays

According to Forgotten Yesterdays, half of the album has not been played live by the band since 1979 and 'Onward' was not played until it was included three times at the San Luis Obispo concerts that were recorded for *Keys To Ascension* in 1996. 'Don't Kill The Whale' is perhaps an obvious candidate for multiple live performances due to its catchy feel. Consequently, it has been played more often than any of the other

---
[62] https://tormatobook.com/forgottenyesterdays

Yes: The Tormato Story

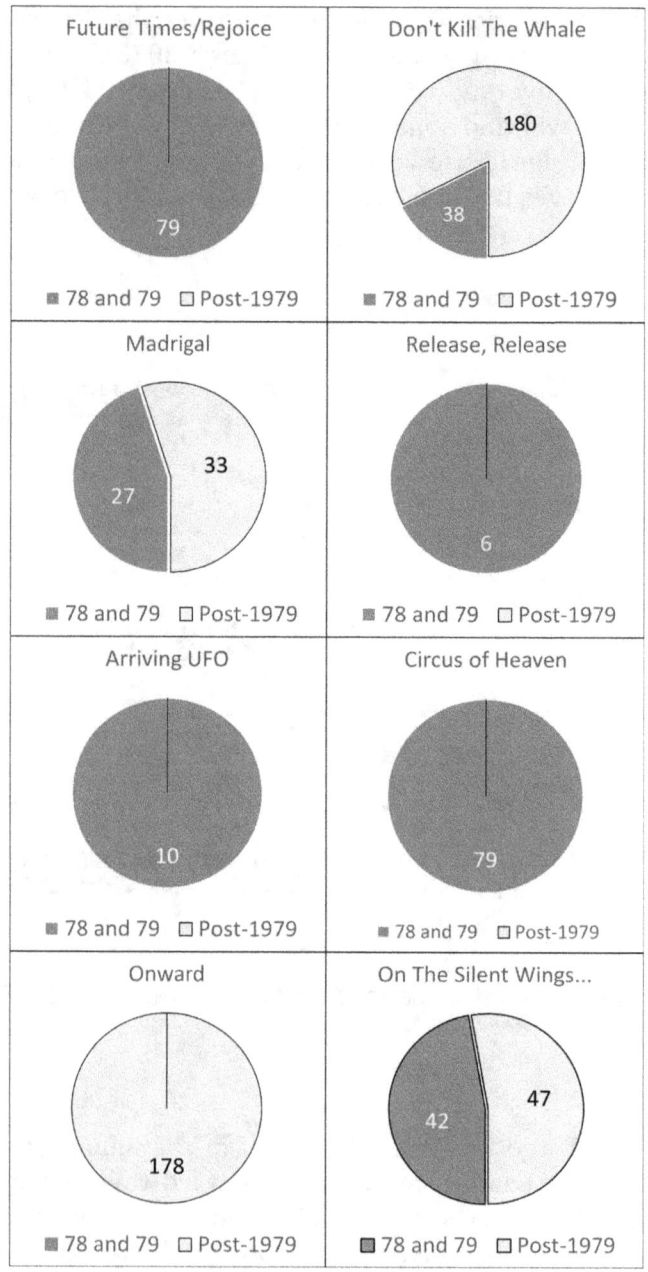

Chart showing the number of times each song from Tormato was played in 1978/9 (dark) and post-1979 to March 2023 (light), data from Forgotten Yesterdays

songs from the record.

In 2022, Yes surprised their fans by including 'On The Silent Wings Of Freedom' in their set list for the *Close To The Edge 50th Anniversary Tour*. I saw the show at The Royal Albert Hall, London, and had the privilege of speaking to Steve Howe about the choice of this Tormato classic on the *Yes Music Podcast* in October 2022.

Firstly, I asked Steve why he thought this was the right time to bring back the song, after forty-three years. He explained that this song had been requested a lot over the years but that were reasons why it hadn't been played live since 1979:

> " ... it's actually incredibly difficult to play on stage ... it was very improvised and a lot of the things were just done, like, spontaneously. So when I played something, it wasn't planned. Nobody said, "Oh, would you come in there?" You know, I just hurtled in because we were improvising. So it became an impossible song to play in its entirety ... [I] couldn't really work out what the heck I was doing in certain parts of the song, or the better, bigger question than that is, "why I was playing like that?""

Steve thinks Billy Sherwood was keen to play the song live, but Steve was not happy with a lot of the guitar parts:

> "[There was] all this stuff all over the track and I didn't like it, you know? And I was not gonna learn it because I'm not gonna learn a guitar part I don't like ... even if they want me to ... There's another option – you design a new part ... which, in part, I've done with songs like 'Parallels' ... and other tracks where I couldn't really ever play exactly the same thing ... as the record, but *Tormato* suffers [even worse] with those problems."

Despite his own misgivings, Steve knew that audiences would appreciate hearing the song live again, so he worked out how it could be done. He played the record and decided that:

> " ... half of this song is great, you know, the other half is not great ... I don't like it at all. So what I did was, I thought about it

from an editing point of view and I thought, well, it should start with something you can grasp, which is the theme ... I moved the theme that came after about five minutes into the beginning of the song ... let's start with something. At least we can all play and agree on what the hell it is."

27

TORMATO OFFICIAL LIVE RELEASES AND COVERS

Unlike the classic *Yessongs*, it is unfortunate that we don't have a filmed version of the band's second live album, *Yesshows*. It's also perhaps a shame, although for entirely understandable reasons, that songs from *Tormato* have featured infrequently on official live releases. Seven out of the eight songs on the album were played live by the band on the 1978/9 tours (see chapter 26) but the major live album from the band, released just a short time after *Tormato*, only includes 'Don't Kill The Whale', taken from the BBC Wembley concert recording. The opportunity to release archive recordings of other *Tormato* songs on the fabulous 2005 collection, *The Word Is Live*, only produced two more – 'Circus Of Heaven' and 'Future Times/Rejoice'.

Chris Squire and Alan White often incorporated the opening figures of 'On The Silent Wings Of Freedom' into their live reworking of 'The Fish', called 'Whitefish'. Despite this, it hasn't been released on as many official live collections as one might expect. This is due to the frequent changes of material in that arrangement, over the years. For example, 'Silent Wings' excerpts were not used in the version of Whitefish on *9012Live – The Solos*. In fact, the only official release of a version containing 'Silent Wings' is on *Live at Montreux 2003*.

'Onward' was not attempted live in 1978/9 but appears on both *Keys To Ascension* from 1996 and *In the Present – Live from Lyon* (2011) where Oliver Wakeman was on keyboards and Benoit David on lead vocals. It was also used as a soundtrack recording for the poignant tribute to Chris Squire before the opening of many concerts after his death in 2015 and these instances are included in the live statistics from Forgotten Yesterdays. The song was subsequently played live again on *The Royal Affair Tour* and recorded on *The Royal Affair Tour: Live from Las Vegas* album (2020). 'Madrigal' also had a late, live resurgence as immortalised on *Yes 50 Live* (2019).

Geoff Bailie (of *The Prog Report*) kindly produced a full survey of releases and cover versions of *Tormato* songs, augmented with the encyclopaedic knowledge of Yes chronicler, Henry Potts:

YES: TORMATO – LIVE AND COVER VERSIONS
by Geoff Bailie with Henry Potts

'Future Times / Rejoice'

Officially released live version by Yes on *The Word Is Live* (2005)

Cover versions:
- 'Rejoice' by Jon Anderson – performed live on his 1980 tour captured on *Lost Tapes 4 – Live in Sheffield* in a live and tour rehearsal version.
- Parallels – on *Awaken* (2022)

'Don't Kill The Whale'

Officially released live versions by Yes on *Yesshows* (1980), *Live At Montreux 2003* (2007), *Live At Glastonbury Festival 2003* (2019)

Cover versions:
- Rick Wakeman – on *Yes's Greatest Hits* (1993)
- Magellan – on *Tales From Yesterday* (2006)
- Aurora Lunare – *Tales From The Edge* (2012)

- Candice Knight/ Billy Sherwood/ Jay Schellen/ Brian Auger – on *A Life In Yes: Chris Squire Tribute* (2018)

'Madrigal'

Officially released live version by Yes on *Yes50 Live* (2019).

Cover version:
- Rick Wakeman – on *Yes's Greatest Hits* (1993)

'Release, Release'

No official live release by Yes

Cover versions:
- Shadow Gallery – on *Tales From Yesterday* (2006)
- Manticore – on *Next Step: Flight 19* (2018)

'Arriving UFO'

No official live release by Yes but the 'Alan White Drum Solo' on *Live at Philadelphia 1979* DVD is taken from the live version of the song.

Also featured on *Yes Remixes* (2003) remixed by The Verge (Virgil Howe).

Cover version:
- Circa: – on *Circa: Live* (2007) – excerpted as part of the 'Chronological Journey' live medley

'Circus of Heaven'

Officially released live version by Yes on *Live In Philadelphia 1979* DVD and *The Word Is Live* (2005)

I could not find any cover versions of this song.

'Onward'

Officially released live versions by Yes on *Keys To Ascension* (1996), *In*

The Present: Live From Lyon (2011), and *The Royal Affair Tour: Live In Las Vegas* (2020)

Cover versions:
- Greenwall – on *Tales From The Edge* (2012)
- Melanie Mau & Martin Schnella on *Gray Matters* (2015)
- Arkady Shilkloper – on *Owner of a Lonely Horn: Symphonic Tribute to Yes* (2015)
- Inventioning – on *Onward* (2016)
- Annie Haslam / Billy Sherwood / Jay Schellen – on *A Life In Yes: Chris Squire Tribute* (2018)
- Parallels (Yes Tribute Band) on *Awaken* (2022)
- Mark Kozelek on *Like Rats* (2013) – also used in the soundtrack for the 2015 film *Youth* and on the soundtrack album for the film
- Logan on *Nuntius* (2010)
- Caballero Reynaldo on *Close To The Lounge* (2015)
- Unitopia on *Covered Mirror Vol 1. – Smooth As Silk* (2012) – excerpted as part of 'Yes Medley'
- Hans Annéllsson on *One More Time for the World Some More* (2002)
- Lil B on *05 Fuck Em* (2013) – sampled on 'Snitch'

'On The Silent Wings Of Freedom'

While there is no full official live release version of this song, it is excerpted in the 'The Fish' on *Live At Montreux* (2003).

Cover versions:
- Circa: on *Circa: Live* (2007) – excerpted as part of the 'Chronological Journey' live medley
- Jon Davison/ Billy Sherwood/ Jay Schellen/ Patrick Moraz – on *A Life In Yes: Chris Squire Tribute* (2018)

LIVE IN PHILADELPHIA 1979 DVD REVIEW

Information about the film shot in Philadelphia on the *Ten True Summers Tour* is surprisingly difficult to find. Yes fan Jon Dee suggested that I should contact author and Grammy-award winning radio producer, Denny Somach who had been involved in arranging the recording of this concert. Denny very kindly replied with the following explanation:

TORMATO OFFICIAL LIVE RELEASES AND COVERS

"Yes: Live in Philadelphia was shot on June 21, 1979 at the Philadelphia Spectrum as they performed in the round on a rotating stage, in the centre of the venue. They were promoting the *Tormato* album. Yes was a huge band in that city, mainly due to a lot of airplay over the years. I was a major DJ on the rock station there and not only my station, WYSP, but the other two rock stations played the hell out the band. They always used to play three nights in Philadelphia (even on the *Drama* Tour) and would sell out instantly.

The video was not planned that far in advance, so it was sort of a last minute thing. We only shot one of the three shows, as I remember, and I still have much of the extra footage. The video release is just under an hour and obviously we picked out what were the best songs. It was originally released on video disc in Japan before coming out in the rest of the world. The quality was not the greatest and we shot using three cameras. I think the band just wanted to have something to document the *Tormato* tour. One thing I remember is that Jon mentioned it was his daughter's birthday when we filmed. It was a great show with an enthusiastic audience. Of course, nobody knew at the time that it would be the last tour with Jon and Rick since they quit while recording the proposed follow up. I was the co-producer/director and close friend of the band members, particularly Chris and Jon.

I didn't see them again until they started recording *Drama* in London in the late spring of 1980. They invited me over to London where I stayed for over three weeks as they recorded at the Town House studios. Part of the time I stayed at Chris's mansion in Suffolk."

Back in 2013, I recorded a review of the DVD version of *Yes Live in Philadelphia 1979*. I released it as episode 85 of the *Yes Music Podcast*. Here is a slightly edited and updated version of my review which now includes more recent statistics and a few corrections.

The DVD entitled *Live in Philadelphia 1979* (see page 276) captures Yes at the end of the main sequence of albums and shortly before the split-up which saw new personnel joining for *Drama*. This live concert

Live In Philadelphia DVD, author's collection

recording should show the band close to their best. Even though this is the tour supporting what many saw as the disappointing *Tormato* album, the concerts themselves were very well received at the time.

According to Discogs, the film was released initially on laserdisc in Japan in 1995 and then as a CD and VCD package in Thailand in 1996. VHS video appeared in Germany in 1996 as well and the first DVD was released in the US in 1998.

The version of the DVD I have seems to be made in Germany and released in 2005. It is pretty basic in terms of its production and packaging. There is no booklet, just a cover which features a version of the Roger Dean painting from the *Classic Yes* album. There is the bubble logo as you'd expect, and some good-quality Dean lettering. The back has some very poor photo stills from the DVD, and the main blurb mentions a duel between Howe and Wakeman, as well as a drum solo from White. The track listing is given as 'Siberian Khatru', 'Circus of Heaven', 'The Ancient', 'Starship Trooper', 'I've Seen all Good People' and 'Roundabout' – so very little beyond the standard repertoire although it will be interesting to see 'Circus of Heaven' from the 1979 tour. The design of the DVD itself is vaguely Dean-inspired in lurid purple and day-glow green.

We have fifty minutes of music to look forward to, as well as some audio commentary from the well-respected author of the book, *The Story of Yes*, Chris Welch, as a DVD Extra. The main menu is well constructed with a Steve Howe guitar loop from 'I've Seen All Good People'. You can choose from 'Track Selection', 'Review', 'Play All', 'Audio Selection' and 'Credits'. The 'Review' section is Chris Welch talking about the video for a couple of minutes. He makes the main points about this being the end of the classic period of the band, says a couple of things about the staging, and makes it clear he thinks this is the band at their peak, especially in the aforementioned music duel and drum solo. It's good to see and hear Mr Welch but it's not exactly a BBC 4 documentary. Clicking on 'Track Selection' takes you to a menu via a tiny, psychedelic trip, with snippets of music and weird graphics flying around. It's interesting to see that Alan White's drum solo is given a track listing of its own here as the last item.

The first in the line-up is called 'Intro and 'Siberian Khatru''. This tour was in the round which meant that the band had to walk through the crowd to reach the stage. This footage begins in almost complete darkness, with the band members appearing out of what looks a bit like an alien spacecraft. It appears to be a tunnel, lit from the inside with bright white light, through which the musicians emerge into an almost completely blacked-out venue, with fans shouting wildly, and some kind of almost inaudible soundtrack playing. It's somewhat bizarre but, then again, this is the most cosmic outfit of all time. I suppose this was their substitute for the idea of appearing on the stage in '11th Illusion' style.

The quality of the footage is pretty poor. In these days of high definition, this looks out of place. There are some shots of the musicians from later in the show which fade in and out before dramatic chords introduce Howe's opening to 'Siberian Khatru', which he takes at a medium to slow pace. Camera work is a little shaky, even making allowances for the constantly turning stage.

Despite all this, it is possible to be drawn in as Anderson begins the vocals and it was clearly a good concert, but unfortunately the audio phases between sides. There are some great shots of Squire as he jumps around in light blue tailcoat and Wakeman's solo comes through nicely. The rotating stage allows different views of the band and the speed of rotation is surprisingly fast. The performance is certainly full of life and energy and the end of the piece seems a bit rushed.

Anderson introduces 'Circus of Heaven' to a rapturous response from the crowd, who have clearly just bought the album. Squire's bass comes through well, and Wakeman pushes the envelope of whimsy even further than on the album. Please, please don't let prog rock critics see this segment. Those of us who understand will understand, but this performance really is bordering on the ridiculous, primarily because of what Wakeman is doing in the first section on the keyboards. As we continue, it becomes closer to the recorded version and begins to build in a pleasing way, especially as Wakeman returns to more recognisable parts. Anderson's voice is assured and cuts through well, and there's no lack of commitment from the band. The recording of the young Anderson is included, and the deliberate chaos of the ending is replicated quite well.

Next up in the running order is 'The Ancient'. Anderson is strumming a guitar and dedicates the song to Jennifer. He then starts a rendition of 'Leaves of Green'. The guitar appears not to be miked up at all, as it's practically inaudible. The only sound from it is coming from Anderson's vocal microphone. I think Wakeman is trying to play along, but it's not really clear. It's a touching tribute but don't expect to hear the whole of 'The Ancient', as advertised.

'Starship Trooper' starts in an appropriately energetic manner. The sound is still rather boomy, and I'm wondering what Alan White's solo will sound like. At least the heavy bass allows us to hear some of the Squire lines which blast out in fine style. This performance is much more enjoyable than previous ones on this disc. The band seem to be more tightly together and appear to have warmed up. Steve Howe's solo finger-picking passage is great, as are the vocal harmonies here. Wakeman adds some slightly odd interjections but, overall, it's great fun. In fact, he launches into a fast, intricate solo which is far removed from Tony Kaye's original part. It's closer to his own 'Six Wives Of Henry VIII' for a few moments, but then Anderson brings the verse in again. The crowd react as Howe starts the epic, repeated guitar pattern for the build up and I'm wondering just how elaborate this version will be. A glance at the track timing reveals that we still have almost six minutes to go, so I'm assuming there's a quite a segment to come. Howe adds improvisations to the line and then drums and rasping bass appear, much earlier than in the studio version. This is to pave the way for Wakeman to mesmerise with those flashing fingers.

His solo is as fast and furious as you'd expect and ends up with a huge glissando, achieved with the turn of a knob at a pitch almost only audible to the local dogs. This leaves Steve Howe room to bring in his cataclysmic solo. The camera pans to reveal Jon Anderson standing at Wakeman's bank of keyboards and the momentary disorientation is cleared by the realisation that Wakeman has strapped on his keytar and joined Howe in the middle of the rotating stage for one of the most startling passages in Yes history. As the two musicians face-off with more and more frenetic playing, it's such fun to see the interplay and the looks on their faces. Wakeman then goes to Chris Squire and the two kneel opposite each other while Howe is atop the plinth, in true guitar-hero mode. The order-out-of-chaos moment is beautifully handled with Howe's guitar suddenly blasting out the main theme and the band all contributing to a tumultuous ending. This is possibly the best performance of 'Starship Trooper' I have seen.

The audience reaction to 'I've seen All Good People' is nothing short of rapturous. Anderson's vocals are on top form and the opening segment comes over very well. The mixing on the backing vocals is a little rough at times, but the actual singing is fine. It's an infectious performance which rolls along in an affecting manner. The addition of drums and Hammond organ adds to the building tension and then the up-tempo rock 'n' roll kicks in with Howe leading the way. As usual for this disc, the musicians are in almost total darkness most of the time, but this doesn't seem to put them off and might be the video recording rather than the reality. This rendition is far more convincing than the opening number and brilliant fun to listen to, despite the audio quality. Howe adds some creative licks to the stripped-down segment and then they career to the end with great panache. A satisfying performance.

In traditional form, this is the last official track in this concert so we get to see the band remove instruments and wave to the audience. Squire is carrying what looks like a can of Pepsi or perhaps something stronger and Wakeman is resplendent in white suit, complete with elaborate, pink embroidery. The five men are the epitome of what passed for style in 1979.

Now the band have re-assembled for 'Roundabout', and Jon Anderson makes a reference to doing many more of these things in the 80s – a comment which is now weighed down with so much baggage it's hardly worth mentioning. I remember he wondered out loud at the first concert I went to on the *Open Your Eyes Tour* whether the band could keep going into the new millennium. However, here we are in 1979 and the band launch into the classic with energy and commitment. The opening has some of the most satisfying shots so far. It appears to be lighter and Chris Squire's technique is visible. It's a great performance with all the elements present and correct. A better mix shows off Wakeman's lines amid the melee, and the tempo is enjoyably fast. The camera angles show Alan White in the foreground and Wakeman viewable beyond Anderson. Another shot shows some aspects of Wakeman's technique not glimpsed previously, as he swaps between keyboards.

The performance is very good with the Wakeman solo causing him to twitch wildly at the keyboard. Howe takes over and the battle continues, bringing a broad smile to the face of this viewer. A classic jousting match between the two is completed by Anderson tossing the tambourine into the air and then away under some convenient equipment. This is exactly the kind of aural mayhem you wish for at a Yes concert. The end is given the rising key treatment followed by a mad frenzy of guitar and drums alongside keyboards screeching up to the essential bash to finish.

The band assemble on the central raised dais again, and eventually walk off into the gloom after a brilliant performance that not even this DVD can spoil.

The last item on the track list is, "drum SOLO". It's just 1 min 58 secs long and starts with cymbal work and little spots of electronics which then grow in intensity. In fact, it turns out that the electronics are being triggered by the acoustic drums (see chapter 7) and overlaying science-fiction sounding tones. It reminds me of the other odd drum moment I witnessed which featured Alan White. On the 35th Anniversary

Tour of 2004, Alan engaged the wonderfully named Reek Havok to create several additional bass drums for his solo, which lit up and played themselves via triggering. I remember I followed the development of these instruments on the creator's blog. In action, Alan White looked a little embarrassed, I recall, and the overall effect was slightly comical.

In order to organise my viewing, I watched individual tracks via the select track section of the DVD. However, there is also the Chris Welch commentary to the full film, which I subsequently switched on and listened to. A highly knowledgeable commentator, Mr Welch tells us he was in the studio when Yes recorded 'I've Seen All Good People'. He points out this was one of the tracks from *The Yes Album* which introduced Yes to the US. He remembers those earliest audiences being stunned by tracks like this one. His commentary is not extensive, but he does share some interesting anecdotes and observations along the way, as they occur to him. He seems to be a calm, quiet and warm personality and his voice reminds me very much of a combination of Dr Brian May from Queen and whispering Bob Harris from the iconic BBC music programme, *The Old Grey Whistle Test*.

Welch mentions the inadequacy of the venue in this video, as well as many stadiums and concert halls Yes frequented during this period, in terms of their lighting and acoustics. He points out that the band had to use enormous monitor speakers so they could hear each other. I imagine this was exacerbated by playing in the round. Other kit he mentions includes Anderson's percussion tree which is sometimes called the 'Bus Stop' and Wakeman's set-up which he says is far simpler and smaller than Keith Emerson's ELP rig of just eight years before, which looked more like a telephone exchange.

Welch also stresses the importance of vocals and vocal harmonies to the group. He says that this is partly what brought Anderson and Squire together in 1968. Both were influenced by groups who had very strong vocal harmonies at the time like The Beatles and The Fifth Dimension. Anderson also always ensured that the vocals were an equal part of the music to the instruments. He singles out Yes and Frank Zappa as the two bands who, in his opinion, succeeded in telling stories through their music. This meant that listening audiences had to put a little effort in, unlike the instant gratification culture of today. Someone who refused to put the effort in when listening to 'Circus of Heaven' in his car was Trevor Horn, according to Welch. It's therefore remarkable to think that, within two years, he was fronting the band himself.

Much more could have been done with the commentary. Maybe a proper interview of Welch could have added a great deal. A skilled interviewer might have been able to coax many more interesting anecdotes and reflections from someone who was, after all, there with the band at some crucial moments in their history and has written a whole book on the subject.

Overall, this collection is important for any Yes fan interested in either *Tormato* or the (arguably) best live touring period of the band's career. It's a shame the quality of the video isn't better but as a record of the event, it is priceless.

28

TOUR BOOKS/PROGRAMMES

Two rather different programmes (tour books) were created for the 1978 live *Tourmato* (or *Tormatour*) dates and the 1979 *Ten True Summers Tour* concerts. As can be seen below, the later programme featured live photos taken on the 1978 tour, whereas the earlier tour book could not, and so opted for different kinds of images.

1978 Tourmato programme, author's collection

Inside the cover of the 1978 programme there is a version (see chapter 12) of Colin Elgie's inner bag map illustration and this programme includes the US dates of the tour as well as the recently added Wembley ones. An earlier version omits the Wembley dates altogether. An article by Dan Hedges (author of *Yes – The Authorised Biography*) explains that the band weren't keen on making any fuss about their tenth anniversary. Each band member is then featured in a double page spread. Jon Anderson's pages includes two paintings by the singer himself, one in which he illustrates the words of 'Awaken' from *Going For The One* and the other is a watercolour of a river winding through a pastoral scene. At the back of the programme is a cartoon drawn by Jeff Cummins. Famed for his illustrations on Doctor Who book covers, Jeff drew the lovely picture of Alan White for the front cover of his solo album, *Ramshackled*. He also drew the portrait of Jon Anderson and his family for the gatefold sleeve of his masterpiece, *Olias Of Sunhillow* (although his name is misspelled as 'Cummings' on the sleeve). The cartoon tells an amusing story of the band's manager, Brian Lane, and an endless round of touring. Entitled 'Torment On A Yes Tour', it shows Jon Anderson in a wheelchair and Rick Wakeman on the floor, after having passed out in front of his keyboards. On the penultimate page is an advertisement for Yes' back catalogue (see chapter 22) and the back cover features a large, squashed tomato.

1979 Ten True Summers Tour programme, author's collection

By the following year, the *Ten True Summers Tour* programme looked very different, although most of the words remained the same. Dan

Hedges did revise his article, but the rest of the main text is unchanged. All the pages (apart from the advertisement at the end) feature photos taken on the 1978 *Tourmato* tour. Anderson's paintings from the previous programme are replaced by a different watercolour showing a flock of Concorde aeroplanes landing at the coast of an undisclosed land. Jeff Cummin's cartoon is replaced with photos of tour crew.

Both programmes are similar in style and contents to the tour books for the 1977 *Going For The One Tour* and the 1980 *Drama Tour*.

At least one other programme was also available on the *Tourmato*, however. Yes fan David Phillips posted the following remarkable item on Twitter and Julian Butler also has a copy from his father's collection. It is a bootleg programme from Wembley 1978. It's not great quality, but certainly an amazing piece of entrepreneurial enterprise by someone. A lot of the content is about *Going For The One*, so there is a suggestion (from some quarters) that it contains mostly material from the bootleg item sold on that previous tour. There also are plenty of errors but I wonder how many of these still exist today.

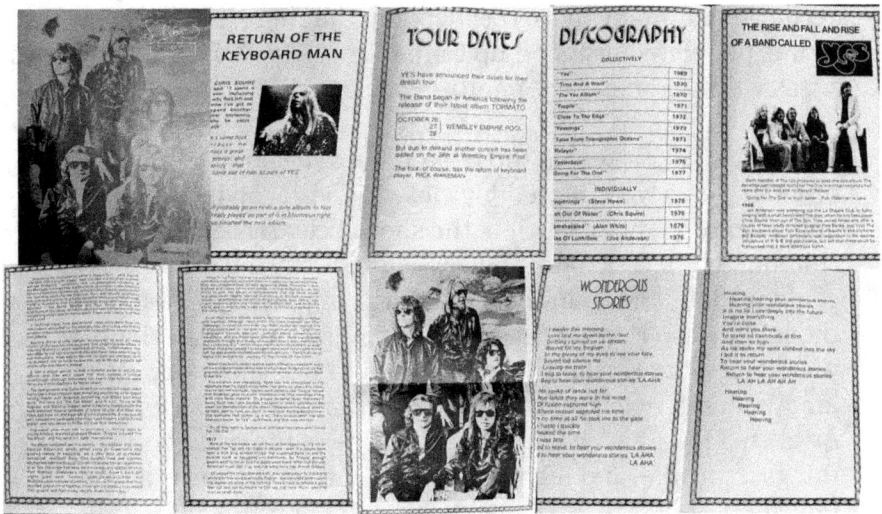

Bootleg tour programme, photos courtesy of David Phillips

29

FAN RECOLLECTIONS

Head over to the extensive database of reviews on Forgotten Yesterdays[63] for many more recollections, but here are just a few from generous people who signed up to the *Yes – The Tormato Story* newsletter, as well as some great photos:

"I had 8th row tickets at the Boston Garden show in August of 1978. Seats were incredibly close to the revolving stage, and I can remember much of the show. I clearly remember running to the rest room shortly before it started – and so I could walk by the soundboard – and saying hello to Mike Tait, though it wasn't until I read the Yes biography by Dan Hedges years later that I realized who that was. I was mesmerized by Jon Anderson who seemed to be in a trance when performing Awaken. I felt I had just experienced one of the most powerful things in my life, and life was certainly never the same after that show!"

Mark S. Jacobsohn

"October 1978, I saw Yes in the round at the Wembley Arena in London – one of four nights at the venue and the only concerts

---

[63] https://tormatobook.com/1978timeline

in the UK that year. This was my fourth Yes gig and came just a year after seeing them at the same venue on the Going For the One tour. Seeing the band in the round was a special treat (to be repeated 13 years later on the Union tour) giving everyone a great view. Unusually the concert started with music from Close Encounters of the Third Kind instead of Firebird but still went straight into Siberian Khatru. I particularly enjoyed the songs from Tormato (five from the album), "the Big Medley" and, my favourite, Awaken. Sadly, I wouldn't see this "classic" version of the band again until 2002."

Ken Fuller

Wembley 1978, photo courtesy of Paul and Julian Butler

"We saw the announcement of the new Yes tour and we grabbed our tickets ASAP. Bill was the friend who first introduced me to Yes, but this would be his first concert (my third). We were thrilled to get sixth row for Yes in the Round at Olympia Stadium in Detroit, September 21, 1978. The new album was to be released the next day. What if it was not good? Would they change their sound? Why did the concert program have tomatoes splattered on it? What is a Tor? What is a Tourmato? We were worried. Then Jon announced they were going to play something from their new album, and they broke into 'Future Times'. Within the first 20 notes, we looked at each other with a big smile. This was going to be good. An amazing show, from an amazing album."

Jamie McQuinn

A photo bought from an unknown photographer by Jamie McQuinn, following a concert he attended in Bloomfield Hills, Michigan, 1978

"My experience from that gig 45 years ago isn't etched into my memory in fine detail but very much an overall impression. It started by hitch-hiking from Durham via Pontefract and Derby. I was pretty hard up and combined my trip with visiting friends en route, which broke up the journey and got me closer. I had some anxious moments on the final leg of the trip, wondering if I'd make it, but arrived at Wembley Empire Pool on time and in hope of buying a ticket. Grasping that precious piece of paper I went into the huge arena.

I did wonder where the seat was in relation to the stage. The year before for the *Going For The One* Tour I hit the jackpot and was in row two in front of Chris Squire. This time I'd no idea they would be playing 'in the round' but again fortune was in my favour. I was seated directly above the stage, though quite a way back. I did though have a 200mm lens which gave me the opportunity to make some decent pictures.

The gig was amazing. The set list was a Yes fan's dream. Along with the new material including 'Circus of Heaven' where there was a mixture of cheers and jeers as Jon's son's voice came in, there were so many 'classics' I'd not heard live before, having been only to the tours of 75 and 77. I was blown away of course, especially by Awaken which almost took the roof off as it had the previous year. The band was in its pomp and loving it. From my vantage point it was so nice to see the interaction of the band as they made the most of their circular playground. The performance I attended was a matinée, but it didn't feel like it. They played again that evening, which was recorded and later broadcast by the BBC."

Jeremy North

Wembley 1978, photos courtesy of Jeremy North

Yes: The Tormato Story

Jeremy North's ticket to the afternoon performance at Wembley 1978, photo courtesy of Jeremy North

"I have many memories as I saw 5 Yes gigs in '78 and 6 in '79, so that's 11 of the 96 US & Canada shows. For the 4th year in a row, I was with the band before or after those concerts, and at select hotels, interviewing them for my then radio shows and hanging out. The '76 shows were the best Yes shows visually with the amazing stage set and lasers, but the in the round shows in '78 and '79 were fantastic for the audiences to see the band from many sides instead of the normal static proscenium stage view. My strongest memories are of the Richfield Coliseum show on Sept. 19, 1978. The Cleveland area has always been very strong for Yes and other prog acts. The band was very happy with their performance after the show. Listen to the FM broadcast recording from the legendary WMMS. I still have my original audiotape recording of the broadcast. The Chicago show on June 9, 1979, was also a barn burner of a show. The concert medley on those tours was very well received and a nice surprise. The band was in great spirits at most shows, although I saw and heard some signs of splintering on the '79 tour."

Doug Curran

"I attended the Yes concert on the *Tormato* tour on the 25th June 1979, at The Omni in Atlanta, Georgia USA. I had just turned 13, and not only was it my first Yes concert, it was my first concert! To say I was blown away would be a huge understatement.

The concert was in the round, and I definitely remember them playing Arriving UFO and this 25-minute song which

FAN RECOLLECTIONS

Ten True Summers Tour, photos courtesy of Charles Kershenblatt

turned out to be the Big Medley. I have seen them about 15 times since and I still have to say this was the best Yes concert I have been to. Everything clicked. The sound was great, the lighting was magical, and the tempo was perfect. Having watched the concert recently on YouTube from this tour I would say they were at their peak with the classic lineup. *Tormato* will always be special to me because it was the album that got me hooked on Yes. Every song on that album is a finely crafted sonic painting."

Doug Dreeman

"I did see yes at Madison Square Garden in 1977 and I was only 14 years old. Then came 1978. This time I wanted to find tickets that were closer to the stage. I did. Walking into Madison Square Garden and seeing the round stage in the middle was very exciting. The show opened up with Siberian Khatru. Steve Howe was on fire jumping around towards the end of the song. Jon was in the very middle singing so beautifully. Yes has always had the best musicians in the world, but Jon was really what made Yes so unique. I am an amateur drummer and seeing Alan White drumming like his life depended on it was something I will never forget. It is hard to really explain what I really experienced that night, but it really changed my life. I finally saw them up close as the round stage gave everyone a closer look. That was around 44 years ago at the time of this writing. I can say I saw the best."

Rob Earley

30
CONCERT MEMORABILIA

A variety of items were produced for concerts, including the usual passes, T-shirts and badges (pins). As always, there are many things to discover on the *Tourmato* tour and *Ten True Summers Tour* pages of Forgotten Yesterdays[64] but here are just a few from my own collection and from kind contributors.

Wembley guest pass, photo courtesy of Doug Curran, crew pass, photo courtesy of David Watkinson and badge (pin), author's collection

---

64 https://tormatobook.com/tourpage

Yes: The Tormato Story

1978 Tour T-shirts, top left – courtesy of Doug Curran, top centre and right – author's collection, bottom – 1979 Tour T-shirt, courtesy of Doug Curran

31

THE 'REVOLUTIONARY' ROTATING STAGE

> "Great fun and enjoyable for all concerned ... we always pushed the boundaries with production and why not?"
> Rick Wakeman on the rotating stage, February 2023

A circular, rotating stage in the middle of a venue is still something of a novelty at a rock concert, although the concept has been used a number of times by different bands. A few venues, such as the NYCB Theatre at Westbury,[65] are even set up like this permanently. Yes performed the last date on the 2022 *Close To The Edge 50th Anniversary Tour* there.

Yes were to play 'in the round' again on their next tour in 1980 in support of *Drama* and on the *Union Tour* in 1991. Possibly the most well-known example of another band using this technique in a rock concert, apart from Yes, is Def Leppard.

In March 2015, the Yes (official) Facebook page posted a photograph[66]

---
65 https://tormatobook.com/westbury
66 https://tormatobook.com/rotatingstage

Yes: The Tormato Story

The stage featured Jon Anderson's Olias of Sunhillow logo on the central dais, photo courtesy of Jeremy North

featuring the stage which was created for the 1978 *Tourmato* tour. Incidentally, the photo used is actually from the 1979 tour because Alan White's kit is not the North hybrid set (see chapter 6) but, instead, the dark wood Ludwig one. The commentary explained how this innovative stage idea was developed, as told by Yes Tour Manager, Michael Tait:

"In America we'd have a three or four truck tour although that is nothing by today's standards. The biggest development was the rotating round stage, which I thought of back in 1976. We were trying to come up with a new stage design and I picked up a can of film I was taking to a studio and was on the seat of my car. I looked at it and I thought, 'That's it!'

I put the idea on paper and showed it to the band. 'Look, we can play in the centre of the arena – in the round.' We'd have Jon in the centre, with Alan behind him. To his left would be Chris and to his right would be Steve which was the normal set-up. The only difference would be the keyboard player would be in front of Jon, but that's how they set up in the studio anyway.

They said it couldn't be done, but I said if it worked in the studio, it would work outside. And it did.

What that rotating round stage did for Yes was to make them a lot of money. The late Seventies were their golden years in

America and Yes were doing big, big business. Sell out business in the round is worth a lot more than sell out business in a proscenium set-up. The front row is 120 feet long instead of sixty! You scale up the tickets and sell more seats.

We broke box office records all over the country, including playing to something like 22,000 people at Madison Square Garden in New York. We were doing the business!"

The rotating stage with suspended lighting and sound rig before the afternoon Wembley concert in 1978, photo courtesy of Jeremy North

The always dependable Geoffrey Mason also found an interview with Michael Tait from May 1979, in the *Edmonton Journal*. Tait explains that Yes gave him permission to create the rotating stage simply to get him to go away and stop disturbing them while they were trying to record *Tormato*. Not only was this circular stage innovative in itself, but the way it was installed in each venue was also new. As pointed out by stage manager, Chip Irwin, this meant that the whole setup could be completed in half-an-hour, compared to the three to four hours needed for a traditional stage. Interviewer Graham Hicks describes the methodology:

"When the 16-man Yes road crew members come into an arena, they string up the lights and sound system on independent, stationary scaffolding in the middle of the arena. At the same time, elsewhere, the revolving stage is set up with the stage equipment. It is then towed under the overhead lighting and PA system, and everything is linked together."

Tait mentions that technicians were positioned under the stage and could occasionally be seen opening grilles in the white-carpeted stage platform (which must have been a nightmare to keep clean) and handing instruments to the musicians. In one concert, a mouse enjoyed wriggling around the carpet until it found its way off. Speaking of soft furnishings, not long into the tour, protestations from the under-stage technicians finally led to carpet being installed beneath the platform to protect their knees.

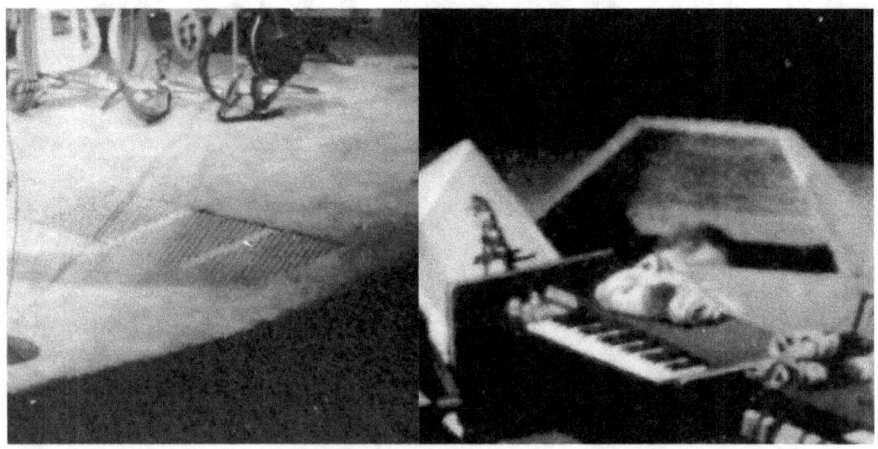

Left – grilles in the white-carpeted stage, right – a hatch in the stage with the top of a technician's head just visible, details from photos courtesy of Jeremy North

Alan White's thoughts[67] on the new stage set up were recorded in an answer to a fan on Yesworld.com in May 2013:

"**Fs. Weller:**

Alan! I saw you in Long Beach during the Tour of The Americas in the Spring of 1979. As a drummer myself, I've wondered if performing on the rotating stage was a challenge,

---

[67] https://tormatobook.com/askyes

THE 'REVOLUTIONARY' ROTATING STAGE

perhaps disorienting over the course of a concert performance or, for that matter, night after night? I would think that the direction of rotation might need to be reversed on occasion! I appreciate your drumming ... both technically and artistically.

Alan White:

The rotating stage was difficult to get used to in the beginning, and you are right, it did turn three times in one direction – clockwise – and then three times counterclockwise, otherwise there would have been a lot of cables messed up under the stage. It seemed to help to some degree, however I was perched on the edge of the stage with my back to the audience most of the time and the stage was in front of me. You were aware that people were looking at your back most of the time, seeing the inner workings of the drum kit. It wasn't easy to get used to, but once the band got used to it, we enjoyed performing on the circular stage—it was something different. I'm not sure, but I think we were one of the first bands to begin using it in that way and people seemed to like it a lot. Who knows, in the future we may do it again."

Image from Wembley 1978 showing the number of fans who could be close to the band due to the circular stage, photo courtesy of Paul and Julian Butler

One fan who witnessed the rotating stage first hand spoke about it on talkbass.com[68] and also mentioned a drawback to the idea:

> **"Tangentmusic:**
>
> Yep – I saw the *Tormato* "in the round tour" at the Long Beach Arena in SoCal. It was truly an innovative stage design for the time. When it started to slowly rotate the crowd went nuts. Then, all of a sudden, it stopped in the middle of a song. We thought it broke down. Then it started to rotate in the opposite direction. Crowd goes nuts again. The only negative aspect of it for me was when you wanted to see Squire or Howe play a particular part and they were on the other side with their backs to you!"

In the same discussion, another contributor recalled what Rick Wakeman said about an occasion on the tour when the rotating mechanism had a glitch:

> **"NealBass:**
>
> [Rick Wakeman] said something like 'One night, in the middle of the show, I noticed the first 3 rows were empty (?). I asked the manager why that was, and the manager told me that the motors that rotate the stage were broken. The manager had the first 3 rows of people in the audience, get under the stage ... and had them all pushing, for the rest of the concert!'"

In Doug Curran's interview with the band in 1978 (see chapter 12), Jon Anderson mentioned they had wanted to be able to appear magically on the stage in the centre of venues on the *Tourmato* tour and *Ten True Summers Tours*, but it was not as easy to accomplish as they had hoped. They ended up walking through the crowd, as can be seen on the *Live In Philadelphia 1979* video (see chapter 27). However, according to Trevor Horn's autobiography, *Adventures In Modern Recording*, it seems the band did manage to create the desired illusion on the *Drama Tour* of 1980. They succeeded by relying on one of the oldest techniques in the magician's arsenal – misdirection.

---

68   https://tormatobook.com/talkbass

The band would congregate at the doors on one side of the arena, and suddenly spotlights would illuminate the doors on the opposite side. The audience's attention was distracted, as they tried to see the band entering through the wrong doors. Yes took this opportunity to make a run for the stage, surrounded by security guards, and threw themselves underneath it. When the opening music, 'The Young Person's Guide To The Orchestra', reached the appropriate point, a cylindrical curtain would descend from the roof and enclose the highest part of the stage, in its centre. The musicians climbed up a short, wooden ladder and emerged inside the curtain, hidden from view. Then there would be a moment of drama (appropriately), as the curtain was raised to reveal the five band members, facing the crowd in a circle, with their backs to each other.[69] As the audience gasped and cheered wildly, they would make their way to their instrumental stations and join in with the end of the introductory music. It sounds like a lot of fun.

---

69   https://tormatobook.com/dramatour

32

WEMBLEY STADIUM RECORDING, 1978

Much more satisfying than the DVD I reviewed in chapter 27, are the *Tormato* songs which appear on the unofficial recordings from Wembley, accessed via Forgotten Yesterdays.[70] One of these combines the BBC 1 broadcast of the evening show on 28th October 1978 with three audience-recorded songs, two of which are of particular interest to us here, namely 'Future Times – Rejoice' and 'Madrigal'. (As pointed out by Yes fan, Jon Dee, the version of this show broadcast on the King Biscuit show in November 1978 featured both the Madrigal and the Rick Wakeman solo recordings in properly recorded format.) Unlike the aforementioned DVD, we can hear in good quality what the following *Tormato* songs sounded like live:

'**Future Times – Rejoice**' (6.58) ++from audience recording++
'**Circus Of Heaven**' (5.17)
'**Don't Kill The Whale**' (4.33)
'**Madrigal**' (0.54) ++from audience recording++
'**Madrigal**' (1.35)
'**On The Silent Wings Of Freedom**' (8.35)

---

[70] https://tormatobook.com/wembleyboot

WEMBLEY STADIUM RECORDING, 1978

I heard from Jon Dee on the topic of this recording. Jon started and ran the Rock Aid Armenia initiative where Chris Squire and Geoff Downes took part in Jon's all-star Rock Aid recording of Smoke on the Water. He spoke via email to Bill Aitken, who worked for the BBC in 1978. Bill was responsible for engineering and mixing this concert for Radio 1. Here is what he said (he makes it sound fairly straightforward, apart from the roof microphone!):

> "I met Nigel Luby at the gig, and took splits from the microphones going in to his front of house mixer. We recorded the show in a 16 track mobile outside and took the tapes back to the BBC studios in Maida Vale.
>
> Funny, but it's always the setting up problems that stick in my mind. This time, I had to sling an audience mic just under the roof of the Wembley Arena. It's a long way up there, and I felt quite queasy making my way along the walkway and feeding a mic down, from on high, into the auditorium.
>
> There were no dramas on this broadcast. Yes seemed to have jettisoned a lot of their earlier control-freakery.
>
> I mixed down the 16-track master onto quarter inch for Tony Wilson in Maida Vale 6 a few days later, and the band sent Nigel Luby down to check the mix. He told us he was happy with what he was hearing and he left after about 30 minutes."

The band decided to play 'Future Times – Rejoice' and then 'Circus Of Heaven' early on in the set, following the openers, 'Siberian Khatru' and 'Heart of the Sunrise'. Jon Anderson introduces 'Future Times – Rejoice' as being from their new album, and the crowd appear to recognise the name. The audio quality is fine, if very treble heavy, despite being one of the audience recordings rather than the professional BBC type. Anderson's voice is clear and strong, with the backing singing and instrumentalists also sounding confident and committed. The snare drum makes it all sound a little bit plodding, but I think that's down to the recording. The arrangement is close to the album version and it rolls along in fine style to 'Rejoice'. Keyboard sounds dodge in and out with the mobile bass line and Howe's guitar. The main theme from Howe comes over well, and the keyboard soloing from Wakeman seems a little bit more compatible with what Howe is doing – perhaps it's a different instrument in the live environment. The vocal melody seems quite high, even for the young Anderson, but the overall impression is a good one.

'Circus of Heaven' is also recognised by the crowd and this benefits from a great-sounding BBC recording. We can hear Squire's bass line properly, and the different parts are appropriately mixed. Again, the arrangement is similar to the album and, even though there are a couple of missed notes from Wakeman, it sounds as good as this song could. It feels like a difficult song to play live. There is a lot of space in the arrangement, and effects which work better on the record, although this group of musicians is probably the only one that could give this a go, even semi-credibly. The comparatively short span of this song always surprises me, but it is a pleasing feature to hear a recording of Damion adding his essential spoken element. The circus music on synth is added with dedication by Wakeman, but it probably requires a lot of studio trickery to make it sound like a departing circus fading into the distance. It is a valiant effort, and it now seems like a significant achievement to have managed to keep playing this undoubtedly difficult song throughout 1978 and 79. In total, the band played 'Circus Of Heaven' seventy-nine times. Maybe it is also significant, however, that it has never been played live since 1979 (see chapter 26).

'Don't Kill The Whale' blasts away right from Howe's opening solo, with Squire's bass thumping and undulating. The vocal harmonies are great, and there's a feeling of positivity in the performance. As always, Alan White's drums are rock solid and Wakeman's keyboards add a few extra elements which work well – perhaps they were just hidden in the studio version. The main feature is Howe's towering electric soloing, but Wakeman's wailing solo also hits the listener firmly between the ears. I'm surprised that the synthesized, sweeping whale noises work so well, but they do and it is a powerful and exciting performance of the song. The audience sound delighted with it.

The first part of 'Madrigal' is from the crowd recording again. It sounds like a piano, voice and acoustic guitar combination, and soon ebbs away for Anderson to introduce Howe for his solo. After 'Clap' and 'Starship Trooper', 'Madrigal' returns on the BBC recording. We can now hear Wakeman's piano in proper quality, combining with

Anderson's peerless vocals, some percussion and some acoustic Howe additions. Suddenly, we realise that the music is morphing into 'On The Silent Wings Of Freedom' and is introduced as such by Anderson.

After hearing this song live in 2022, and asking Steve Howe about it on the *Yes Music Podcast*, I'm intrigued to see what Squire and the others do at the beginning, which was omitted from the version on the *Close To The Edge 50th Anniversary Tour*. The opening certainly does have the bass solo – in fact, Squire plays it even faster than on the record and White supports him brilliantly. Despite Steve not wanting to preserve this preamble in 2022, it comes over here as a powerful, exciting romp. There are effective cascades of electric guitar from Howe, and Wakeman also adds in some interjections. Howe's part certainly isn't clearly defined, which is probably why he didn't want to repeat it recently, but it all sounds fabulous to my ears. Anderson's high vocals split the texture and the big refrains have an irresistible forward motion. Squire swoops and sweeps around his Rickenbacker, and everything coalesces perfectly into the quiet middle section. Yes have always been masters of recreating the most dramatic contrasts in songs on record and live, and this is no exception. Where a lot of bands seem to sound essentially the same throughout a concert, the poise, variety, precision and control of Yes in 1978 is staggering. Wakeman throws in fast soloing as the charge to the end of the song begins, still with moments of hiatus and suspension to come. Guitar and bass play furiously in unison beneath an immense, additional Wakeman semi-improvised sounding solo, and the final notes are timed to perfection, bringing a sudden and climactic end to the song.

This recording shows what the band were capable of at their peak. The earlier songs from *Tormato* are good (perhaps apart from 'Circus Of Heaven') but everything takes a huge leap when 'On The Silent Wings Of Freedom' appears. It's an exhausting and wonderful rush for the listener, and quite possibly the most exciting song I have ever experienced the band performing, recorded or live.

PART 7 - EPILOGUE

33

EPILOGUE

Author: "When you heard the record, were you disappointed with the overall sound?"

Rick Wakeman: "It would have been better mixed on a food mixer."

Author: "Would you like to see it re-mixed?"

Rick Wakeman: "Yes … if I could do it with my co-producer, Erik Jordan."

Every fan (and Yes musician) has their own view of the overall effectiveness of *Tormato* as a Yes album. Here's what guitarist Fernando Perdomo said when we asked him the question on the *Yes Music Podcast*:

"When you listen to it in 2022, 'quirky' is the word, and they weren't going for 'quirky'. They were actually trying to convince the audience that it was still Yes, but with sound adapted for the times. This was clear with synthesizers now being polyphonic, electronics and guitar synths in the mix and the drums being recorded in a completely different way to all other Yes records – there's no sustain at all which makes it sound 'off'."

As you will be aware after reading this book, I cannot hear the deficiencies of the album clearly, and perhaps, if everyone could experience the sonic delights of *Tormato* in the new MQA-CD format, a lot more sceptics would join me in my love for the record – or maybe not. In any case, the intention of writing this book has always been to use *Tormato* as a gateway to finding out as much as possible about Yes and how they created albums at this time. I hope you have enjoyed reading it as much as I have enjoyed researching and assembling it.

Finally, I'd like to thank Simon Barrow (author of *Solid Mental Grace: Listening to the Music of Yes*, and the forthcoming *Yes in the 1990s*) once again for his help and encouragement throughout the process of producing this book and I'll leave the final word to him, as he considers the place of *Tormato* in the story of Yes.

WHY TORMATO MATTERS by Simon Barrow

When people consider key turning points in Yes history, the most likely candidates are *The Yes Album* (birth of the classic sound), *Close to the Edge* (widely considered a landmark album in progressive rock) and *90125* (the band's hit-making best seller, which catapulted them to a new level of fame). In recent years, *Drama* has also gained in recognition, and rightly so. But the most overlooked and dismissed 'hinge point' of all, I would argue, is *Tormato* – which, back in 1978, prophetically prefigured the disruptive transition from 1970s Yes to the sound of the 80s and beyond.

All the signs of this are present on the physical record. The cover includes the traditional, iconic Roger Dean logo, which had adorned every Yes album since the ground-breaking *Close to the Edge* in 1972. But it sits atop a controversial Hipgnosis cover that represents a clear break with the recent past, and a tomato splattering which indicates the deeper rupture which was about to take place. Again, the band photo depicts the classic line-up, but their be-leathered appearance signals both the emerging post-punk, New Wave era, and also the 1960s – both 'beyond and before' classic Yes, you might say.

Most important is the music, of course. There are eight full band tracks for the first time since *Time and a Word*, which was put together at the end of 1969 and released in 1970, and the band's 1969 eponymous debut. You can hear Yes pulling in different directions across these new tracks. The punchy, processed bass of 'On the Silent Wings of Freedom' is a fresh take on the 70s legacy, but with a rocky feel that draws on *Going for the One*, where the real return to roots began. 'Release, Release' embodies the harder-edged sound that White and Squire, in particular, were looking for. 'Don't Kill the Whale' ventures into hit territory, and would not be that out of place on 1988's *Big Generator*. Meanwhile, 'Madrigal', with its polytime rhythms and its combination of harpsichord and acoustic guitar, has very much a 1970s feel, connecting back to 'Wonderous Stories'.

Then we have the Anderson-led 'Circus of Heaven', displaying that soft, playful, almost childlike approach that marked a growing tension between Jon and Rick's softer side, and Steve, Chris and Alan wanting to break free and rock out on the other wing. 'Arriving UFO' with its adventurous instrumental patterns and whimsical lyrics is perhaps the closest they get to holding these different poles together. It is a track which is often regarded as nothing more than an oddity, but which actually combines New Age sentiment and musical experimentalism in a fascinating way.

Last but not least we have 'Onward', and the composite opener, 'Future Times/Rejoice'. The former is a song which echoes back both to Chris Squire's majestic 1975 solo outing *Fish Out of Water*, orchestrated by the incredibly talented Andrew Pryce Jackman, and to the first use of an orchestra on *Time and a Word*. Yet its pop sensibility is also one that Yes would lean into in the 1980s, even though it is nothing like what would eventually emerge as *90125* in 1983. 'Future 'Times/Rejoice', meanwhile, encapsulates many of the divergent musical tendencies across the album as a whole. Mixed in a churchy ambience it wouldn't have sounded out of place on the preceding *Going For The One*. Vamped up and simplified, you could imagine it traversing the next decade comfortably. Instead, tragically, it has been lost as a 'deep cut' for aficionados only.

Altogether then, *Tormato* offers us mini-telegrams and musical amalgams from both the past and the future, as well as having its own distinctive ethos and featuring a one-off curiosity in the use of the Birotron. The album also bequeathed us one of the great live tours in Yes history, where the territory of the past and the beckoning of the future was very much present. This is an album and a moment in time which very much needs revisiting, so I am particularly pleased that Kevin Mulryne has done so in such devoted detail. He has succeeded not just in producing an informative book on an underrated and overlooked album, but he has done so in a way that casts further light on the whole process of 'Yes at work' and the band's wider musical legacy.

ACKNOWLEDGEMENTS

I'd like to thank the following people for their help writing this book:

Alan White (RIP), Rick Wakeman, Jon Anderson, Steve Howe and Chris Squire (RIP) for creating this wonderful album.

Sarah, William, Edward and Charlotte Mulryne for putting up with my *Tormato* obsession and finding it funny rather than odd.

William Mulryne, in addition to the above, for his brilliant photos on *My Own Tourmato* as well as his expert photo restoration.

Edward Mulryne, in addition to the above, for his expert proofreading, word-wrangling and interest in the project.

Oliver Wakeman for his instant agreement to writing the foreword, his approachable nature and time as Yes keyboardist.

Steve Howe and Rick Wakeman for being happy to talk to me about *Tormato*.

Simon Barrow for his essential encouragement, help and advice – not to mention proofreading and providing expert content.

Jon Dee for expert proofreading, fantastic additional content, research and image restoration.

David Watkinson for lending me his unique items, his recollections and his time through many years (and for happily meeting up with me at Blow-Up Bridge).

Mark Anthony K for his friendship, knowledge and many happy hours spent together recording the *Yes Music Podcast*.

Geoff Bailie for his proofreading, expert content, generosity and willingness to be involved with whatever mad scheme I think of next.

Henry Potts for everything he does for me and all Yes fans as well as his cheerful and expert fact checking and proofreading.

Doug Curran for unique artefacts, content, resources and generous help.

Miguel Falcão for his expert knowledge of Chris Squire's bass, his unwavering generosity and his expert content.

Peter Woolliscroft for his generosity in sharing his recollections of his time at Advision including his detailed memories of the *Tormato* recording.

Chris Dale for extensive continued help, expert knowledge and his work to preserve the Birotron.

Jeremy North for his amazing photos of Wembley 1978 and long-term friendship.

Bob Carling for expert production management and friendly advice.

Izsi Lawrence for expert cover artwork.

Geoffrey Mason for keeping the Yes research flame burning and for his knowledgeable assistance.

Jim Halley for his behind-the-scenes knowledge, unique photos and willingness to search for answers to my often bizarre questions.

Pete Whipple, and latterly Steve Sullivan, for establishing and nurturing the amazing Forgotten Yesterdays website.

Sam Ashworth, Gerard Bassols, Rob Brimson, Paul Butler, Julian Butler, Sharon Chevin, Paul Cobb, Joseph Cottrell, Martin Darvill, Roger Dean, Derek Dearden, Doug Dreeman, Tim Durling, Rob Earley, Colin Elgie, John Ford, Ken Fuller, Ryan Gallagher, James Gardner, Jan Halley, Dan Hedges, John Holden, Chris Hoskins, Henry Jackman, Mark S. Jacobsohn, Brian Kehew, Charles Kershenblatt, Chris Kimball, Jon Kirkman, Catherine Koureas, Brian Lane, Paul Laue, Jaime Martin, Sean McCarthy, Jamie McQuinn, Tim Morse, Thomas J. Mosbø, Brian Neeson, Fernando Perdomo, Steve Perry, Hogne Bø Pettersen, David Phillips, Barry Plummer, Aubrey Powell, Kevin Pyne, Clive Richardson, Andrew Pryce Jackman (RIP), Geoff Young (RIP), Billy Sherwood, Denny Somach, Michael Tait, Chris Welch, Adam Wildi, all *Yes Music Podcast* producers, patrons and listeners.

www.ingramcontent.com/pod-product-compliance
Lightning Source LLC
Chambersburg PA
CBHW071332080526
44587CB00017B/2816